Table of Contents

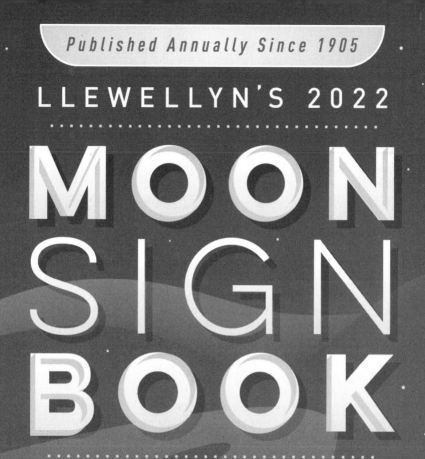

Published Annually Since 1905

LLEWELLYN'S 2022
MOON SIGN BOOK

Plan Your Life by the Cycles of the Moon

Llewellyn's 2022 Moon Sign Book®

ISBN 978-0-7387-6048-3

Cover design by Kevin R. Brown
Editing by Hanna Grimson
Stock photography models used for illustrative purposes only and may not endorse or represent the book's subject.
Interior photographs: Getty Images
Typography owned by Llewellyn Worldwide Ltd.

Weekly tips by Penny Kelly, Lupa, and Shelby Deering.

Any internet references contained in this work are current at publication time, but the publisher cannot guarantee that a specific location will continue to be maintained.

A special thanks to Beth Rosato for astrological proofreading.

Astrological data compiled and programmed by Rique Pottenger. Based on the earlier work of Neil F. Michelsen.

You can order Llewellyn annuals and books from *New Worlds*, Llewellyn's catalog. To request a free copy of the catalog, call toll-free 1-877-NEW-WRLD or visit our website at www.llewellyn.com.

Llewellyn Publications is a registered trademark of Llewellyn Worldwide Ltd.
2143 Wooddale Drive, Woodbury, MN 55125-2989 USA
Moon Sign Book® is registered in U.S. Patent and Trademark Office.
Moon Sign Book is a trademark of Llewellyn Worldwide Ltd. (Canada).

Llewellyn Publications
A Division of Llewellyn Worldwide Ltd.
2143 Wooddale Drive
Woodbury, MN 55125-2989
www.llewellyn.com

Printed in the United States of America

The Methods of the
Moon Sign Book

Whether we live in simple, primitive times or a time of high technology and mass communication, we need our connection to Mother Nature and an understanding of how all of her systems work together—soil, sun, wind, water, plants, animals, people, and planets.

The connections among elements of nature become especially relevant when we recognize that many energies—both subtle and obvious—flow through our world and affect all things. Ancient civilizations knew about these changing energies and were much more attuned to the subtle effects that they had on us.

In the world of unseen energies, it has long been accepted in many quarters that the position of the planets makes a difference in the energy flowing around planet Earth. Those who question these energy flows are often sadly divorced from nature.

Imagine placing a large rock in the waters of a flowing stream or creek. Immediately you would notice numerous changes in the flow of the water moving over, around, and past the rock.

It is no different with our solar system. We live on a planet that floats in a solar sea of energies and frequency waves. As the planets move around the sun, the currents of energy flowing through the solar sea change in the same way that flowing water changes around the rock placed in a creek or stream…and we are affected by those changes at every level—physically, mentally, emotionally, and spiritually.

The ability to detect these changes and their effect on us has long been organized into knowledge systems, and the *Moon Sign Book* has always been a stable anchor in maintaining this knowledge and recognizing its importance. We call these organized methods of gaining knowledge *astrology*, and ancient cultures around the globe used this as their science. It was how they found and maintained a sense of prediction, control, and security, something we are still striving for even today as we try to anticipate the cycles and events of our daily lives.

Although there are several ways of organizing and assessing these energy flows based on planetary positions, the *Moon Sign Book* uses the tropical system, which says that spring officially begins when the Sun is directly over the equator at noon, something that occurs around March 20 to 21 every year. Once that moment has been determined, the rest of the zodiac calendar is laid out at thirty-degree intervals. This allows us to be precise, but also flex with the changing nature of all things, including our solar system. We support a knowledge base that upholds the ancient wisdom and teaches it to all who are interested. We invite you to read what we have written here and to celebrate the interactions of these energies with the plants, animals, earth, and stars that share this time and space with us.

Weekly Almanac

Your Guide to
Lunar Gardening
& Good Timing for Activities

♑ January

December 26–January 1

When the whole world is silent, even one voice becomes
powerful.   ~MALALA YOUSAFZAI

Date	Qtr.	Sign	Activity
Dec. 28, 4:16 pm– Dec. 30, 6:08 pm	4th	Scorpio	Plant biennials, perennials, bulbs and roots. Prune. Irrigate. Fertilize (organic).

Even if it's chilly, it's important to get outside in the sun as much as you can. It helps your body make vitamin D, something that's essential to boosting low moods and building strong bones. It will properly set your circadian rhythm, resulting in restful sleep. It can even improve immune systems. Just be sure to wear some sunscreen! You'll still reap the benefits.

December 26
9:24 pm EST

JANUARY

S	M	T	W	T	F	S
						1
2	3	4	5	6	7	8
9	10	11	12	13	14	15
16	17	18	19	20	21	22
23	24	25	26	27	28	29
30	31					

January 2–8   ♑

In the depth of winter, I finally learned that there was in me
an invincible summer.   ~ALBERT CAMUS

Date	Qtr.	Sign	Activity
Jan. 2, 1:33 pm– Jan. 3, 5:44 pm	1st	Capricorn	Graft or bud plants. Trim to increase growth.
Jan. 5, 7:17 pm– Jan. 8, 12:26 am	1st	Pisces	Plant grains, leafy annuals. Fertilize (chemical). Graft or bud plants. Irrigate. Trim to increase growth.

Go to the hardware store and get some potting soil, a couple
of pots at least 12 inches deep, and some herbs and flower
seeds. Fill the pots with soil and plant the flowers in one pot, the
herbs in the other. The flowers will germinate within a week, the
herbs will take up to three weeks, and you'll feel that winter is
over. You'll also have a head start on your garden!

_____

_____

_____

_____

●
January 2
1:33 pm EST

JANUARY

S	M	T	W	T	F	S
						1
2	3	4	5	6	7	8
9	10	11	12	13	14	15
16	17	18	19	20	21	22
23	24	25	26	27	28	29
30	31					

♉ January 9–15

This is the world of light and speech, and I shall take leave to tell you that you are very dear.   ~GEORGE ELIOT

Date	Qtr.	Sign	Activity
Jan. 10, 9:47 am – Jan. 12, 10:08 pm	2nd	Taurus	Plant annuals for hardiness. Trim to increase growth.
Jan. 15, 11:11 am– Jan. 17, 6:48 pm	2nd	Cancer	Plant grains, leafy annuals. Fertilize (chemical). Graft or bud plants. Irrigate. Trim to increase growth.

Read a book on the history, myths, and culture of a different people in another part of the world. Their stories range from amazing to gripping, and you will learn a lot about issues that we all face as well as how other people see the world.

◑

January 9
1:11 pm EST

JANUARY

S	M	T	W	T	F	S
						1
2	3	4	5	6	7	8
9	10	11	12	13	14	15
16	17	18	19	20	21	22
23	24	25	26	27	28	29
30	31					

January 16–22 ♑

I am out with lanterns, looking for myself.

~EMILY DICKINSON

Date	Qtr.	Sign	Activity
Jan. 17, 6:48 pm– Jan. 17, 11:03 pm	3rd	Cancer	Plant biennials, perennials, bulbs and roots. Prune. Irrigate. Fertilize (organic).
Jan. 17, 11:03 pm– Jan. 20, 9:02 am	3rd	Leo	Cultivate. Destroy weeds and pests. Harvest fruits and root crops for food. Trim to retard growth.
Jan. 20, 9:02 am– Jan. 22, 5:03 pm	3rd	Virgo	Cultivate, especially medicinal plants. Destroy weeds and pests. Trim to retard growth.

Air plants are great starter plants! You can put them in any sort of a container or even open on a shelf, since they don't need soil. Choose a room that doesn't get too cold or hot. Keep them near a sunny window but not in direct sunlight. Soak them in room temperature water for a few hours every two weeks; add fertilizer in spring and fall. Let them dry thoroughly on a towel afterward.

○
January 17
6:48 pm EST

JANUARY

S	M	T	W	T	F	S
						1
2	3	4	5	6	7	8
9	10	11	12	13	14	15
16	17	18	19	20	21	22
23	24	25	26	27	28	29
30	31					

∼∼∼ **January 23–January 29**

Courage doesn't always roar. Sometimes courage is the quiet voice at the end of the day saying, (whispering), "I will try again tomorrow."
                                    ∼MARY ANNE RADMACHER

Date	Qtr.	Sign	Activity
Jan. 24, 10:57 pm– Jan. 25, 8:41 am	3rd	Scorpio	Plant biennials, perennials, bulbs and roots. Prune. Irrigate. Fertilize (organic).
Jan. 25, 8:41 am– Jan. 27, 2:34 am	4th	Scorpio	Plant biennials, perennials, bulbs and roots. Prune. Irrigate. Fertilize (organic).
Jan. 27, 2:34 am– Jan. 29, 4:09 am	4th	Sagittarius	Cultivate. Destroy weeds and pests. Harvest fruits and root crops for food. Trim to retard growth.
Jan. 29, 4:09 am– Jan. 31, 4:43 am	4th	Capricorn	Plant potatoes and tubers. Trim to retard growth.

Treat yourself to a spa day at home by buying a luxury conditioner for your hair, putting it on, and combing it through. Soak your feet in warm water with a few drops of lavender oil while you let the conditioner work on your hair. You'll feel renewed from head to toe.

_____

_____

_____

_____

January 25
8:41 am EST

JANUARYY

S	M	T	W	T	F	S
						1
2	3	4	5	6	7	8
9	10	11	12	13	14	15
16	17	18	19	20	21	22
23	24	25	26	27	28	29
30	31					

February ≈≈

January 30–February 5

One's friends are that part of the human race with which one
can be human. ~GEORGE SANTAYANA

Date	Qtr.	Sign	Activity
Jan. 31, 4:43 am– Feb. 1, 12:46 am	4th	Aquarius	Cultivate. Destroy weeds and pests. Harvest fruits and root crops for food. Trim to retard growth.
Feb. 2, 6:00 am– Feb. 4, 9:57 am	1st	Pisces	Plant grains, leafy annuals. Fertilize (chemical). Graft or bud plants. Irrigate. Trim to increase growth.

If you happen to have some seashells on hand from past vacations, take them out of the box and give them a vibrant makeover. Using paints in kaleidoscopic hues or metallics to make them modern, paint swirls and stripes all over the shells. Then show them off in a bowl, a vase, or in a pot alongside a houseplant.

●

February 1
12:46 am EST

FEBRUARY

S	M	T	W	T	F	S
		1	2	3	4	5
6	7	8	9	10	11	12
13	14	15	16	17	18	19
20	21	22	23	24	25	26
27	28					

〰 February 6–12

I have been impressed with the urgency of doing. Knowing is not enough; we must apply. Being willing is not enough; we must do.   ～LEONARDO DA VINCI

Date	Qtr.	Sign	Activity
Feb. 6, 5:52 pm– Feb. 8, 8:50 am	1st	Taurus	Plant annuals for hardiness. Trim to increase growth.
Feb. 8, 8:50 am– Feb. 9, 5:27 am	2nd	Taurus	Plant annuals for hardiness. Trim to increase growth.
Feb. 11, 6:27 pm– Feb. 14, 6:17 am	2nd	Cancer	Plant grains, leafy annuals. Fertilize (chemical). Graft or bud plants. Irrigate. Trim to increase growth.

Want more birds in your life? Support your local insect population, which provides them with a lot of their food, especially in nesting season. By planting native plants that insects are more likely to be able to eat, removing unnecessary non-native species, and laying off the pesticides, you create a bug-friendly— and therefore bird-friendly—habitat!

◐
February 8
8:50 am EST

FEBRUARY

S	M	T	W	T	F	S
		1	2	3	4	5
6	7	8	9	10	11	12
13	14	15	16	17	18	19
20	21	22	23	24	25	26
27	28					

February 13–19 〜〜〜

Limit your "always" and your "nevers."

~AMY POEHLER

Date	Qtr.	Sign	Activity
Feb. 16, 11:56 am– Feb. 16, 3:42 pm	3rd	Leo	Cultivate. Destroy weeds and pests. Harvest fruits and root crops for food. Trim to retard growth.
Feb. 16, 3:42 pm– Feb. 18, 10:51 pm	3rd	Virgo	Cultivate, especially medicinal plants. Destroy weeds and pests. Trim to retard growth.

Ferns are vibrantly green, resilient plants that look lovely indoors and out. Although there are thousands of fern varieties in the world, maidenhair ferns and staghorn ferns often do well inside while Boston ferns and Japanese painted ferns love the outdoors. Plant several of them together in dappled shade to make your backyard look like a forest glen, or give one the spotlight in an indoor pot.

○
February 16
11:56 am EST

FEBRUARY

S	M	T	W	T	F	S
		1	2	3	4	5
6	7	8	9	10	11	12
13	14	15	16	17	18	19
20	21	22	23	24	25	26
27	28					

♓ February 20–26

*The decision to make the present moment into your friend is
the end of the ego.* ~ECKHART TOLLE

Date	Qtr.	Sign	Activity
Feb. 21, 4:19 am– Feb. 23, 8:29 am	3rd	Scorpio	Plant biennials, perennials, bulbs and roots. Prune. Irrigate. Fertilize (organic).
Feb. 23, 8:29 am– Feb. 23, 5:32 pm	3rd	Sagittarius	Cultivate. Destroy weeds and pests. Harvest fruits and root crops for food. Trim to retard growth.
Feb. 23, 5:32 pm– Feb. 25, 11:27 am	4th	Sagittarius	Cultivate. Destroy weeds and pests. Harvest fruits and root crops for food. Trim to retard growth.
Feb. 25, 11:27 am– Feb. 27, 1:36 pm	4th	Capricorn	Plant potatoes and tubers. Trim to retard growth.

If you sew, make several old-fashioned kitchen aprons that are simple yet attractive. Cooking and kitchen duties seem easier and you'll find you do a better and more complete job when you have the right "uniform." Aprons also make good gifts for Christmas and birthdays.

_____

_____

_____

_____

◑
*February 23
5:32 pm EST*

FEBRUARY

S	M	T	W	T	F	S
		1	2	3	4	5
6	7	8	9	10	11	12
13	14	15	16	17	18	19
20	21	22	23	24	25	26
27	28					

March ♓

February 27–March 5

Nature gives to every time and season some beauties of its own.   ∼Charles Dickens

Date	Qtr.	Sign	Activity
Feb. 27, 1:36 pm–Mar. 1, 3:53 pm	4th	Aquarius	Cultivate. Destroy weeds and pests. Harvest fruits and root crops for food. Trim to retard growth.
Mar. 1, 3:53 pm–Mar. 2, 12:35 pm	4th	Pisces	Plant biennials, perennials, bulbs and roots. Prune. Irrigate. Fertilize (organic).
Mar. 2, 12:35 pm–Mar. 3, 7:52 pm	1st	Pisces	Plant grains, leafy annuals. Fertilize (chemical). Graft or bud plants. Irrigate. Trim to increase growth.

It may be tempting to buy all your garden supplies from online marketplaces, but keep in mind that it's also great to support your local mom-and-pop garden shops. Unlike a website, experienced staff will be on hand to answer any of your questions, and you'll feel good knowing that you're supporting a small business.

March 2
12:35 pm EST

March

S	M	T	W	T	F	S
		1	2	3	4	5
6	7	8	9	10	11	12
13	14	15	16	17	18	19
20	21	22	23	24	25	26
27	28	29	30	31		

March 6–12

Never limit yourself because of others' limited imagination;
never limit others because of your own limited imagination.

~Mae Jemison

Date	Qtr.	Sign	Activity
Mar. 6, 3:00 am–Mar. 8, 1:40 pm	1st	Taurus	Plant annuals for hardiness. Trim to increase growth.
Mar. 11, 2:24 am–Mar. 13, 3:32 pm	2nd	Cancer	Plant grains, leafy annuals. Fertilize (chemical). Graft or bud plants. Irrigate. Trim to increase growth.

Several vegetables can be grown from leftover ends, including carrot tops, green onion roots and bulbs, and the bottoms of celery bunches. Put these in a dish with an inch or two of water (don't drown them!) until they start showing fresh growth, then transfer to a pot of soil. Once they've outgrown the pot, you can put them outside if it's warm enough, or continue to grow them in larger containers indoors.

_____

_____

_____

_____

◐
March 10
5:45 am EST

MARCH

S	M	T	W	T	F	S
		1	2	3	4	5
6	7	8	9	10	11	12
13	14	15	16	17	18	19
20	21	22	23	24	25	26
27	28	29	30	31		

March 13–19 ♓

The challenge is not to be perfect. It's to be whole.

~JANE FONDA

Date	Qtr.	Sign	Activity
Mar. 18, 3:18 am– Mar. 18, 7:26 am	3rd	Virgo	Cultivate, especially medicinal plants. Destroy weeds and pests. Trim to retard growth.

If you're searching for something new to collect, how about vintage photos? They tend to be inexpensive and can be easily found at flea markets and antique stores. Even if you don't know the people in the photos, it's fun to imagine what their lives were like. Group several of them together on a wall for visual impact, tuck them in among tchotchkes, or hang them alongside vintage oil paintings for a unique gallery wall.

*Daylight Saving Time
begins March 13, 2:00 am*

○
*March 18
3:18 am EDT*

MARCH

S	M	T	W	T	F	S
		1	2	3	4	5
6	7	8	9	10	11	12
13	14	15	16	17	18	19
20	21	22	23	24	25	26
27	28	29	30	31		

♈ **March 20–26**

*I think Nature's imagination is so much greater than man's,
she's never going to let us relax!*   ~RICHARD FEYNMAN

Date	Qtr.	Sign	Activity
Mar. 20, 11:45 am– Mar. 22, 2:59 pm	3rd	Scorpio	Plant biennials, perennials, bulbs and roots. Prune. Irrigate. Fertilize (organic).
Mar. 22, 2:59 pm– Mar. 24, 5:54 pm	3rd	Sagittarius	Cultivate. Destroy weeds and pests. Harvest fruits and root crops for food. Trim to retard growth.
Mar. 24, 5:54 pm– Mar. 25, 1:37 am	3rd	Capricorn	Plant potatoes and tubers. Trim to retard growth.
Mar. 25, 1:37 am– Mar. 26, 8:55 pm	4th	Capricorn	Plant potatoes and tubers. Trim to retard growth.
Mar. 26, 8:55 pm– Mar. 29, 12:32 am	4th	Aquarius	Cultivate. Destroy weeds and pests. Harvest fruits and root crops for food. Trim to retard growth.

Exercise is nonnegotiable because it generates electricity in the body that powers the thousands of chemical transactions that must go on every day. Create a small stretch and exercise program for yourself and stick to it. Even if it's only 15 minutes, you'll feel like a different person!

March 25
1:37 am EDT

MARCH

S	M	T	W	T	F	S
		1	2	3	4	5
6	7	8	9	10	11	12
13	14	15	16	17	18	19
20	21	22	23	24	25	26
27	28	29	30	31		

April ♈

March 27–April 2

Most powerful is he who has himself in his own power.

~Lucius Annaeus Seneca

Date	Qtr.	Sign	Activity
Mar. 29, 12:32 am–Mar. 31, 5:30 am	4th	Pisces	Plant biennials, perennials, bulbs and roots. Prune. Irrigate. Fertilize (organic).
Mar. 31, 5:30 am–Apr. 1, 2:24 am	4th	Aries	Cultivate. Destroy weeds and pests. Harvest fruits and root crops for food. Trim to retard growth.
Apr. 2, 12:50 pm–Apr. 4, 11:04 pm	1st	Taurus	Plant annuals for hardiness. Trim to increase growth.

If you have a small business that you run from the kitchen table, consider creating a small office area that is bright, uncluttered, and has everything you need to smoothly handle the "business" end of the business—a desk or table, comfortable chair, wired internet connection, perhaps a cupboard, drawers, and shelves.

●

April 1
2:24 am EDT

APRIL

S	M	T	W	T	F	S
					1	2
3	4	5	6	7	8	9
10	11	12	13	14	15	16
17	18	19	20	21	22	23
24	25	26	27	28	29	30

♈ **April 3–9**

Never forget that justice is what love looks like in public.

~Dr. Cornel West

Date	Qtr.	Sign	Activity
Apr. 7, 11:30 am– Apr. 9, 2:48 am	1st	Cancer	Plant grains, leafy annuals. Fertilize (chemical). Graft or bud plants. Irrigate. Trim to increase growth.
Apr. 9, 2:48 am– Apr. 10, 12:00 am	2nd	Cancer	Plant grains, leafy annuals. Fertilize (chemical). Graft or bud plants. Irrigate. Trim to increase growth.

You may be surprised to learn that there's another floral scent beyond lavender that can alleviate feelings of depression and anxiety. The scent of rose has been scientifically proven to gently lift and soften moods. Use rose essential oil in a diffuser. Light a rose-scented candle as soon as you wake up. Drop rose petals into a bath or walk out to your backyard to literally stop and smell the roses.

_____

_____

_____

_____

◑

April 9
2:48 am EDT

APRIL

S	M	T	W	T	F	S
					1	2
3	4	5	6	7	8	9
10	11	12	13	14	15	16
17	18	19	20	21	22	23
24	25	26	27	28	29	30

April 10–16 ♈

*Like art, revolutions come from combining what exists into
what has never existed before.*   ∼GLORIA STEINEM

Date	Qtr.	Sign	Activity
Apr. 14, 4:46 pm– Apr. 16, 2:55 pm	2nd	Libra	Plant annuals for fragrance and beauty. Trim to increase growth.
Apr. 16, 8:23 pm– Apr. 18, 10:16 pm	3rd	Scorpio	Plant biennials, perennials, bulbs and roots. Prune. Irrigate. Fertilize (organic).

If you find a nest of baby rabbits in the spring and you think they may be abandoned, put a circle of flour or a tic-tac-toe of yarn around them. The mother will disturb the yarn or flour when she returns. If it has not been disturbed after twenty-four hours, call a wildlife rehabilitation center and ask whether to bring them in. Baby rabbits are very fragile and should only be cared for by professionals.

_____

_____

_____

○
April 16
2:55 pm EDT

APRIL

S	M	T	W	T	F	S
					1	2
3	4	5	6	7	8	9
10	11	12	13	14	15	16
17	18	19	20	21	22	23
24	25	26	27	28	29	30

♈ April 17–23

For solitude sometimes is best society.   ∼JOHN MILTON

Date	Qtr.	Sign	Activity
Apr. 18, 10:16 pm– Apr. 20, 11:52 pm	3rd	Sagittarius	Cultivate. Destroy weeds and pests. Harvest fruits and root crops for food. Trim to retard growth.
Apr. 20, 11:52 pm– Apr. 23, 2:17 am	3rd	Capricorn	Plant potatoes and tubers. Trim to retard growth.
Apr. 23, 2:17 am– Apr. 23, 7:56 am	3rd	Aquarius	Cultivate. Destroy weeds and pests. Harvest fruits and root crops for food. Trim to retard growth.
Apr. 23, 7:56 am– Apr. 25, 6:15 am	4th	Aquarius	Cultivate. Destroy weeds and pests. Harvest fruits and root crops for food. Trim to retard growth.

A fairy garden is simply magical, and it's fun to imagine those little beings visiting your own backyard, even if its most frequent visitors might be ladybugs and butterflies. Starting with a planter and fairy-garden-friendly plants like succulents and mini violets, look for small objects around your house to complete the whimsy. Think childhood dollhouse furniture, miniature animal figurines, and multicolored glass pebbles.

◑
April 23
7:56 am EDT

APRIL

S	M	T	W	T	F	S
					1	2
3	4	5	6	7	8	9
10	11	12	13	14	15	16
17	18	19	20	21	22	23
24	25	26	27	28	29	30

April 24–30 ♉

Do something today that communicates to your body that you desire to care for it. Tomorrow is not promised.

~JADA PINKETT SMITH

Date	Qtr.	Sign	Activity
Apr. 25, 6:15 am– Apr. 27, 12:10 pm	4th	Pisces	Plant biennials, perennials, bulbs and roots. Prune. Irrigate. Fertilize (organic).
Apr. 27, 12:10 pm– Apr. 29, 8:19 pm	4th	Aries	Cultivate. Destroy weeds and pests. Harvest fruits and root crops for food. Trim to retard growth.
Apr. 29, 8:19 pm– Apr. 30, 4:28 pm	4th	Taurus	Plant potatoes and tubers. Trim to retard growth.
Apr. 30, 4:28 pm– May 2, 6:47 am	1st	Taurus	Plant annuals for hardiness. Trim to increase growth.

Once a month, plan a meal in which you set the table with table linens and flowers. Cook from a thoughtful, healthy menu, invite spouse, child, or friend to share, and eat slowly and without hurry. You will discover the joy of what it means to share food and life.

●

April 30
4:28 pm EDT

APRIL

S	M	T	W	T	F	S
					1	2
3	4	5	6	7	8	9
10	11	12	13	14	15	16
17	18	19	20	21	22	23
24	25	26	27	28	29	30

♉ May

May 1–7

The best time to plant a tree was twenty years ago. The second best time is now.   ~CHINESE PROVERB

Date	Qtr.	Sign	Activity
May 4, 7:05 pm– May 7, 7:50 am	1st	Cancer	Plant grains, leafy annuals. Fertilize (chemical). Graft or bud plants. Irrigate. Trim to increase growth.

Many botanical gardens and arboretums hold classes for the public. Sign up for a class and you'll get the chance to soak up knowledge from a master gardener who will share tips and tricks you can take home with you. Your backyard might look just as stunning as your favorite botanical garden in no time.

_____

_____

_____

_____

MAY

S	M	T	W	T	F	S
	1	2	3	4	5	6	7
8	9	10	11	12	13	14
15	16	17	18	19	20	21
22	23	24	25	26	27	28
29	30	31				

May 8–14

Stay close to any sounds that make you glad you are alive.

~HAFEZ

Date	Qtr.	Sign	Activity
May 12, 2:34 am–May 14, 6:34 am	2nd	Libra	Plant annuals for fragrance and beauty. Trim to increase growth.
May 14, 6:34 am–May 16, 12:14 am	2nd	Scorpio	Plant grains, leafy annuals. Fertilize (chemical). Graft or bud plants. Irrigate. Trim to increase growth.

Make a porch area something special by painting the floor a soothing color, arranging a wicker rocker and small table on it, and filling the surrounding space with potted trees and plants. You'll have a retreat area that is cool, restful, and always inviting.

May 8
8:21 pm EDT

MAY

S	M	T	W	T	F	S
1	2	3	4	5	6	7
8	9	10	11	12	13	14
15	16	17	18	19	20	21
22	23	24	25	26	27	28
29	30	31				

May 15–21

Sadness is but a wall between two gardens.

~KHALIL GIBRAN

Date	Qtr.	Sign	Activity
May 16, 12:14 am– May 16, 7:50 am	3rd	Scorpio	Plant biennials, perennials, bulbs and roots. Prune. Irrigate. Fertilize (organic).
May 16, 7:50 am– May 18, 8:02 am	3rd	Sagittarius	Cultivate. Destroy weeds and pests. Harvest fruits and root crops for food. Trim to retard growth.
May 18, 8:02 am– May 20, 8:53 am	3rd	Capricorn	Plant potatoes and tubers. Trim to retard growth.
May 20, 8:53 am– May 22, 11:49 am	3rd	Aquarius	Cultivate. Destroy weeds and pests. Harvest fruits and root crops for food. Trim to retard growth.

Instead of coating yourself in chemical-heavy bug spray before gardening or heading out for a hike, consider dabbing on an essential oil instead. On your pulse points, paying special attention to your ankles, use cedarwood or lavender essential oils or lemon eucalyptus oil (not essential oil) to keep those bugs at bay. It'll smell great to you but not so great to the insects.

_____

_____

_____

_____

○
May 16
12:14 am EDT

MAY

S	M	T	W	T	F	S
1	2	3	4	5	6	7
8	9	10	11	12	13	14
15	16	17	18	19	20	21
22	23	24	25	26	27	28
29	30	31				

May 22–May 28 ♊

Whatever the problem, be part of the solution. Don't just sit around raising questions and pointing out obstacles.

~TINA FEY

Date	Qtr.	Sign	Activity
May 22, 11:49 am– May 22, 2:43 pm	3rd	Pisces	Plant biennials, perennials, bulbs and roots. Prune. Irrigate. Fertilize (organic).
May 22, 2:43 pm– May 24, 5:39 pm	4th	Pisces	Plant biennials, perennials, bulbs and roots. Prune. Irrigate. Fertilize (organic).
May 24, 5:39 pm– May 27, 2:22 am	4th	Aries	Cultivate. Destroy weeds and pests. Harvest fruits and root crops for food. Trim to retard growth.
May 27, 2:22 am– May 29, 1:23 pm	4th	Taurus	Plant potatoes and tubers. Trim to retard growth.

Learn something about our planet this year. Study the stars, oceans, perhaps geological history, the sun, rivers, mountains, or anything that presents a new set of facts and information. Start with books that are mostly pictures and progress to books with more substantial information in them.

◑
May 22
2:43 pm EDT

MAY

S	M	T	W	T	F	S
1	2	3	4	5	6	7
8	9	10	11	12	13	14
15	16	17	18	19	20	21
22	23	24	25	26	27	28
29	30	31				

♊ June

May 29–June 4

A surplus of effort could overcome a deficit of confidence.

~SONIA SOTOMAYOR

Date	Qtr.	Sign	Activity
May 29, 1:23 pm– May 30, 7:30 am	4th	Gemini	Cultivate. Destroy weeds and pests. Harvest fruits and root crops for food. Trim to retard growth.
Jun. 1, 1:49 am– Jun. 3, 2:38 pm	1st	Cancer	Plant grains, leafy annuals. Fertilize (chemical). Graft or bud plants. Irrigate. Trim to increase growth.

To create a quick and easy compost container for large amounts of compost, get four wood pallets and stand them on their ends in a square, open end facing up. Drive T-posts into the ground in the space between the two layers of wood in each pallet, at least two posts per pallet. You can still stir the compost from outside; if you need to remove a large amount of compost, just remove one pallet.

_____

_____

_____

_____

●
May 30
7:30 am EDT

JUNE

S	M	T	W	T	F	S
			1	2	3	4
5	6	7	8	9	10	11
12	13	14	15	16	17	18
19	20	21	22	23	24	25
26	27	28	29	30		

June 5–11 ♊

Few things help an individual more than to place responsibility upon him, and to let him know that you trust him.

~Booker T. Washington

Date	Qtr.	Sign	Activity
Jun. 8, 11:23 am–Jun. 10, 4:41 pm	2nd	Libra	Plant annuals for fragrance and beauty. Trim to increase growth.
Jun. 10, 4:41 pm–Jun. 12, 6:31 pm	2nd	Scorpio	Plant grains, leafy annuals. Fertilize (chemical). Graft or bud plants. Irrigate. Trim to increase growth.

Many people have trouble sleeping during the three days before the full moon. Instead of tossing, turning, and feeling frustrated, roll onto your back and practice healing yourself by breathing slowly and deeply into various areas of your body, envisioning those areas filled with beautiful golden light and feeling bones, muscles, and organs relax.

◐

June 7
10:48 am EDT

June

S	M	T	W	T	F	S
			1	2	3	4
5	6	7	8	9	10	11
12	13	14	15	16	17	18
19	20	21	22	23	24	25
26	27	28	29	30		

♊ June 12–18

I need to listen well so that I hear what is not said.

~Thuli Madonsela

Date	Qtr.	Sign	Activity
Jun. 14, 7:52 am– Jun. 14, 6:14 pm	3rd	Sagittarius	Cultivate. Destroy weeds and pests. Harvest fruits and root crops for food. Trim to retard growth.
Jun. 14, 6:14 pm– Jun. 16, 5:44 pm	3rd	Capricorn	Plant potatoes and tubers. Trim to retard growth.
Jun. 16, 5:44 pm– Jun. 18, 7:01 pm	3rd	Aquarius	Cultivate. Destroy weeds and pests. Harvest fruits and root crops for food. Trim to retard growth.
Jun. 18, 7:01 pm– Jun. 20, 11:11 pm	3rd	Pisces	Plant biennials, perennials, bulbs and roots. Prune. Irrigate. Fertilize (organic).

To make it feel as if you've added another room onto your house, consider creating an outdoor living room. Taking it beyond basic patio furniture, decorate a deck or veranda with an upholstered, waterproof sofa, a footstool or two, side tables with tabletop décor, an outdoor rug, and perhaps even a bar cart for a twilight cocktail hour.

○
June 14
7:52 am EDT

JUNE

S	M	T	W	T	F	S
			1	2	3	4
5	6	7	8	9	10	11
12	13	14	15	16	17	18
19	20	21	22	23	24	25
26	27	28	29	30		

June 19–25 ♊

*Give me but one firm spot on which to stand, and I shall move
the earth.*   ~ARCHIMEDES

Date	Qtr.	Sign	Activity
Jun. 20, 11:11 pm– Jun. 20, 11:37 pm	4th	Pisces	Plant biennials, perennials, bulbs and roots. Prune. Irrigate. Fertilize (organic).
Jun. 20, 11:37 pm– Jun. 23, 7:58 am	4th	Aries	Cultivate. Destroy weeds and pests. Harvest fruits and root crops for food. Trim to retard growth.
Jun. 23, 7:58 am– Jun. 25, 7:13 pm	4th	Taurus	Plant potatoes and tubers. Trim to retard growth.
Jun. 25, 7:13 pm– Jun. 28, 7:53 am	4th	Gemini	Cultivate. Destroy weeds and pests. Harvest fruits and root crops for food. Trim to retard growth.

Feel stressed, anxious, or otherwise ungrounded? Go outside and start counting individual species of plant, fungus, and animal that you see. It doesn't matter if you don't know all their names; just notice what makes each one unique from the rest. This will help to distract you from whatever's got you worked up, and it helps you get to know your nearby nature better!

◑
June 20
11:11 pm EDT

JUNE

S	M	T	W	T	F	S
			1	2	3	4
5	6	7	8	9	10	11
12	13	14	15	16	17	18
19	20	21	22	23	24	25
26	27	28	29	30		

♋ July

June 26–July 2

When you are inspired by some great purpose, some extraordinary project, all your thoughts break their bonds.

.~~Patanjali

Date	Qtr.	Sign	Activity
Jun. 28, 7:53 am– Jun. 28, 10:52 pm	4th	Cancer	Plant biennials, perennials, bulbs and roots. Prune. Irrigate. Fertilize (organic).
Jun. 28, 10:52 pm– Jun. 30, 8:40 pm	1st	Cancer	Plant grains, leafy annuals. Fertilize (chemical). Graft or bud plants. Irrigate. Trim to increase growth.

When the garden is producing cucumbers prodigiously, consider making a small batch of sweet pickles using a favorite family recipe. Skip the canning in order to preserve top-quality nutrition. They will keep in the fridge for weeks and remain crunchy and fresh.

●

June 28
10:52 pm EDT

			July			
S	M	T	W	T	F	S
					1	2
3	4	5	6	7	8	9
10	11	12	13	14	15	16
17	18	19	20	21	22	23
24	25	26	27	28	29	30
31						

July 3–9 ♋

The sun, with all those planets revolving around it and
dependent upon it, can still ripen a bunch of grapes as if it
had nothing else in the universe to do.   ~GALILEO GALILEI

Date	Qtr.	Sign	Activity
Jul. 5, 6:25 pm– Jul. 6, 10:14 pm	1st	Libra	Plant annuals for fragrance and beauty. Trim to increase growth.
Jul. 6, 10:14 pm– Jul. 8, 1:15 am	2nd	Libra	Plant annuals for fragrance and beauty. Trim to increase growth.
Jul. 8, 1:15 am– Jul. 10, 4:34 am	2nd	Scorpio	Plant grains, leafy annuals. Fertilize (chemical). Graft or bud plants. Irrigate. Trim to increase growth.

Garden orbs are a wonderful way to add interest to your garden without overwhelming the visuals. You can always buy vintage orbs (easily found at most flea markets) or you can purchase new ones at home goods stores. Drape them in solar fairy lights, vary the sizes, and space out several of them for a modern, eye-catching vibe.

◖

July 6
10:14 pm EDT

JULY

S	M	T	W	T	F	S
					1	2
3	4	5	6	7	8	9
10	11	12	13	14	15	16
17	18	19	20	21	22	23
24	25	26	27	28	29	30
31						

July 10–16

I have only to break into the tightness of a strawberry, and I see summer—its dust and lowering skies.

~ Toni Morrison

Date	Qtr.	Sign	Activity
Jul. 12, 5:01 am– Jul. 13, 2:38 pm	2nd	Capricorn	Graft or bud plants. Trim to increase growth.
Jul. 13, 2:38 pm– Jul. 14, 4:13 am	3rd	Capricorn	Plant potatoes and tubers. Trim to retard growth.
Jul. 14, 4:13 am– Jul. 16, 4:18 am	3rd	Aquarius	Cultivate. Destroy weeds and pests. Harvest fruits and root crops for food. Trim to retard growth.
Jul. 16, 4:18 am– Jul. 18, 7:17 am	3rd	Pisces	Plant biennials, perennials, bulbs and roots. Prune. Irrigate. Fertilize (organic).

Butterflies are expert pollinators, something our planet needs in order for all those gorgeous flowers and fruit trees to thrive. Welcome butterflies into your garden with blooms they're sure to love, like sedum, phlox, snapdragons, verbena, and coneflowers. The butterflies will enjoy the buffet of sweet treats as you sit back and watch them flit and flutter.

O
July 13
2:38 pm EDT

JULY

S	M	T	W	T	F	S
					1	2
3	4	5	6	7	8	9
10	11	12	13	14	15	16
17	18	19	20	21	22	23
24	25	26	27	28	29	30
31						

July 17–23 ♋

An expert is a person who has found out by his own painful experience all the mistakes that one can make in a very narrow field.

~NIELS BOHR

Date	Qtr.	Sign	Activity
Jul. 18, 7:17 am– Jul. 20, 10:19 am	3rd	Aries	Cultivate. Destroy weeds and pests. Harvest fruits and root crops for food. Trim to retard growth.
Jul. 20, 10:19 am– Jul. 20, 2:23 pm	4th	Aries	Cultivate. Destroy weeds and pests. Harvest fruits and root crops for food. Trim to retard growth.
Jul. 20, 2:23 pm– Jul. 23, 1:11 am	4th	Taurus	Plant potatoes and tubers. Trim to retard growth.
Jul. 23, 1:11 am– Jul. 25, 1:54 pm	4th	Gemini	Cultivate. Destroy weeds and pests. Harvest fruits and root crops for food. Trim to retard growth.

There are several ways to make a trellis pop, even without climbing flowers. If a trellis has seen better days, spray-paint it a bright turquoise or sunny yellow. Cover it in twinkling white lights. Hang a few vintage Christmas ornaments for a colorful look that'll inspire smiles all year round.

◐

July 20
10:19 am EDT

JULY

S	M	T	W	T	F	S
					1	2
3	4	5	6	7	8	9
10	11	12	13	14	15	16
17	18	19	20	21	22	23
24	25	26	27	28	29	30
31						

♌ July 24–July 30

True life is not lived where great external changes take place—where people move about, clash, fight, and slay one another—but it is lived only where these tiny, tiny, infinitesimally small changes occur.   ～Leo Tolstoy

Date	Qtr.	Sign	Activity
Jul. 25, 1:54 pm– Jul. 28, 2:36 am	4th	Cancer	Plant biennials, perennials, bulbs and roots. Prune. Irrigate. Fertilize (organic).
Jul. 28, 2:36 am– Jul. 28, 1:55 pm	4th	Leo	Cultivate. Destroy weeds and pests. Harvest fruits and root crops for food. Trim to retard growth.

Keep your technological skills current. Buy a computer and learn to use it. Buy new software and do something creative with it. Whether you write, work with photos, play with landscape design, or something else, there is software out there to help you avoid the pitfall of not keeping up with the time you live in.

●
July 28
1:55 pm EDT

July

S	M	T	W	T	F	S
					1	2
3	4	5	6	7	8	9
10	11	12	13	14	15	16
17	18	19	20	21	22	23
24	25	26	27	28	29	30
31						

August ♌

July 31–August 6

Art is a personal act of courage, something one human does
that creates change in another.   ～SETH GODIN

Date	Qtr.	Sign	Activity
Aug. 2, 12:06 am– Aug. 4, 7:47 am	1st	Libra	Plant annuals for fragrance and beauty. Trim to increase growth.
Aug. 4, 7:47 am– Aug. 5, 7:07 am	1st	Scorpio	Plant grains, leafy annuals. Fertilize (chemical). Graft or bud plants. Irrigate. Trim to increase growth.
Aug. 5, 7:07 am– Aug. 6, 12:39 pm	2nd	Scorpio	Plant grains, leafy annuals. Fertilize (chemical). Graft or bud plants. Irrigate. Trim to increase growth.

To transform your backyard into a peaceful oasis that feels far away from the rest of the world, create a bit more privacy. Metal screens with beautiful patterns are an option, along with planters complete with mini trellises and plants that climb, like clematis and morning glories. A bamboo screen or two is a way to add privacy with a tropical feel.

◐

August 5
7:07 am EDT

AUGUST

S	M	T	W	T	F	S
		1	2	3	4	5	6
7	8	9	10	11	12	13
14	15	16	17	18	19	20
21	22	23	24	25	26	27
28	29	30	31			

♌ August 7–13

Remember no effort that we make to attain something beautiful is ever lost. Sometime, somewhere, somehow we shall find that which we seek. ~HELEN KELLER

Date	Qtr.	Sign	Activity
Aug. 8, 2:39 pm– Aug. 10, 2:45 pm	2nd	Capricorn	Graft or bud plants. Trim to increase growth.
Aug. 11, 9:36 pm– Aug. 12, 2:44 pm	3rd	Aquarius	Cultivate. Destroy weeds and pests. Harvest fruits and root crops for food. Trim to retard growth.
Aug. 12, 2:44 pm– Aug. 14, 4:43 pm	3rd	Pisces	Plant biennials, perennials, bulbs and roots. Prune. Irrigate. Fertilize (organic).

Deer are beautiful animals, but keep your distance. Does with fawns can be very protective, and their hooves are sharp. In autumn rutting season, bucks may be more aggressive, including toward humans. Instead of feeding them, grow native plants that they like to eat, and keep your garden well fenced-off. Deer that are afraid of humans are less likely to be injured or killed by us, our dogs, and our cars.

○
August 11
9:36 pm EDT

AUGUST

S	M	T	W	T	F	S
	1	2	3	4	5	6
7	8	9	10	11	12	13
14	15	16	17	18	19	20
21	22	23	24	25	26	27
28	29	30	31			

August 14–20 ♌

And there is nothing which so instructs a reasonable creature
as the exercise and experience of many different things.

~CHRISTINE DE PIZAN

Date	Qtr.	Sign	Activity
Aug. 14, 4:43 pm– Aug. 16, 10:22 pm	3rd	Aries	Cultivate. Destroy weeds and pests. Harvest fruits and root crops for food. Trim to retard growth.
Aug. 16, 10:22 pm– Aug. 19, 12:36 am	3rd	Taurus	Plant potatoes and tubers. Trim to retard growth.
Aug. 19, 12:36 am– Aug. 19, 8:06 am	4th	Taurus	Plant potatoes and tubers. Trim to retard growth.
Aug. 19, 8:06 am– Aug. 21, 8:29 pm	4th	Gemini	Cultivate. Destroy weeds and pests. Harvest fruits and root crops for food. Trim to retard growth.

Before school starts, survey your space and then give yourself the best chance for success by creating a study and research space that is clean, uncluttered, and comfortable and has pens, pencils, internet hookups, a shelf for important references, and other things you will need.

◐

August 19
12:36 am EDT

AUGUST

S	M	T	W	T	F	S
	1	2	3	4	5	6
7	8	9	10	11	12	13
14	15	16	17	18	19	20
21	22	23	24	25	26	27
28	29	30	31			

♌ August 21–27

You can't fail if you do something and it doesn't work out.
That's success. Maybe it wasn't to the point of success where
you wanted to do it, but it's still success.

~SERENA WILLIAMS

Date	Qtr.	Sign	Activity
Aug. 21, 8:29 pm– Aug. 24, 9:09 am	4th	Cancer	Plant biennials, perennials, bulbs and roots. Prune. Irrigate. Fertilize (organic).
Aug. 24, 9:09 am– Aug. 26, 8:25 pm	4th	Leo	Cultivate. Destroy weeds and pests. Harvest fruits and root crops for food. Trim to retard growth.
Aug. 26, 8:25 pm– Aug. 27, 4:17 am	4th	Virgo	Cultivate, especially medicinal plants. Destroy weeds and pests. Trim to retard growth.

If you have a wooden floor that is looking beat up, consider renting a sander from your local hardware store. Give the floor a once-over with a fine-grit sandpaper, then cover with several coats of polyurethane. The transformation of the room will be amazing.

● *August 27*
4:17 am EDT

AUGUST

S	M	T	W	T	F	S
		1	2	3	4	5	6
7	8	9	10	11	12	13
14	15	16	17	18	19	20
21	22	23	24	25	26	27
28	29	30	31			

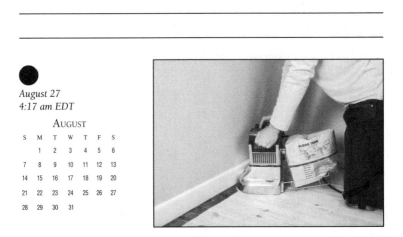

September ♍

August 28–September 3

Be there for others, but never leave yourself behind.

~Dodinsky

Date	Qtr.	Sign	Activity
Aug. 29, 5:45 am– Aug. 31, 1:11 pm	1st	Libra	Plant annuals for fragrance and beauty. Trim to increase growth.
Aug. 31, 1:11 pm– Sep. 2, 6:39 pm	1st	Scorpio	Plant grains, leafy annuals. Fertilize (chemical). Graft or bud plants. Irrigate. Trim to increase growth.

Rattan has been used in home décor for thousands of years, manifesting as popular furniture in the Victorian period and the 1970s. Today, it's back again, and you can decorate with it in many ways. Place a small rattan stool alongside your bathtub as a spot to hold bath salts and a dry brush. Display greenery in rattan planters. Find a rattan pendant light to weave a fresh, easygoing feel into a room.

◐

September 3
2:08 pm EDT

SEPTEMBER

S	M	T	W	T	F	S
				1	2	3
4	5	6	7	8	9	10
11	12	13	14	15	16	17
18	19	20	21	22	23	24
25	26	27	28	29	30	

♍ September 4–10

*Love is the voice under all silences, the hope which has
no opposite in fear; the strength so strong mere force is
feebleness: the truth more first than sun more last than star.*

~E. E. CUMMINGS

Date	Qtr.	Sign	Activity
Sep. 4, 10:03 pm– Sep. 6, 11:41 pm	2nd	Capricorn	Graft or bud plants. Trim to increase growth.
Sep. 9, 12:42 am– Sep. 10, 5:59 am	2nd	Pisces	Plant grains, leafy annuals. Fertilize (chemical). Graft or bud plants. Irrigate. Trim to increase growth.
Sep. 10, 5:59 am– Sep. 11, 2:47 am	3rd	Pisces	Plant biennials, perennials, bulbs and roots. Prune. Irrigate. Fertilize (organic).

Fall is a fabulous time for mushroom hunting! If you are lucky enough to find edible mushrooms, carry them out in a mesh bag so that you can spread spores as you go along, helping them increase their population. Either eat or preserve your mushrooms as soon as possible to protect both flavor and nutrients.

_____

_____

_____

_____

○
*September 10
5:59 am EDT*

SEPTEMBER

S	M	T	W	T	F	S
				1	2	3
4	5	6	7	8	9	10
11	12	13	14	15	16	17
18	19	20	21	22	23	24
25	26	27	28	29	30	

September 11–17 ♍

Time, as it grows old, teaches all things.   ~AESCHYLUS

Date	Qtr.	Sign	Activity
Sep. 11, 2:47 am– Sep. 13, 7:39 am	3rd	Aries	Cultivate. Destroy weeds and pests. Harvest fruits and root crops for food. Trim to retard growth.
Sep. 13, 7:39 am– Sep. 15, 4:16 pm	3rd	Taurus	Plant potatoes and tubers. Trim to retard growth.
Sep. 15, 4:16 pm– Sep. 17, 5:52 pm	3rd	Gemini	Cultivate. Destroy weeds and pests. Harvest fruits and root crops for food. Trim to retard growth.
Sep. 17, 5:52 pm– Sep. 18, 3:59 am	4th	Gemini	Cultivate. Destroy weeds and pests. Harvest fruits and root crops for food. Trim to retard growth.

If you have a small walkway area that gets muddy every time it rains, buy a bag of ready-mix cement and try your hand at making pavers or a small cement sidewalk. It's not difficult and is very rewarding because you don't have to walk through the mud anymore.

_____

_____

_____

_____

◗

September 17
5:52 pm EDT

SEPTEMBER

S	M	T	W	T	F	S
				1	2	3
4	5	6	7	8	9	10
11	12	13	14	15	16	17
18	19	20	21	22	23	24
25	26	27	28	29	30	

♍ September 18–24

Remember always that you have not only the right to be an individual; you have an obligation to be one.

~ELEANOR ROOSEVELT

Date	Qtr.	Sign	Activity
Sep. 18, 3:59 am– Sep. 20, 4:38 pm	4th	Cancer	Plant biennials, perennials, bulbs and roots. Prune. Irrigate. Fertilize (organic).
Sep. 20, 4:38 pm– Sep. 23, 3:53 am	4th	Leo	Cultivate. Destroy weeds and pests. Harvest fruits and root crops for food. Trim to retard growth.
Sep. 23, 3:53 am– Sep. 25, 12:43 pm	4th	Virgo	Cultivate, especially medicinal plants. Destroy weeds and pests. Trim to retard growth.

Your outdoor space isn't the only place for your beloved plants. Many varieties like the hardy snake plant or parlor palm are begging to be brought indoors. Place them on a bookshelf to green up your literary collection. Put them in brightly colored pots to punch up a neutral space. Use a set of wall planters to turn them into a work of art. Just be sure to give them plenty of water, sunlight, and love.

SEPTEMBER

S	M	T	W	T	F	S
				1	2	3
4	5	6	7	8	9	10
11	12	13	14	15	16	17
18	19	20	21	22	23	24
25	26	27	28	29	30	

October ♎

September 25–October 1

When we're growing up there are all sorts of people telling us what to do when really what we need is space to work out who to be.
                                                    ~ELLIOT PAGE

Date	Qtr.	Sign	Activity
Sep. 25, 5:55 pm– Sep. 27, 7:15 pm	1st	Libra	Plant annuals for fragrance and beauty. Trim to increase growth.
Sep. 27, 7:15 pm– Sep. 30, 12:03 am	1st	Scorpio	Plant grains, leafy annuals. Fertilize (chemical). Graft or bud plants. Irrigate. Trim to increase growth.

To boost your nutrition, learn to make green smoothies. Add 2–3 vegetables (spinach, carrot, cauliflower, or sprouts), 2–3 kinds of fruits (strawberries, peaches, blueberries, or banana), some yogurt, 1 tbsp. flaxseed oil, a dash of cinnamon, ½ tsp. spirulina, ¼ tsp. cardamom, and a bit of water if needed. Blend and drink!

●
September 25
5:55 pm EDT

OCTOBER

S	M	T	W	T	F	S
						1
2	3	4	5	6	7	8
9	10	11	12	13	14	15
16	17	18	19	20	21	22
23	24	25	26	27	28	29
30	31					

♎ October 2–8

I've dreamt in my life, dreams that have stayed with me ever after and changed my ideas; they've gone through and through me like wine through water, and altered the color of my mind.   ∼EMILY BRONTË

Date	Qtr.	Sign	Activity
Oct. 2, 3:38 am– Oct. 2, 8:14 pm	1st	Capricorn	Graft or bud plants. Trim to increase growth.
Oct. 2, 8:14 pm– Oct. 4, 6:20 am	2nd	Capricorn	Graft or bud plants. Trim to increase growth.
Oct. 6, 8:47 am– Oct. 8, 11:57 am	2nd	Pisces	Plant grains, leafy annuals. Fertilize (chemical). Graft or bud plants. Irrigate. Trim to increase growth.

Visit estate sales to look for old crocks, big pots, and old-fashioned double boilers used to make large batches of tomato sauce, jams and jellies, potions, lotions, and personal care products. You will be more self-sufficient and keep old skills alive.

_____

_____

_____

_____

◗
October 2
8:14 pm EDT

OCTOBER

S	M	T	W	T	F	S
						1
2	3	4	5	6	7	8
9	10	11	12	13	14	15
16	17	18	19	20	21	22
23	24	25	26	27	28	29
30	31					

October 9–15

All careers go up and down like friendships, like marriages,
like anything else, and you can't bat a thousand all the time.

~Julie Andrews

Date	Qtr.	Sign	Activity
Oct. 9, 4:55 pm–Oct. 10, 5:04 pm	3rd	Aries	Cultivate. Destroy weeds and pests. Harvest fruits and root crops for food. Trim to retard growth.
Oct. 10, 5:04 pm–Oct. 13, 1:08 am	3rd	Taurus	Plant potatoes and tubers. Trim to retard growth.
Oct. 13, 1:08 am–Oct. 15, 12:11 pm	3rd	Gemini	Cultivate. Destroy weeds and pests. Harvest fruits and root crops for food. Trim to retard growth.
Oct. 15, 12:11 pm–Oct. 17, 1:15 pm	3rd	Cancer	Plant biennials, perennials, bulbs and roots. Prune. Irrigate. Fertilize (organic).

After you dry the lavender from your garden, there are lots of things you can do with it. Add it to some homemade bath salts for a flower-filled, calming bath. Drop buds into a sachet to breathe in the soothing aroma even in the middle of winter. If it's edible, add it to a favorite cookie recipe for an unexpected flavor.

_____

_____

_____

_____

October 9
4:55 pm EDT

October

S	M	T	W	T	F	S
						1
2	3	4	5	6	7	8
9	10	11	12	13	14	15
16	17	18	19	20	21	22
23	24	25	26	27	28	29
30	31					

♎ October 16–22

I believe I'm here for a reason. And I think a little bit of the reason is to throw little torches out to the next step to lead people through the dark. ∼WHOOPI GOLDBERG

Date	Qtr.	Sign	Activity
Oct. 17, 1:15 pm–Oct. 18, 12:45 am	4th	Cancer	Plant biennials, perennials, bulbs and roots. Prune. Irrigate. Fertilize (organic).
Oct. 18, 12:45 am–Oct. 20, 12:25 pm	4th	Leo	Cultivate. Destroy weeds and pests. Harvest fruits and root crops for food. Trim to retard growth.
Oct. 20, 12:25 pm–Oct. 22, 9:24 pm	4th	Virgo	Cultivate, especially medicinal plants. Destroy weeds and pests. Trim to retard growth.

When was the last time you went stargazing? Pick a night with a new moon, head to a low-lit area, and take in the illuminated sky. You can always take a constellation guide with you—or you can spot some planets that are visible to the naked eye. For example, depending on the time of year, Mercury and Venus can be viewed at dusk. See if you can spy satellites crossing the sky too.

October 17
1:15 pm EDT

OCTOBER

S	M	T	W	T	F	S
						1
2	3	4	5	6	7	8
9	10	11	12	13	14	15
16	17	18	19	20	21	22
23	24	25	26	27	28	29
30	31					

October 23–29 ♏

How many lessons of faith and beauty we should lose if there was no winter in our year!

~THOMAS WENTWORTH HIGGINSON

Date	Qtr.	Sign	Activity
Oct. 25, 3:18 am– Oct. 25, 6:49 am	4th	Scorpio	Plant biennials, perennials, bulbs and roots. Prune. Irrigate. Fertilize (organic).
Oct. 25, 6:49 am– Oct. 27, 6:55 am	1st	Scorpio	Plant grains, leafy annuals. Fertilize (chemical). Graft or bud plants. Irrigate. Trim to increase growth.
Oct. 29, 9:21 am– Oct. 31, 11:43 am	1st	Capricorn	Graft or bud plants. Trim to increase growth.

Restore an old table using furniture restoration wax or refinish an old dresser with paint and one of the exquisite floral transfers for furniture that are now available. The results are stunning and will often become a family treasure.

●

October 25
6:49 am EDT

OCTOBER

S	M	T	W	T	F	S
						1
2	3	4	5	6	7	8
9	10	11	12	13	14	15
16	17	18	19	20	21	22
23	24	25	26	27	28	29
30	31					

♏ November

October 30–November 5

I'm a legit snack.

~ELEANOR SHELLSTROP, *THE GOOD PLACE*

Date	Qtr.	Sign	Activity
Nov. 2, 2:46 pm–Nov. 4, 7:07 pm	2nd	Pisces	Plant grains, leafy annuals. Fertilize (chemical). Graft or bud plants. Irrigate. Trim to increase growth.

Invest in a fruit juice steam extractor, and when harvest season comes along, get a bushel of grapes or apples from a U-pick, some quart jars, and some canning lids so you can make your own juice. You'll be stunned at the rich taste of real juice, and you'll have a useful piece of equipment for years to come.

◖
November 1
2:37 am EDT

NOVEMBER

S	M	T	W	T	F	S
		1	2	3	4	5
6	7	8	9	10	11	12
13	14	15	16	17	18	19
20	21	22	23	24	25	26
27	28	29	30			

November 6–12 ♏

Tolerance, inter-cultural dialogue and respect for diversity are more essential than ever in a world where peoples are becoming more and more closely interconnected.

~Kofi Annan

Date	Qtr.	Sign	Activity
Nov. 7, 12:15 am– Nov. 8, 6:02 am	2nd	Taurus	Plant annuals for hardiness. Trim to increase growth.
Nov. 8, 6:02 am– Nov. 9, 8:37 am	3rd	Taurus	Plant potatoes and tubers. Trim to retard growth.
Nov. 9, 8:37 am– Nov. 11, 7:22 pm	3rd	Gemini	Cultivate. Destroy weeds and pests. Harvest fruits and root crops for food. Trim to retard growth.
Nov. 11, 7:22 pm– Nov. 14, 7:48 am	3rd	Cancer	Plant biennials, perennials, bulbs and roots. Prune. Irrigate. Fertilize (organic).

Looking for a new perspective? Do something different and interesting by getting a numerology reading or having an astrology chart drawn up for yourself. It will change your view of yourself and your outlook on life.

*Daylight Saving Time
ends November 6, 2:00 am*

○

November 8
6:02 am EST

NOVEMBER

S	M	T	W	T	F	S
		1	2	3	4	5
6	7	8	9	10	11	12
13	14	15	16	17	18	19
20	21	22	23	24	25	26
27	28	29	30			

♏ November 13–19

Life is an unfoldment, and the further we travel the more truth we can comprehend.   ~HYPATIA OF ALEXANDRIA

Date	Qtr.	Sign	Activity
Nov. 14, 7:48 am– Nov. 16, 8:27 am	3rd	Leo	Cultivate. Destroy weeds and pests. Harvest fruits and root crops for food. Trim to retard growth.
Nov. 16, 8:27 am– Nov. 16, 8:04 pm	4th	Leo	Cultivate. Destroy weeds and pests. Harvest fruits and root crops for food. Trim to retard growth.
Nov. 16, 8:04 pm– Nov. 19, 5:58 am	4th	Virgo	Cultivate, especially medicinal plants. Destroy weeds and pests. Trim to retard growth.

Spending time with your pets every day is good for you! In addition to being good company, they also represent a bridge between humanity and the rest of nature right in your own home. Physical contact with them can boost your mood, and with some pets like dogs and cats, you both get a beneficial dose of oxytocin. But even watching a tank of fish can be a stress-buster on a bad day!

_____

_____

_____

_____

◗
November 16
8:27 am EST

NOVEMBER

S	M	T	W	T	F	S
		1	2	3	4	5
6	7	8	9	10	11	12
13	14	15	16	17	18	19
20	21	22	23	24	25	26
27	28	29	30			

November 20–26 ♏ ♐

The battles that count aren't the ones for gold medals. The struggles within yourself—the invisible, inevitable battles inside all of us—that's where it's at. ~JESSE OWENS

Date	Qtr.	Sign	Activity
Nov. 21, 12:16 pm–Nov. 23, 3:16 pm	4th	Scorpio	Plant biennials, perennials, bulbs and roots. Prune. Irrigate. Fertilize (organic).
Nov. 23, 3:16 pm–Nov. 23, 5:57 pm	4th	Sagittarius	Cultivate. Destroy weeds and pests. Harvest fruits and root crops for food. Trim to retard growth.
Nov. 25, 4:18 pm–Nov. 27, 5:07 pm	1st	Capricorn	Graft or bud plants. Trim to increase growth.

If your library has a book club, consider joining. You will read some fantastic books, meet some interesting people, and help build and deepen a sense of community—all while expanding yourself and your perspective.

●

November 23
5:57 pm EST

NOVEMBER

S	M	T	W	T	F	S
		1	2	3	4	5
6	7	8	9	10	11	12
13	14	15	16	17	18	19
20	21	22	23	24	25	26
27	28	29	30			

↗ December

November 27–December 3

Everything was beginning to be snug and cosy again.

~Laura Ingalls Wilder

Date	Qtr.	Sign	Activity
Nov. 29, 7:15 pm– Nov. 30, 9:37 am	1st	Pisces	Plant grains, leafy annuals. Fertilize (chemical). Graft or bud plants. Irrigate. Trim to increase growth.
Nov. 30, 9:37 am– Dec. 1, 11:41 pm	2nd	Pisces	Plant grains, leafy annuals. Fertilize (chemical). Graft or bud plants. Irrigate. Trim to increase growth.

Spruce and pine needles make a tasty tea full of vitamin C! You can harvest the needles year-round, but fresh spring growth has a milder flavor. Steep a twig of needles in hot water for at least 15 minutes or longer for stronger tea. You can also cut up the needles for even more flavor. Add honey or maple syrup for sweetness. Make sure you have a spruce or pine; some conifers, like yew, are toxic!

_____

_____

_____

_____

◑

November 30
9:37 am EST

December

S	M	T	W	T	F	S
				1	2	3
4	5	6	7	8	9	10
11	12	13	14	15	16	17
18	19	20	21	22	23	24
25	26	27	28	29	30	31

December 4–10

If you want others to be happy, practice compassion. If you want to be happy, practice compassion. ~DALAI LAMA

Date	Qtr.	Sign	Activity
Dec. 4, 6:38 am–Dec. 6, 3:49 pm	2nd	Taurus	Plant annuals for hardiness. Trim to increase growth.
Dec. 7, 11:08 pm–Dec. 9, 2:49 am	3rd	Gemini	Cultivate. Destroy weeds and pests. Harvest fruits and root crops for food. Trim to retard growth.
Dec. 9, 2:49 am–Dec. 11, 3:09 pm	3rd	Cancer	Plant biennials, perennials, bulbs and roots. Prune. Irrigate. Fertilize (organic).

Looking for a special Christmas gift? Consider creating a book of family photos showing as many generations as you can. Gather photos going back into your heritage, upload them to a site like Shutterfly, create a caption for each, and voila! You will have captured your family history forever.

○
December 7
11:08 pm EST

DECEMBER

S	M	T	W	T	F	S
				1	2	3
4	5	6	7	8	9	10
11	12	13	14	15	16	17
18	19	20	21	22	23	24
25	26	27	28	29	30	31

December 11–17

One kind word can warm three winter months.

~JAPANESE PROVERB

Date	Qtr.	Sign	Activity
Dec. 11, 3:09 pm– Dec. 14, 3:45 am	3rd	Leo	Cultivate. Destroy weeds and pests. Harvest fruits and root crops for food. Trim to retard growth.
Dec. 14, 3:45 am– Dec. 16, 3:56 am	3rd	Virgo	Cultivate, especially medicinal plants. Destroy weeds and pests. Trim to retard growth.
Dec. 16, 3:56 am– Dec. 16, 2:49 pm	4th	Virgo	Cultivate, especially medicinal plants. Destroy weeds and pests. Trim to retard growth.

Remember those classic books from your childhood, the ones that might be gathering dust in your attic or basement? You're never too old to read stories that warm your heart. After reading these treasured tomes, don't put them back in storage. Place them on a bookshelf or coffee table to relive those memories whenever you see them.

_____

_____

_____

_____

December 16
3:56 am EST

DECEMBER

S	M	T	W	T	F	S
				1	2	3
4	5	6	7	8	9	10
11	12	13	14	15	16	17
18	19	20	21	22	23	24
25	26	27	28	29	30	31

December 18–24

> *But today, our very survival depends on our ability to stay awake, to adjust to new ideas, to remain vigilant and to face the challenge of change.*

~MARTIN LUTHER KING JR.

Date	Qtr.	Sign	Activity
Dec. 18, 10:31 pm–Dec. 21, 2:12 am	4th	Scorpio	Plant biennials, perennials, bulbs and roots. Prune. Irrigate. Fertilize (organic).
Dec. 21, 2:12 am–Dec. 23, 2:49 am	4th	Sagittarius	Cultivate. Destroy weeds and pests. Harvest fruits and root crops for food. Trim to retard growth.
Dec. 23, 2:49 am–Dec. 23, 5:17 am	4th	Capricorn	Plant potatoes and tubers. Trim to retard growth.
Dec. 23, 5:17 am–Dec. 25, 2:14 am	1st	Capricorn	Graft or bud plants. Trim to increase growth.

Flowers are beautiful and beauty brings joy, so treat yourself to a bouquet of flowers every month, especially in the long, drab days of winter. Grow a variety of flowers in summer and you'll have beauty and joy year-round.

●

December 23
5:17 am EST

DECEMBER

S	M	T	W	T	F	S
				1	2	3
4	5	6	7	8	9	10
11	12	13	14	15	16	17
18	19	20	21	22	23	24
25	26	27	28	29	30	31

♑ December 25–31

To see the world, things dangerous to come to, to see behind walls, to draw closer, to find each other and to feel. That is the purpose of life. ∼THE SECRET LIFE OF WALTER MITTY

Date	Qtr.	Sign	Activity
Dec. 27, 2:34 am– Dec. 29, 5:36 am	1st	Pisces	Plant grains, leafy annuals. Fertilize (chemical). Graft or bud plants. Irrigate. Trim to increase growth.

Our dreams can certainly tell us a lot, which is why it can be eye-opening to keep a dream journal. Place it on your nightstand and jot down the details of your dream as soon as you wake up, when you'll remember it best. A dream dictionary can help you decode the most memorable portions of your dream.

◖ December 29
8:21 pm EST

DECEMBER

S	M	T	W	T	F	S
				1	2	3
4	5	6	7	8	9	10
11	12	13	14	15	16	17
18	19	20	21	22	23	24
25	26	27	28	29	30	31

Gardening by the Moon

Welcome to the world of gardening by the Moon! Unlike most gardening advice, this article is not about how to garden, it's about when to garden. Timing is everything; if you know how to use the Moon, you'll not only be in sync with nature but you can sit back and watch your garden grow beyond your wildest dreams.

Gardening by the Moon is nothing new. It's been around since ancient times when people used both the Sun and the Moon to predict the tides, as well as fertility and growth cycles for plants and animals.

Lunar gardening is simple and the results are immediate. It doesn't matter whether you're a beginner gardener with a single pot or an old hand with years of master gardening experience—your garden will grow bigger and better if you follow the cycles of the Moon and match up the right time with the right garden activity. When the temperature has dropped and the sun is low on the horizon, you can apply what you've learned to your indoor plants as well.

The sky is a celestial clock, with the Sun and the Moon as the "hands" that tell the time. The Sun tells the season, and the light and location of the Moon tell the best times for birth, growth, and death in the garden. The Moon doesn't generate any light by itself, but as it circles the Earth it reflects the light of the Sun, which makes the Moon look like it's getting bigger and smaller. The cyclical increases and decreases in the light of the Moon are phases and tell times of growth.

Moon Phases

The theory behind gardening by the Moon is "as the Moon goes, so goes the garden." The Earth circles around the Sun once a year, but the Moon has a much shorter "life span" of twenty-eight to thirty days. Every month, as the light of the Moon increases and decreases, it mirrors the cycle of birth, growth, and death in the garden. After adjusting your garden activities to the light of the Moon, you'll be amazed to see how well your garden grows.

The **waxing phase** is the growth cycle in the garden. It begins with the New Moon and lasts for two weeks. Each month the Moon is "born" at the New Moon (day one) and grows bigger and brighter until it reaches maturity at the Full Moon (day fourteen). When the light of the Moon is increasing, it's the best time of the month to sow seeds, plant leafy annuals, and cut back or prune plants to encourage bigger growth.

The **waning phase** is the declining cycle in the garden. It begins with the Full Moon (day fourteen) and lasts for two weeks. The Moon grows older after the Full Moon as the light begins to decrease, until it disappears or "dies" at day twenty-eight. The decreasing light of the Moon is the time to plant bulbs, root vegetables, and perennials that store their energy underground. The waning Moon phase is also a good time for garden maintenance, including weeding, raking, deadheading, mowing, working the soil, destroying insects, and burning brush.

How can you tell if the Moon is waxing or waning?

Cup your right hand into a C shape and look up into the sky. If the crescent Moon fits into the closed part of your right hand, it's a waxing Moon.

Cup your left hand into a C shape and look up into the sky. If the crescent Moon fits into the closed part of your left hand, it's a waning Moon.

New Moon and Full Moon

Every month, the Moon takes one day off. This time-out between waning and waxing is called the New Moon. The time-out between waxing and waning is called the Full Moon. When the Moon reaches either of these stopping points, it's time for you to follow its example and take a one-day break from the garden.

Moon Signs

Once you know the Moon phases, the next step is to locate where the Moon is in the zodiac. The Moon hangs out in each of the zodiac signs for two to three days per month.

There's no such thing as a "bad" time in the garden, but there are Moon signs that are better for growth and others that are better for digging and weeding. Growth times alternate every two to three days with maintenance times. The trick is knowing which one is which.

The grow signs are Taurus, Cancer, Libra, Scorpio, Capricorn, and Pisces. When the Moon is in these signs, it's time to seed and plant.

The no-grow/maintenance signs are Aries, Gemini, Leo, Virgo, Sagittarius, and Aquarius. When the Moon is in these signs, it's time for digging, weeding, mowing, and pruning.

Remember: It's always a good time to garden something!

Putting It All Together

In order to get started, you'll need three tools: a calendar with New and Full Moons, the Moon tables (pg. 136), and the Moon phases and signs below.

Then follow these simple steps:

1. Mark your calendar with your time frame for gardening.

2. Figure out when the Moon is waxing (1st and 2nd quarters) and waning (3rd and 4th quarters). Use the tables in the Weekly Almanac section.

3. Locate the Moon by zodiac sign.

4. Check out the gardening advice below, which takes into account the Moon's phase and sign.

Moon Phases and Signs

Note: Can be applied to any calendar year.

Waxing Aries Moon (October–April)

Aries is one of the three fire signs that is hot and barren. Seeds planted under a waxing Aries Moon tend to be bitter or bolt quickly, but if you're feeling lucky, you could try your hand at hot and spicy peppers or herbs that thrive in dry heat.

Waning Aries Moon (April–October)

The decreasing light of the waning Aries Moon makes these two to three days a good time to focus on harvesting, cutting back, mowing the lawn, and getting rid of pests.

Waxing Taurus Moon (November–May)

Taurus is one of the three semi-fruitful earth signs. These days are perfect ones to establish your garden by planting or fertilizing annuals. Annuals with outside seeds like lettuces, cabbage, corn, and broccoli grow faster when planted under a waxing Taurus Moon that is one to seven days old. Vegetables with inside seeds like cucumbers, melons, squash, tomatoes, and beans should be planted when the Moon is seven to twelve days old. Annual flowers can be planted any time during this two-week phase.

Waning Taurus Moon (May–November)

The decreasing light of this semi-fruitful waning Taurus Moon gives you a perfect two- or three-day window for planting perennials or digging in root vegetables and flower bulbs.

Waxing Gemini Moon (December–June)

Gemini is one of the three dry and barren signs. But with the light of the Moon increasing, you can use these two to three days to prune or cut back plants you want to flourish and grow bigger.

Waning Gemini Moon (June–December)

Gemini can be all over the place, so use these couple of dry and barren days when the light is decreasing to weed invasive plants that are out of control.

Waxing Cancer Moon (January–July)

Cancer is one of the three wet and fruitful signs, so when the Moon is waxing in Cancer it's the perfect time to plant seeds or set out seedlings and annual flowers that live for only one season. Annuals with outside seeds grow faster when planted under a Moon that is one to seven days old. Vegetables with inside seeds should be planted when the Moon is seven to twelve days old. Annual flowers can be planted any time during these two weeks.

Waning Cancer Moon (July–January)

Plant perennials, root vegetables, and bulbs to your heart's content under the decreasing light of this fruitful Moon.

Waxing Leo Moon (February–August)

The light of the Moon is increasing, but Leo is one of the three hot and barren fire signs. Use the two or three days of this waxing Leo Moon to cut and prune the plants and shrubs you want to be the king or queen of your garden.

Waning Leo Moon (August–February)

With the light of the Moon decreasing, this Leo Moon is a good period to dig the soil, destroy pests and insects, and burn brush.

Waxing Virgo Moon (March–September)

Virgo is a semi-barren sign, which is good for fertilizing (Virgo is a "greenie" type that loves organics) and for planting woody vines and hardy herbs.

Waning Virgo Moon (September–March)

With the light of this semi-barren Moon decreasing for a couple of days, plan to hoe those rows and get rid of your weeds. Harvest Moon in September.

Waxing Libra Moon (October–April)

Libra is a semi-fruitful sign focused on beauty. Because the Moon is growing brighter in Libra, these two to three days are a great time to give your flower garden some heavy-duty TLC.

Waning Libra Moon (April–October)

If you want to encourage re-blooming, try deadheading your vegetables and flowers under the light of this decreasing Libra Moon. Harvest your flowers.

Waxing Scorpio Moon (November–May)

Scorpio is one of the three wet and fruitful signs. When the Moon is waxing in Scorpio, it's the perfect time for planting annuals that have a bite, like arugula and hot peppers. Annuals with outside seeds grow faster when planted under a Moon that is one to seven days old. Vegetables with inside seeds should be planted when the Moon is seven to twelve days old. Annual flowers can be planted anytime during this two-week phase.

Waning Scorpio Moon (May–November)

With the light of the Moon decreasing in Scorpio, a sign that likes strong and intense flavors, this is the perfect period to plant hardy perennials, garlic bulbs, and onion sets.

Waxing Sagittarius Moon (June–December)

Sagittarius is one of the three hot and barren signs. Because Sagittarius prefers roaming to staying still, this waxing Moon is not a good time for planting. But you can encourage growth during the two or three days when the light is increasing by cutting back, mowing, and pruning.

Waning Sagittarius Moon (December–June)

It's time to discourage growth during the days when the light of the Moon is decreasing in Sagittarius. Cut back, mow the lawn, prune, and destroy pests and insects you never want to darken your garden again.

Waxing Capricorn Moon (July–January)

Capricorn is a semi-fruitful earth sign. The couple of days when the light of the Moon is increasing in Capricorn are good for getting the garden into shape, setting out plants and transplants, and fertilizing.

Waning Capricorn Moon (January–July)

The decreasing light of this fruitful Capricorn Moon is the perfect window for digging and dividing bulbs and pinching back suckers to encourage bigger blooms on your flowers and vegetables.

Waxing Aquarius Moon (August–February)

Aquarius is a dry and barren sign. However, the increasing light of the Aquarian Moon makes this a good opportunity to experiment by pruning or cutting back plants you want to flourish.

Waning Aquarius Moon (February–August)

The light of the Moon is decreasing. Use this time to harvest or to weed, cut back, and prune the shrubs and plants that you want to banish forever from your garden. Harvest vegetables.

Waxing Pisces Moon (September–March)

When the Moon is increasing in fruitful Pisces, it's a perfect period for planting seeds and annuals. Annuals with outside seeds grow faster when planted under a Moon that is one to seven days old. Vegetables with inside seeds should be planted when the Moon is seven to twelve days old. Annual flowers can be planted any time during these two weeks.

Waning Pisces Moon (March–September)

With the light of the Moon decreasing, it's time to plant all perennials, bulbs, and root vegetables except potatoes. Garden lore has it that potatoes planted under a Pisces Moon tend to grow bumps or "toes" because Pisces is associated with the feet.

Here's hoping that this has inspired you to give gardening by the Moon a try. Not only is it the secret ingredient that will make your garden more abundant, but you can use it as long as the Sun is in the sky and the Moon circles the Earth!

A Guide to Planting

Plant	Quarter	Sign
Annuals	1st or 2nd	
Apple tree	2nd or 3rd	Cancer, Pisces, Virgo
Artichoke	1st	Cancer, Pisces
Asparagus	1st	Cancer, Scorpio, Pisces
Aster	1st or 2nd	Virgo, Libra
Barley	1st or 2nd	Cancer, Pisces, Libra, Capricorn, Virgo
Beans (bush & pole)	2nd	Cancer, Taurus, Pisces, Libra
Beans (kidney, white & navy)	1st or 2nd	Cancer, Pisces
Beech tree	2nd or 3rd	Virgo, Taurus
Beets	3rd	Cancer, Capricorn, Pisces, Libra
Biennials	3rd or 4th	
Broccoli	1st	Cancer, Scorpio, Pisces, Libra
Brussels sprouts	1st	Cancer, Scorpio, Pisces, Libra
Buckwheat	1st or 2nd	Capricorn
Bulbs	3rd	Cancer, Scorpio, Pisces
Bulbs for seed	2nd or 3rd	
Cabbage	1st	Cancer, Scorpio, Pisces, Taurus, Libra
Canes (raspberry, blackberry & gooseberry)	2nd	Cancer, Scorpio, Pisces
Cantaloupe	1st or 2nd	Cancer, Scorpio, Pisces, Taurus, Libra
Carrots	3rd	Cancer, Scorpio, Pisces, Taurus, Libra
Cauliflower	1st	Cancer, Scorpio, Pisces, Libra
Celeriac	3rd	Cancer, Scorpio, Pisces
Celery	1st	Cancer, Scorpio, Pisces
Cereals	1st or 2nd	Cancer, Scorpio, Pisces, Libra
Chard	1st or 2nd	Cancer, Scorpio, Pisces
Chicory	2nd or 3rd	Cancer, Scorpio, Pisces
Chrysanthemum	1st or 2nd	Virgo
Clover	1st or 2nd	Cancer, Scorpio, Pisces

Plant	Quarter	Sign
Coreopsis	2nd or 3rd	Libra
Corn	1st	Cancer, Scorpio, Pisces
Corn for fodder	1st or 2nd	Libra
Cosmos	2nd or 3rd	Libra
Cress	1st	Cancer, Scorpio, Pisces
Crocus	1st or 2nd	Virgo
Cucumber	1st	Cancer, Scorpio, Pisces
Daffodil	1st or 2nd	Libra, Virgo
Dahlia	1st or 2nd	Libra, Virgo
Deciduous trees	2nd or 3rd	Cancer, Scorpio, Pisces, Virgo, Libra
Eggplant	2nd	Cancer, Scorpio, Pisces, Libra
Endive	1st	Cancer, Scorpio, Pisces, Libra
Flowers	1st	Cancer, Scorpio, Pisces, Libra, Taurus, Virgo
Garlic	3rd	Libra, Taurus, Pisces
Gladiola	1st or 2nd	Libra, Virgo
Gourds	1st or 2nd	Cancer, Scorpio, Pisces, Libra
Grapes	2nd or 3rd	Cancer, Scorpio, Pisces, Virgo
Hay	1st or 2nd	Cancer, Scorpio, Pisces, Libra, Taurus
Herbs	1st or 2nd	Cancer, Scorpio, Pisces
Honeysuckle	1st or 2nd	Scorpio, Virgo
Hops	1st or 2nd	Scorpio, Libra
Horseradish	1st or 2nd	Cancer, Scorpio, Pisces
Houseplants	1st	Cancer, Scorpio, Pisces, Libra
Hyacinth	3rd	Cancer, Scorpio, Pisces
Iris	1st or 2nd	Cancer, Virgo
Kohlrabi	1st or 2nd	Cancer, Scorpio, Pisces, Libra
Leek	2nd or 3rd	Sagittarius
Lettuce	1st	Cancer, Scorpio, Pisces, Libra, Taurus
Lily	1st or 2nd	Cancer, Scorpio, Pisces
Maple tree	2nd or 3rd	Taurus, Virgo, Cancer, Pisces
Melon	2nd	Cancer, Scorpio, Pisces
Moon vine	1st or 2nd	Virgo

Plant	Quarter	Sign
Morning glory	1st or 2nd	Cancer, Scorpio, Pisces, Virgo
Oak tree	2nd or 3rd	Taurus, Virgo, Cancer, Pisces
Oats	1st or 2nd	Cancer, Scorpio, Pisces, Libra
Okra	1st or 2nd	Cancer, Scorpio, Pisces, Libra
Onion seed	2nd	Cancer, Scorpio, Sagittarius
Onion set	3rd or 4th	Cancer, Pisces, Taurus, Libra
Pansies	1st or 2nd	Cancer, Scorpio, Pisces
Parsley	1st	Cancer, Scorpio, Pisces, Libra
Parsnip	3rd	Cancer, Scorpio, Taurus, Capricorn
Peach tree	2nd or 3rd	Cancer, Taurus, Virgo, Libra
Peanuts	3rd	Cancer, Scorpio, Pisces
Pear tree	2nd or 3rd	Cancer, Scorpio, Pisces, Libra
Peas	2nd	Cancer, Scorpio, Pisces, Libra
Peony	1st or 2nd	Virgo
Peppers	2nd	Cancer, Scorpio, Pisces
Perennials	3rd	
Petunia	1st or 2nd	Libra, Virgo
Plum tree	2nd or 3rd	Cancer, Pisces, Taurus, Virgo
Poppies	1st or 2nd	Virgo
Portulaca	1st or 2nd	Virgo
Potatoes	3rd	Cancer, Scorpio, Libra, Taurus, Capricorn
Privet	1st or 2nd	Taurus, Libra
Pumpkin	2nd	Cancer, Scorpio, Pisces, Libra
Quince	1st or 2nd	Capricorn
Radishes	3rd	Cancer, Scorpio, Pisces, Libra, Capricorn
Rhubarb	3rd	Cancer, Pisces
Rice	1st or 2nd	Scorpio
Roses	1st or 2nd	Cancer, Virgo
Rutabaga	3rd	Cancer, Scorpio, Pisces, Taurus
Saffron	1st or 2nd	Cancer, Scorpio, Pisces
Sage	3rd	Cancer, Scorpio, Pisces

Plant	Quarter	Sign
Salsify	1st	Cancer, Scorpio, Pisces
Shallot	2nd	Scorpio
Spinach	1st	Cancer, Scorpio, Pisces
Squash	2nd	Cancer, Scorpio, Pisces, Libra
Strawberries	3rd	Cancer, Scorpio, Pisces
String beans	1st or 2nd	Taurus
Sunflowers	1st or 2nd	Libra, Cancer
Sweet peas	1st or 2nd	Any
Tomatoes	2nd	Cancer, Scorpio, Pisces, Capricorn
Trees, shade	3rd	Taurus, Capricorn
Trees, ornamental	2nd	Libra, Taurus
Trumpet vine	1st or 2nd	Cancer, Scorpio, Pisces
Tubers for seed	3rd	Cancer, Scorpio, Pisces, Libra
Tulips	1st or 2nd	Libra, Virgo
Turnips	3rd	Cancer, Scorpio, Pisces, Taurus, Capricorn, Libra
Valerian	1st or 2nd	Virgo, Gemini
Watermelon	1st or 2nd	Cancer, Scorpio, Pisces, Libra
Wheat	1st or 2nd	Cancer, Scorpio, Pisces, Libra

Companion Planting Guide

Plant	Companions	Hindered by
Asparagus	Tomatoes, parsley, basil	None known
Beans	Tomatoes, carrots, cucumbers, garlic, cabbage, beets, corn	Onions, gladiolas
Beets	Onions, cabbage, lettuce, mint, catnip	Pole beans
Broccoli	Beans, celery, potatoes, onions	Tomatoes
Cabbage	Peppermint, sage, thyme, tomatoes	Strawberries, grapes
Carrots	Peas, lettuce, chives, radishes, leeks, onions, sage	Dill, anise
Citrus trees	Guava, live oak, rubber trees, peppers	None known
Corn	Potatoes, beans, peas, melon, squash, pumpkin, sunflowers, soybeans	Quack grass, wheat, straw, mulch
Cucumbers	Beans, cabbage, radishes, sunflowers, lettuce, broccoli, squash	Aromatic herbs
Eggplant	Green beans, lettuce, kale	None known
Grapes	Peas, beans, blackberries	Cabbage, radishes
Melons	Corn, peas	Potatoes, gourds
Onions, leeks	Beets, chamomile, carrots, lettuce	Peas, beans, sage
Parsnip	Peas	None known
Peas	Radishes, carrots, corn, cucumbers, beans, tomatoes, spinach, turnips	Onion, garlic
Potatoes	Beans, corn, peas, cabbage, hemp, cucumbers, eggplant, catnip	Raspberries, pumpkins, tomatoes, sunflowers
Radishes	Peas, lettuce, nasturtiums, cucumbers	Hyssop
Spinach	Strawberries	None known
Squash/ Pumpkin	Nasturtiums, corn, mint, catnip	Potatoes
Tomatoes	Asparagus, parsley, chives, onions, carrots, marigolds, nasturtiums, dill	Black walnut roots, fennel, potatoes
Turnips	Peas, beans, brussels sprouts	Potatoes

Plant	Companions	Uses
Anise	Coriander	Flavor candy, pastry, cheeses, cookies
Basil	Tomatoes	Dislikes rue; repels flies and mosquitoes
Borage	Tomatoes, squash	Use in teas
Buttercup	Clover	Hinders delphinium, peonies, monkshood, columbine
Catnip		Repels flea beetles
Chamomile	Peppermint, wheat, onions, cabbage	Roman chamomile may control damping-off disease; use in herbal sprays
Chervil	Radishes	Good in soups and other dishes
Chives	Carrots	Use in spray to deter black spot on roses
Coriander	Plant anywhere	Hinders seed formation in fennel
Cosmos		Repels corn earworms
Dill	Cabbage	Hinders carrots and tomatoes
Fennel	Plant in borders	Disliked by all garden plants
Horseradish		Repels potato bugs
Horsetail		Makes fungicide spray
Hyssop		Attracts cabbage flies; harmful to radishes
Lavender	Plant anywhere	Use in spray to control insects on cotton, repels clothes moths
Lovage		Lures horn worms away from tomatoes
Marigolds		Pest repellent; use against Mexican bean beetles and nematodes
Mint	Cabbage, tomatoes	Repels ants, flea beetles, cabbage worm butterflies
Morning glory	Corn	Helps melon germination
Nasturtium	Cabbage, cucumbers	Deters aphids, squash bugs, pumpkin beetles
Okra	Eggplant	Attracts leafhopper (lure insects from other plants)
Parsley	Tomatoes, asparagus	Freeze chopped-up leaves to flavor foods
Purslane		Good ground cover
Rosemary		Repels cabbage moths, bean beetles, carrot flies
Savory		Plant with onions for added sweetness
Tansy		Deters Japanese beetles, striped cucumber beetles, squash bugs
Thyme		Repels cabbage worms
Yarrow		Increases essential oils of neighbors

Moon Void-of-Course

Kim Rogers-Gallagher

The Moon circles the Earth in about twenty-eight days, moving through each zodiac sign in two and a half days. As she passes through the thirty degrees of each sign, she "visits" with the planets in numerical order, forming aspects with them. Because she moves one degree in just two to two and a half hours, her influence on each planet lasts only a few hours. She eventually reaches the planet that's in the highest degree of any sign and forms what will be her final aspect before leaving the sign. From this point until she enters the next sign, she is referred to as void-of-course.

Think of it this way: the Moon is the emotional "tone" of the day, carrying feelings with her particular to the sign she's "wearing" at the moment. After she has contacted each of the planets, she symbolically "rests" before changing her costume, so her instinct is temporarily on hold. It's during this time that many people feel "fuzzy" or "vague." Plans or decisions made now often do not pan out. Without the instinctual "knowing" the Moon provides as she touches each planet, we tend to be unrealistic or exercise poor judgment. The traditional definition of the void Moon is that "nothing will come of this." Actions initiated under a void Moon are often wasted, irrelevant, or incorrect—usually because information is hidden, missing, or has been overlooked.

Although it's not a good time to initiate plans, routine tasks seem to go along just fine. This period is ideal for reflection. On the lighter side, remember there are good uses for the void Moon. It is the period when the universe seems to be most open to loopholes. It's a great time to make plans you don't want to fulfill or schedule things you don't want to do. See the tables on pages 76–81 for a schedule of the Moon's void-of-course times.

Last Aspect   **Moon Enters New Sign**

		January			
1	3:16 am	1	Capricorn	6:02 pm
3	11:21 am	3	Aquarius	5:44 pm
4	7:45 pm	5	Pisces	7:17 pm
7	5:23 pm	8	Aries	12:26 am
10	2:23 am	10	Taurus	9:47 am
12	2:39 pm	12	Gemini	10:08 pm
14	9:22 pm	15	Cancer	11:11 am
17	6:48 pm	17	Leo	11:03 pm
20	3:15 am	20	Virgo	9:02 am
22	2:46 pm	22	Libra	5:03 pm
24	5:10 pm	24	Scorpio	10:57 pm
27	12:28 am	27	Sagittarius	2:34 am
28	2:00 pm	29	Capricorn	4:09 am
30	11:44 pm	31	Aquarius	4:43 am
		February			
1	6:01 am	2	Pisces	6:00 am
4	4:41 am	4	Aries	9:57 am
6	12:21 pm	6	Taurus	5:52 pm
8	11:48 pm	9	Gemini	5:27 am
11	3:23 am	11	Cancer	6:27 pm
14	5:27 am	14	Leo	6:17 am
16	11:56 am	16	Virgo	3:42 pm
18	6:20 pm	18	Libra	10:51 pm
21	12:02 am	21	Scorpio	4:19 am
23	4:24 am	23	Sagittarius	8:29 am
24	10:24 pm	25	Capricorn	11:27 am
27	9:49 am	27	Aquarius	1:36 pm
28	9:01 pm	1	Pisces	3:53 pm

Last Aspect   Moon Enters New Sign

		March		
3	4:45 pm	3	Aries	7:52 pm
5	11:02 pm	6	Taurus	3:00 am
8	9:35 am	8	Gemini	1:40 pm
10	11:43 am	11	Cancer	2:24 am
13	11:44 am	13	Leo	3:32 pm
15	6:56 am	16	Virgo	12:59 am
18	4:11 am	18	Libra	7:26 am
20	8:40 am	20	Scorpio	11:45 am
22	12:01 pm	22	Sagittarius	2:59 pm
24	8:59 am	24	Capricorn	5:54 pm
26	7:51 pm	26	Aquarius	8:55 pm
28	10:11 am	29	Pisces	12:32 am
31	2:37 am	31	Aries	5:30 am
		April		
2	9:51 am	2	Taurus	12:50 pm
4	9:53 pm	4	Gemini	11:04 pm
6	11:15 pm	7	Cancer	11:30 am
9	9:01 pm	10	Leo	12:00 am
12	6:16 am	12	Virgo	10:07 am
14	2:11 pm	14	Libra	4:46 pm
16	5:57 pm	16	Scorpio	8:23 pm
18	7:55 pm	18	Sagittarius	10:16 pm
20	4:56 pm	20	Capricorn	11:52 pm
22	11:53 pm	23	Aquarius	2:17 am
24	8:33 pm	25	Pisces	6:15 am
27	9:36 am	27	Aries	12:10 pm
29	5:38 pm	29	Taurus	8:19 pm

Last Aspect   **Moon Enters New Sign**

		May		
2	6:13 am	2	Gemini	6:47 am
4	4:37 pm	4	Cancer	7:05 pm
7	6:26 am	7	Leo	7:50 am
9	8:39 am	9	Virgo	6:53 pm
12	12:00 am	12	Libra	2:34 am
14	4:07 am	14	Scorpio	6:34 am
16	5:28 am	16	Sagittarius	7:50 am
17	11:59 pm	18	Capricorn	8:02 am
20	8:00 am	20	Aquarius	8:53 am
22	3:19 am	22	Pisces	11:49 am
24	5:33 pm	24	Aries	5:39 pm
26	11:20 pm	27	Taurus	2:22 am
29	10:11 am	29	Gemini	1:23 pm
31	4:10 pm	1	Cancer	1:49 am
		June		
3	11:15 am	3	Leo	2:38 pm
5	7:12 pm	6	Virgo	2:22 am
8	8:09 am	8	Libra	11:23 am
10	1:36 pm	10	Scorpio	4:41 pm
12	5:40 pm	12	Sagittarius	6:31 pm
14	10:58 am	14	Capricorn	6:14 pm
16	2:41 pm	16	Aquarius	5:44 pm
18	2:50 pm	18	Pisces	7:01 pm
20	11:11 pm	20	Aries	11:37 pm
23	4:02 am	23	Taurus	7:58 am
25	3:02 pm	25	Gemini	7:13 pm
27	10:38 pm	28	Cancer	7:53 am
30	4:14 pm	30	Leo	8:40 pm

Last Aspect   Moon Enters New Sign

		July		
3	5:59 am	3	Virgo	8:31 am
5	2:04 pm	5	Libra	6:25 pm
7	9:04 pm	8	Scorpio	1:15 am
10	12:34 am	10	Sagittarius	4:34 am
11	9:42 pm	12	Capricorn	5:01 am
14	12:17 am	14	Aquarius	4:13 am
16	12:36 am	16	Pisces	4:18 am
18	2:43 am	18	Aries	7:17 am
20	10:19 am	20	Taurus	2:23 pm
22	7:45 pm	23	Gemini	1:11 am
25	4:14 am	25	Cancer	1:54 pm
27	8:54 pm	28	Leo	2:36 am
30	12:29 am	30	Virgo	2:11 pm
		August		
1	6:29 pm	2	Libra	12:06 am
4	2:20 am	4	Scorpio	7:47 am
6	7:24 am	6	Sagittarius	12:39 pm
8	6:30 am	8	Capricorn	2:39 pm
10	12:39 pm	10	Aquarius	2:45 pm
12	7:07 am	12	Pisces	2:44 pm
14	11:11 am	14	Aries	4:43 pm
16	4:18 pm	16	Taurus	10:22 pm
19	7:06 am	19	Gemini	8:06 am
21	6:06 pm	21	Cancer	8:29 pm
24	5:40 am	24	Leo	9:09 am
26	2:55 am	26	Virgo	8:25 pm
28	11:08 pm	29	Libra	5:45 am
31	6:43 am	31	Scorpio	1:11 pm

Last Aspect   Moon Enters New Sign

		September		
2	1:22 pm	2	Sagittarius	6:39 pm
4	9:51 pm	4	Capricorn	10:03 pm
6	5:43 pm	6	Aquarius	11:41 pm
8	8:34 am	9	Pisces	12:42 am
10	8:29 pm	11	Aries	2:47 am
13	12:53 am	13	Taurus	7:39 am
15	8:59 am	15	Gemini	4:16 pm
17	5:52 pm	18	Cancer	3:59 am
20	11:57 am	20	Leo	4:38 pm
22	7:07 am	23	Virgo	3:53 am
25	8:49 am	25	Libra	12:43 pm
27	12:21 pm	27	Scorpio	7:15 pm
29	5:20 pm	30	Sagittarius	12:03 am
		October		
1	5:46 pm	2	Capricorn	3:38 am
3	11:49 pm	4	Aquarius	6:20 am
5	6:46 pm	6	Pisces	8:47 am
8	7:10 am	8	Aries	11:57 am
10	10:02 am	10	Taurus	5:04 pm
12	5:42 pm	13	Gemini	1:08 am
15	12:11 am	15	Cancer	12:11 pm
17	4:56 pm	18	Leo	12:45 am
20	6:35 am	20	Virgo	12:25 pm
22	2:17 pm	22	Libra	9:24 pm
24	8:36 pm	25	Scorpio	3:18 am
27	12:27 am	27	Sagittarius	6:55 am
29	9:10 am	29	Capricorn	9:21 am
31	11:14 am	31	Aquarius	11:43 am

Last Aspect   **Moon Enters New Sign**

		November			
2	7:08 am	2		Pisces	2:46 pm
4	6:05 pm	4		Aries	7:07 pm
6	5:30 pm	7		Taurus	12:15 am
9	7:00 am	9		Gemini	8:37 am
11	5:28 pm	11		Cancer	7:22 pm
14	5:41 am	14		Leo	7:48 am
16	6:55 pm	16		Virgo	8:04 pm
19	3:47 am	19		Libra	5:58 am
21	6:14 am	21		Scorpio	12:16 pm
23	1:16 pm	23		Sagittarius	3:16 pm
25	2:22 pm	25		Capricorn	4:18 pm
27	3:11 pm	27		Aquarius	5:07 pm
29	1:53 am	29		Pisces	7:15 pm
		December			
1	9:44 pm	1		Aries	11:41 pm
4	12:46 am	4		Taurus	6:38 am
6	2:02 pm	6		Gemini	3:49 pm
9	1:13 am	9		Cancer	2:49 am
11	1:49 pm	11		Leo	3:09 pm
13	10:52 am	14		Virgo	3:45 am
16	2:13 pm	16		Libra	2:49 pm
18	5:35 pm	18		Scorpio	10:31 pm
20	9:45 pm	21		Sagittarius	2:12 am
22	3:16 pm	23		Capricorn	2:49 am
24	10:11 pm	25		Aquarius	2:14 am
26	1:19 pm	27		Pisces	2:34 am
29	1:21 am	29		Aries	5:36 am
31	7:44 am	31		Taurus	12:08 pm

The Moon's Rhythm

The Moon journeys around Earth in an elliptical orbit that takes about 27.33 days, which is known as a sidereal month (period of revolution of one body about another). She can move up to 15 degrees or as few as 11 degrees in a day, with the fastest motion occurring when the Moon is at perigee (closest approach to Earth). The Moon is never retrograde, but when her motion is slow, the effect is similar to a retrograde period.

Astrologers have observed that people born on a day when the Moon is fast will process information differently from those who are born when the Moon is slow in motion. People born when the Moon is fast process information quickly and tend to react quickly, while those born during a slow Moon will be more deliberate.

The time from New Moon to New Moon is called the synodic month (involving a conjunction), and the average time span between this Sun-Moon alignment is 29.53 days. Since 29.53 won't divide into 365 evenly, we can have a month with two Full Moons or two New Moons.

Moon Aspects

The aspects the Moon will make during the times you are considering are also important. A trine or sextile, and sometimes a conjunction, are considered favorable aspects. A trine or sextile between the Sun and Moon is an excellent foundation for success. Whether or not a conjunction is considered favorable depends upon the planet the Moon is making a conjunction to. If it's joining the Sun, Venus, Mercury, Jupiter, or even Saturn, the aspect is favorable. If the Moon joins Pluto or Mars, however, that would not be considered favorable. There may be exceptions, but it would depend on what you are electing to do. For example, a trine to Pluto might hasten the end of a relationship you want to be free of.

It is important to avoid times when the Moon makes an aspect to or is conjoining any retrograde planet, unless, of course, you want the thing started to end in failure.

After the Moon has completed an aspect to a planet, that planetary energy has passed. For example, if the Moon squares Saturn at 10:00 am, you can disregard Saturn's influence on your activity if it will occur after that time. You should always look ahead at aspects the Moon will make on the day in question, though, because if the Moon opposes Mars at 11:30 pm on that day, you can expect events that stretch into the evening to be affected by the Moon-Mars aspect. A testy conversation might lead to an argument, or more.

Moon Signs

Much agricultural work is ruled by earth signs—Virgo, Capricorn, and Taurus. The air signs—Gemini, Aquarius, and Libra—rule flying and intellectual pursuits.

Each planet has one or two signs in which its characteristics are enhanced or "dignified," and the planet is said to "rule" that sign. The Sun rules Leo and the Moon rules Cancer, for example. The ruling planet for each sign is listed below. These should not be considered complete lists. We recommend that you purchase a book of planetary rulerships for more complete information.

Aries Moon

The energy of an Aries Moon is masculine, dry, barren, and fiery. Aries provides great start-up energy, but things started at this time may be the result of impulsive action that lacks research or necessary support. Aries lacks staying power.

Use this assertive, outgoing Moon sign to initiate change, but have a plan in place for someone to pick up the reins when you're impatient to move on to the next thing. Work that requires skillful but not necessarily patient use of tools—cutting down trees, hammering, etc.—is appropriate in Aries. Expect things to occur rapidly but to also quickly pass. If you are prone to injury or accidents, exercise caution and good judgment in Aries-related activities.

RULER: Mars
IMPULSE: Action
RULES: Head and face

Taurus Moon

A Taurus Moon's energy is feminine, semi-fruitful, and earthy. The Moon is exalted—very strong—in Taurus. Taurus is known as the farmer's sign because of its associations with farmland and precipitation that is the typical day-long "soaker" variety. Taurus energy is good to incorporate into your plans when patience, practicality, and perseverance are needed. Be aware, though, that you may also experience stubbornness in this sign.

Things started in Taurus tend to be long lasting and to increase in value. This can be very supportive energy in a marriage election. On the downside, the fixed energy of this sign resists change or the letting go of even the most difficult situations. A divorce following a marriage that occurred during a Taurus Moon may be difficult and costly to end. Things begun now tend to become habitual and hard to alter. If you want to make changes in something you started, it would be better to wait for Gemini. This is a good time to get a loan, but expect the people in charge of money to be cautious and slow to make decisions.

RULER: Venus

IMPULSE: Stability

RULES: Neck, throat, and voice

Gemini Moon

A Gemini Moon's energy is masculine, dry, barren, and airy. People are more changeable than usual and may prefer to follow intellectual pursuits and play mental games rather than apply themselves to practical concerns.

This sign is not favored for agricultural matters, but it is an excellent time to prepare for activities, to run errands, and write letters. Plan to use a Gemini Moon to exchange ideas, meet people, go on vacations that include walking or biking, or be in situations that require versatility and quick thinking on your feet.

RULER: Mercury

IMPULSE: Versatility

RULES: Shoulders, hands, arms, lungs, and nervous system

Cancer Moon

A Cancer Moon's energy is feminine, fruitful, moist, and very strong. Use this sign when you want to grow things—flowers, fruits, vegetables, commodities, stocks, or collections—for example. This sensitive sign stimulates rapport between people. Considered the most fertile of the signs, it is often associated with mothering. You can use this moontime to build personal friendships that support mutual growth.

Cancer is associated with emotions and feelings. Prominent Cancer energy promotes growth, but it can also turn people pouty and prone to withdrawing into their shells.

RULER: The Moon

IMPULSE: Tenacity

RULES: Chest area, breasts, and stomach

Leo Moon

A Leo Moon's energy is masculine, hot, dry, fiery, and barren. Use it whenever you need to put on a show, make a presentation, or entertain colleagues or guests. This is a proud yet playful energy that exudes self-confidence and is often associated with romance.

This is an excellent time for fundraisers and ceremonies or to be straightforward, frank, and honest about something. It is advisable not to put yourself in a position of needing public approval or where you might have to cope with underhandedness, as trouble in these areas can bring out the worst Leo traits. There is a tendency in this sign to become arrogant or self-centered.

RULER: The Sun

IMPULSE: I am

RULES: Heart and upper back

Virgo Moon

A Virgo Moon is feminine, dry, barren, earthy energy. It is favorable for anything that needs painstaking attention—especially those things where exactness rather than innovation is preferred.

Use this sign for activities when you must analyze information or when you must determine the value of something. Virgo is the sign of bargain hunting. It's friendly toward agricultural matters with an emphasis on animals and harvesting vegetables. It is an excellent time to care for animals, especially training them and veterinary work.

This sign is most beneficial when decisions have already been made and now need to be carried out. The inclination here is to see details rather than the bigger picture.

There is a tendency in this sign to overdo. Precautions should be taken to avoid becoming too dull from all work and no play. Build relaxation and pleasure into your routine from the beginning.

RULER: Mercury

IMPULSE: Discriminating

RULES: Abdomen and intestines

Libra Moon

A Libra Moon's energy is masculine, semi-fruitful, and airy. This energy will benefit any attempt to bring beauty to a place or thing. Libra is considered good energy for starting things of an intellectual nature. Libra is the sign of partnership and unions, which makes it an excellent time to form partnerships of any kind, to make agreements, and to negotiate. Even though this sign is good for initiating things, it is crucial to work with a partner who will provide incentive and encouragement. A Libra Moon accentuates teamwork (particularly teams of two) and artistic work (especially work that involves color). Make use of this sign when you are decorating your home or shopping for better-quality clothing.

RULER: Venus

IMPULSE: Balance

RULES: Lower back, kidneys, and buttocks

Scorpio Moon

The Scorpio Moon is feminine, fruitful, cold, and moist. It is useful when intensity (that sometimes borders on obsession) is needed. Scorpio is considered a very psychic sign. Use this Moon sign when you must back up something you strongly believe in, such as union or employer relations. There is strong group loyalty here, but a Scorpio Moon is also a good time to end connections thoroughly. This is also a good time to conduct research.

The desire nature is so strong here that there is a tendency to manipulate situations to get what one wants or to not see one's responsibility in an act.

RULER: Pluto, Mars (traditional)

IMPULSE: Transformation

RULES: Reproductive organs, genitals, groin, and pelvis

Sagittarius Moon

The Moon's energy is masculine, dry, barren, and fiery in Sagittarius, encouraging flights of imagination and confidence in the flow of life. Sagittarius is the most philosophical sign. Candor and honesty are enhanced when the Moon is here. This is an excellent time to "get things off your chest" and to deal with institutions of higher learning, publishing companies, and the law. It's also a good time for sport and adventure.

Sagittarians are the crusaders of this world. This is a good time to tackle things that need improvement, but don't try to be the diplomat while influenced by this energy. Opinions can run strong, and the tendency to proselytize is increased.

RULER: Jupiter

IMPULSE: Expansion

RULES: Thighs and hips

Capricorn Moon

In Capricorn the Moon's energy is feminine, semi-fruitful, and earthy. Because Cancer and Capricorn are polar opposites, the Moon's energy is thought to be weakened here. This energy encourages the need for structure, discipline, and organization. This is a good time to set goals and plan for the future, tend to family business, and to take care of details requiring patience or a businesslike manner. Institutional activities are favored. This sign should be avoided if you're seeking favors, as those in authority can be insensitive under this influence.

RULER: Saturn

IMPULSE: Ambitious

RULES: Bones, skin, and knees

Aquarius Moon

An Aquarius Moon's energy is masculine, barren, dry, and airy. Activities that are unique, individualistic, concerned with humanitarian issues, society as a whole, and making improvements are favored under this Moon. It is this quality of making improvements that has caused this sign to be associated with inventors and new inventions.

An Aquarius Moon promotes the gathering of social groups for friendly exchanges. People tend to react and speak from an intellectual rather than emotional viewpoint when the Moon is in this sign.

RULER: Uranus and Saturn

IMPULSE: Reformer

RULES: Calves and ankles

Pisces Moon

A Pisces Moon is feminine, fruitful, cool, and moist. This is an excellent time to retreat, meditate, sleep, pray, or make that dreamed-of escape into a fantasy vacation. However, things are not always what they seem to be with the Moon in Pisces. Personal boundaries tend to be fuzzy, and you may not be seeing things clearly. People tend to be idealistic under this sign, which can prevent them from seeing reality.

There is a live-and-let-live philosophy attached to this sign, which in the idealistic world may work well enough, but chaos is frequently the result. That's why this sign is also associated with alcohol and drug abuse, drug trafficking, and counterfeiting. On the lighter side, many musicians and artists are ruled by Pisces. It's only when they move too far away from reality that the dark side of substance abuse, suicide, or crime takes away life.

RULER: Jupiter and Neptune

IMPULSE: Empathetic

RULES: Feet

More About Zodiac Signs

Element (Triplicity)

Each of the zodiac signs is classified as belonging to an element; these are the four basic elements:

Fire Signs

Aries, Sagittarius, and Leo are action-oriented, outgoing, energetic, and spontaneous.

Earth Signs

Taurus, Capricorn, and Virgo are stable, conservative, practical, and oriented to the physical and material realm.

Air Signs

Gemini, Aquarius, and Libra are sociable and critical, and they tend to represent intellectual responses rather than feelings.

Water Signs

Cancer, Scorpio, and Pisces are emotional, receptive, intuitive, and can be very sensitive.

Quality (Quadruplicity)

Each zodiac sign is further classified as being cardinal, mutable, or fixed. There are four signs in each quadruplicity, one sign from each element.

Cardinal Signs

Aries, Cancer, Libra, and Capricorn represent beginnings and newly initiated action. They initiate each new season in the cycle of the year.

Fixed Signs

Taurus, Leo, Scorpio, and Aquarius want to maintain the status quo through stubbornness and persistence; they represent that "between" time. For example, Leo is the month when summer really feels like summer.

Mutable Signs

Pisces, Gemini, Virgo, and Sagittarius adapt to change and tolerate situations. They represent the last month of each season, when things are changing in preparation for the coming season.

Nature and Fertility

In addition to a sign's element and quality, each sign is further classified as either fruitful, semi-fruitful, or barren. This classification is the most important for readers who use the gardening information in the *Moon Sign Book* because the timing of most events depends on the fertility of the sign occupied by the Moon. The water signs of Cancer, Scorpio, and Pisces are the most fruitful. The semi-fruitful signs are the earth signs Taurus and Capricorn, and the air sign Libra. The barren signs correspond to fire-signs Aries, Leo, and Sagittarius; air-signs Gemini and Aquarius; and earth-sign Virgo.

Good Timing

Sharon Leah

Electional astrology is the art of electing times to begin any undertaking. Say, for example, you want to start a business. That business will experience ups and downs, as well as reach its potential, according to the promise held in the universe at the time the business was started—its birth time. The horoscope (birth chart) set for the date, time, and place that a business starts would indicate the outcome—its potential to succeed.

So, you might ask yourself the question: If the horoscope for a business start can show success or failure, why not begin at a time that is more favorable to the venture? Well, you can.

While no time is perfect, there are better times and better days to undertake specific activities. There are thousands of examples that prove electional astrology is not only practical, but that it can make a difference in our lives. There are rules for electing times to begin various activities—even shopping. You'll find detailed instructions about how to make elections beginning on page 107.

Personalizing Elections

The election rules in this almanac are based upon the planetary positions at the time for which the election is made. They do not depend on any type of birth chart. However, a birth chart based upon the time, date, and birthplace of an event has advantages. No election is effective for every person. For example, you may leave home to begin a trip at the same time as a friend, but each of you will have a different experience according to whether or not your birth chart favors the trip.

Not all elections require a birth chart, but the timing of very important events—business starts, marriages, etc.—would benefit from the additional accuracy a birth chart provides. To order a birth chart for yourself or a planned event, visit our website at www.llewellyn.com.

Some Things to Consider

You've probably experienced good timing in your life. Maybe you were at the right place at the right time to meet a friend whom you hadn't seen in years. Frequently, when something like that happens, it is the result of following an intuitive impulse—that "gut instinct." Consider for a moment that you were actually responding to planetary energies. Electional astrology is a tool that can help you to align with energies, present and future, that are available to us through planetary placements.

Significators

Decide upon the important significators (planet, sign, and house ruling the matter) for which the election is being made. The Moon is the most important significator in any election, so the Moon should always be fortified (strong by sign and making favorable aspects to other planets). The Moon's aspects to other planets are more important than the sign the Moon is in.

Other important considerations are the significators of the Ascendant and Midheaven—the house ruling the election matter and the ruler of the sign on that house cusp. Finally, any planet or sign that has a general rulership over the matter in question should be taken into consideration.

Nature and Fertility

Determine the general nature of the sign that is appropriate for your election. For example, much agricultural work is ruled by the earth signs of Virgo, Capricorn, and Taurus; while the air signs—Gemini, Aquarius, and Libra—rule intellectual pursuits.

One Final Comment

Use common sense. If you must do something, like plant your garden or take an airplane trip on a day that doesn't have the best aspects, proceed anyway, but try to minimize problems. For example, leave early for the airport to avoid being left behind due to delays in the security lanes. When you have no other choice, do the best that you can under the circumstances at the time.

If you want to personalize your elections, please turn to page 107 for more information. If you want a quick and easy answer, you can refer to Llewellyn's Astro Almanac on the following pages.

Llewellyn's Astro Almanac

The Astro Almanac tables, beginning on the next page, can help you find the dates best suited to particular activities. The dates provided are determined from the Moon's sign, phase, and aspects to other planets. Please note that the Astro Almanac does not take personal factors, such as your Sun and Moon sign, into account. The dates are general, and they will apply for everyone. Some activities will not have ideal dates during a particular month.

Activity	January
Animals (Neuter or spay)	1, 2, 27–30
Animals (Sell or buy)	10
Automobile (Buy)	2, 13, 14, 21, 29, 30
Brewing	25
Build (Start foundation)	no ideal dates
Business (Conducting for self and others)	7, 12, 22, 27
Business (Start new)	10
Can Fruits and Vegetables	25
Can Preserves	25
Concrete (Pour)	18, 19
Construction (Begin new)	1, 10, 12, 15, 22, 27, 29
Consultants (Begin work with)	1, 3, 5, 8, 10, 13, 15, 22, 25, 27, 29, 30
Contracts (Bid on)	3, 5, 8, 10, 13, 15
Cultivate	31
Decorating	3–5, 13–15
Demolition	18, 19, 27, 28
Electronics (Buy)	3, 13, 22
Entertain Guests	11
Floor Covering (Laying new)	18–24, 31
Habits (Break)	1, 29, 30
Hair (Cut to increase growth)	6, 7, 10–14, 17
Hair (Cut to decrease growth)	1, 2, 27–30
Harvest (Grain for storage)	18,–20, 23
Harvest (Root crops)	1, 18, 19, 27, 28
Investments (New)	12, 22
Loan (Ask for)	10–12
Massage (Relaxing)	11
Mow Lawn (Decrease growth)	1, 18–30
Mow Lawn (Increase growth)	3–16
Mushrooms (Pick)	16–18
Negotiate (Business for the elderly)	23
Prune for Better Fruit	1, 24–28
Prune to Promote Healing	2, 29–31
Wean Children	1–5, 27–31
Wood Floors (Installing)	1, 2, 29–31
Write Letters or Contracts	2, 3, 6, 16, 21, 29, 30

Activity	February
Animals (Neuter or spay)	23–27
Animals (Sell or buy)	3, 7
Automobile (Buy)	10, 17, 26
Brewing	22
Build (Start foundation)	no ideal dates
Business (Conducting for self and others)	5, 11, 21, 26
Business (Start new)	7
Can Fruits and Vegetables	22
Can Preserves	22
Concrete (Pour)	28
Construction (Begin new)	5, 7, 11, 12, 26
Consultants (Begin work with)	7, 8, 12, 19, 22, 24, 26, 28
Contracts (Bid on)	2, 3, 7, 8, 12
Cultivate	28
Decorating	1, 2, 9, 10, 11
Demolition	23, 24
Electronics (Buy)	19, 28
Entertain Guests	7
Floor Covering (Laying new)	17–21, 27, 28
Habits (Break)	25–28
Hair (Cut to increase growth)	3, 6–10, 14
Hair (Cut to decrease growth)	23–26
Harvest (Grain for storage)	23
Harvest (Root crops)	16, 23, 24, 27, 28
Investments (New)	11, 21
Loan (Ask for)	6–9, 14, 15
Massage (Relaxing)	7
Mow Lawn (Decrease growth)	17–28
Mow Lawn (Increase growth)	2–15
Mushrooms (Pick)	15–17
Negotiate (Business for the elderly)	5, 10, 24
Prune for Better Fruit	21–24
Prune to Promote Healing	25–27
Wean Children	1, 2, 23–28
Wood Floors (Installing)	25, 26, 27
Write Letters or Contracts	3, 12, 17, 26

Activity	March
Animals (Neuter or spay)	1, 2, 25, 26, 29–31
Animals (Sell or buy)	3, 7
Automobile (Buy)	10, 16, 25, 26
Brewing	21, 22, 29, 30
Build (Start foundation)	no ideal dates
Business (Conducting for self and others)	7, 12, 22, 27
Business (Start new)	7, 17
Can Fruits and Vegetables	2, 21, 29, 30
Can Preserves	21
Concrete (Pour)	27
Construction (Begin new)	7, 12, 22, 26, 27
Consultants (Begin work with)	2, 5, 7, 11, 12, 21, 26, 30, 31
Contracts (Bid on)	5, 7, 11, 12
Cultivate	23, 24, 27, 28, 31
Decorating	8–10
Demolition	22, 23, 31
Electronics (Buy)	no ideal dates
Entertain Guests	8, 19
Floor Covering (Laying new)	1, 19, 20, 27, 28
Habits (Break)	25, 26, 27, 28
Hair (Cut to increase growth)	6–10, 13
Hair (Cut to decrease growth)	2, 22–25, 29, 30
Harvest (Grain for storage)	22–24, 26
Harvest (Root crops)	22–24
Investments (New)	12, 22
Loan (Ask for)	6–8, 13–15
Massage (Relaxing)	19, 28
Mow Lawn (Decrease growth)	1, 19–30
Mow Lawn (Increase growth)	3–17
Mushrooms (Pick)	17–19
Negotiate (Business for the elderly)	19
Prune for Better Fruit	20–24
Prune to Promote Healing	25, 26
Wean Children	23–28
Wood Floors (Installing)	25, 26
Write Letters or Contracts	2, 12, 16, 25, 29, 31

Activity	April
Animals (Neuter or spay)	25–27
Animals (Sell or buy)	2
Automobile (Buy)	6, 12, 13, 21, 22
Brewing	17, 18, 26, 27
Build (Start foundation)	no ideal dates
Business (Conducting for self and others)	6, 11, 21, 25
Business (Start new)	4, 14
Can Fruits and Vegetables	17, 18, 26
Can Preserves	17, 18
Concrete (Pour)	23, 24
Construction (Begin new)	4, 6, 9, 11, 21, 22
Consultants (Begin work with)	4, 6, 9, 12, 18, 22, 27
Contracts (Bid on)	4, 6, 9, 12
Cultivate	19, 23, 24, 28, 29
Decorating	6, 7, 15, 16
Demolition	19, 28
Electronics (Buy)	6
Entertain Guests	7
Floor Covering (Laying new)	23, 24
Habits (Break)	24, 28, 29
Hair (Cut to increase growth)	2– 4, 6
Hair (Cut to decrease growth)	19–22, 26, 29, 30
Harvest (Grain for storage)	18–20
Harvest (Root crops)	19, 20, 23, 24, 28, 29
Investments (New)	11, 21
Loan (Ask for)	3, 4, 10, 11, 12, 29, 30
Massage (Relaxing)	7
Mow Lawn (Decrease growth)	17–29
Mow Lawn (Increase growth)	2–4, 6–15
Mushrooms (Pick)	15–17
Negotiate (Business for the elderly)	1, 6, 16, 20, 29
Prune for Better Fruit	16–20
Prune to Promote Healing	21, 22
Wean Children	19–24
Wood Floors (Installing)	21, 22
Write Letters or Contracts	8, 13, 21, 26

Activity	May
Animals (Neuter or spay)	22–24
Animals (Sell or buy)	2, 7
Automobile (Buy)	2, 4, 10, 19, 31
Brewing	23, 24
Build (Start foundation)	no ideal dates
Business (Conducting for self and others)	6, 11, 20, 25
Business (Start new)	2
Can Fruits and Vegetables	23, 24
Can Preserves	27, 28
Concrete (Pour)	21, 27, 28
Construction (Begin new)	2, 6, 7, 11, 16, 20, 25, 29
Consultants (Begin work with)	2, 7, 12, 16, 20, 24, 29
Contracts (Bid on)	2, 7, 12
Cultivate	17, 25, 26
Decorating	2–4, 12–14, 30, 31
Demolition	16, 17, 24, 25, 26
Electronics (Buy)	2, 12, 20
Entertain Guests	2, 7
Floor Covering (Laying new)	20, 21, 27, 28, 29
Habits (Break)	24–26, 29
Hair (Cut to increase growth)	1–3, 7, 30, 31
Hair (Cut to decrease growth)	17–19, 23, 27–29
Harvest (Grain for storage)	17, 18, 20
Harvest (Root crops)	16, 17, 20, 21, 24–26, 29
Investments (New)	11, 20
Loan (Ask for)	1, 2, 7–9
Massage (Relaxing)	2, 7, 21
Mow Lawn (Decrease growth)	17–29
Mow Lawn (Increase growth)	1–14, 31
Mushrooms (Pick)	15–17
Negotiate (Business for the elderly)	13, 17, 26, 31
Prune for Better Fruit	16, 17
Prune to Promote Healing	18–20
Wean Children	16–22
Wood Floors (Installing)	18–20
Write Letters or Contracts	2, 6, 19, 23, 29

Activity	June
Animals (Neuter or spay)	20
Animals (Sell or buy)	3, 13
Automobile (Buy)	7, 8, 15, 27
Brewing	19, 20
Build (Start foundation)	no ideal dates
Business (Conducting for self and others)	4, 9, 18, 23
Business (Start new)	no ideal dates
Can Fruits and Vegetables	19, 20
Can Preserves	24, 25
Concrete (Pour)	17, 18, 24, 25
Construction (Begin new)	3, 4, 9, 13, 17, 18, 23, 26
Consultants (Begin work with)	3, 8, 13, 16, 17, 21, 26, 27
Contracts (Bid on)	3, 8, 13
Cultivate	14, 21, 22, 26, 27
Decorating	8, 9, 10
Demolition	21, 22
Electronics (Buy)	16, 27
Entertain Guests	26
Floor Covering (Laying new)	16–18, 23–27
Habits (Break)	21–23, 26, 27
Hair (Cut to increase growth)	3, 12, 13, 30
Hair (Cut to decrease growth)	15, 19, 23–27
Harvest (Grain for storage)	16–18, 20
Harvest (Root crops)	14, 16–18, 21, 22, 26, 27
Investments (New)	9, 18
Loan (Ask for)	3–5, 30
Massage (Relaxing)	1
Mow Lawn (Decrease growth)	15–27
Mow Lawn (Increase growth)	1–13, 29, 30
Mushrooms (Pick)	13–15
Negotiate (Business for the elderly)	10, 14, 22, 27
Prune for Better Fruit	no ideal dates
Prune to Promote Healing	15, 16
Wean Children	13–18
Wood Floors (Installing)	14–16
Write Letters or Contracts	2, 7, 15, 20, 27, 29

Activity	July
Animals (Neuter or spay)	no ideal dates
Animals (Sell or buy)	1, 7, 10, 31
Automobile (Buy)	4, 13, 23, 25
Brewing	17, 26
Build (Start foundation)	no ideal dates
Business (Conducting for self and others)	4, 9, 17, 23
Business (Start new)	12
Can Fruits and Vegetables	17, 26
Can Preserves	21, 26
Concrete (Pour)	15, 21
Construction (Begin new)	1, 4, 10, 14, 23, 28
Consultants (Begin work with)	1, 3, 8, 10, 14, 18, 23, 28, 29
Contracts (Bid on)	1, 3, 8, 10, 29
Cultivate	20, 23–25, 28
Decorating	5–7
Demolition	18, 19, 28
Electronics (Buy)	23
Entertain Guests	1, 7, 26
Floor Covering (Laying new)	14, 15, 21–25
Habits (Break)	23–25
Hair (Cut to increase growth)	10–13
Hair (Cut to decrease growth)	17, 20–24
Harvest (Grain for storage)	14, 15, 18, 19
Harvest (Root crops)	14, 15, 18, 19, 20, 23–25
Investments (New)	9, 17
Loan (Ask for)	1, 2, 3, 29, 30
Massage (Relaxing)	1, 7, 16, 20, 26
Mow Lawn (Decrease growth)	14–27
Mow Lawn (Increase growth)	1–12, 29–31
Mushrooms (Pick)	12–14
Negotiate (Business for the elderly)	7, 11
Prune for Better Fruit	no ideal dates
Prune to Promote Healing	13, 14
Wean Children	10–16
Wood Floors (Installing)	13, 14
Write Letters or Contracts	4, 13, 17, 27

Activity	August
Animals (Neuter or spay)	no ideal dates
Animals (Sell or buy)	6, 7, 31
Automobile (Buy)	1, 9, 21, 28
Brewing	13, 14, 22, 23
Build (Start foundation)	no ideal dates
Business (Conducting for self and others)	2, 7, 16, 21
Business (Start new)	9
Can Fruits and Vegetables	13, 14, 22, 23
Can Preserves	17, 18, 22, 23
Concrete (Pour)	17, 18, 25, 26
Construction (Begin new)	2, 7, 11, 16, 19, 21, 25
Consultants (Begin work with)	4, 7, 9, 11, 15, 18, 19, 24, 25, 29
Contracts (Bid on)	4, 7, 9, 11, 29
Cultivate	20, 21, 25, 26
Decorating	2–4, 11, 29–31
Demolition	14, 15, 24, 25
Electronics (Buy)	29
Entertain Guests	20, 25, 31
Floor Covering (Laying new)	12, 17–21, 24–27
Habits (Break)	19–21, 24–26
Hair (Cut to increase growth)	6–9
Hair (Cut to decrease growth)	13, 16–20, 24
Harvest (Grain for storage)	14–16
Harvest (Root crops)	12, 14–16, 19–21, 24–26
Investments (New)	7, 16
Loan (Ask for)	no ideal dates
Massage (Relaxing)	25, 31
Mow Lawn (Decrease growth)	12–26
Mow Lawn (Increase growth)	1–10, 28–31
Mushrooms (Pick)	10–12
Negotiate (Business for the elderly)	3, 30
Prune for Better Fruit	no ideal dates
Prune to Promote Healing	no ideal dates
Wean Children	7–12
Wood Floors (Installing)	no ideal dates
Write Letters or Contracts	1, 9, 13, 23, 28, 29

Activity	September
Animals (Neuter or spay)	no ideal dates
Animals (Sell or buy)	4, 7, 30
Automobile (Buy)	6, 16, 17, 24, 25
Brewing	18–20
Build (Start foundation)	no ideal dates
Business (Conducting for self and others)	1, 5, 15, 20, 30
Business (Start new)	5
Can Fruits and Vegetables	18–20
Can Preserves	14, 15, 18–20
Concrete (Pour)	14, 15, 21, 22
Construction (Begin new)	3, 5, 7, 15, 16, 20, 21, 30
Consultants (Begin work with)	3, 7, 11, 16, 20, 21, 25, 29, 30
Contracts (Bid on)	3, 7, 11, 29, 30
Cultivate	21–25
Decorating	7, 8, 25–27
Demolition	11, 12, 20–23
Electronics (Buy)	7, 16
Entertain Guests	14, 19
Floor Covering (Laying new)	13–17, 21–25
Habits (Break)	20–23
Hair (Cut to increase growth)	2–5, 9, 30
Hair (Cut to decrease growth)	13–17, 20
Harvest (Grain for storage)	11, 12, 15–17
Harvest (Root crops)	11, 12, 16, 17, 20–22
Investments (New)	5, 15
Loan (Ask for)	no ideal dates
Massage (Relaxing)	14, 19
Mow Lawn (Decrease growth)	11–24
Mow Lawn (Increase growth)	1–9, 26–30
Mushrooms (Pick)	9–11
Negotiate (Business for the elderly)	12, 26
Prune for Better Fruit	no ideal dates
Prune to Promote Healing	no ideal dates
Wean Children	3–8, 30
Wood Floors (Installing)	no ideal dates
Write Letters or Contracts	6, 10, 19, 24, 25

Activity	October
Animals (Neuter or spay)	no ideal dates
Animals (Sell or buy)	4, 27, 31
Automobile (Buy)	3, 13, 14, 21, 30
Brewing	16
Build (Start foundation)	no ideal dates
Business (Conducting for self and others)	5, 14, 20, 29
Business (Start new)	2, 31
Can Fruits and Vegetables	16, 25
Can Preserves	11, 16, 25
Concrete (Pour)	11, 18, 19
Construction (Begin new)	4, 5, 13, 14, 18, 20, 27, 29, 31
Consultants (Begin work with)	3, 4, 8, 13, 18, 19, 24, 27, 29, 31
Contracts (Bid on)	3, 4, 8, 27, 29, 31
Cultivate	19, 20–22
Decorating	4–6, 31
Demolition	9, 18, 19
Electronics (Buy)	13, 24
Entertain Guests	14, 20
Floor Covering (Laying new)	11–15, 18–24
Habits (Break)	18–20
Hair (Cut to increase growth)	1–3, 7, 27–30
Hair (Cut to decrease growth)	10–14
Harvest (Grain for storage)	10, 13, 14
Harvest (Root crops)	10, 13–15, 18–20
Investments (New)	5, 14
Loan (Ask for)	no ideal dates
Massage (Relaxing)	4, 20
Mow Lawn (Decrease growth)	10–24
Mow Lawn (Increase growth)	1–8, 26–31
Mushrooms (Pick)	8–10
Negotiate (Business for the elderly)	1, 9, 14, 28
Prune for Better Fruit	25
Prune to Promote Healing	no ideal dates
Wean Children	1–6, 27–31
Wood Floors (Installing)	no ideal dates
Write Letters or Contracts	3, 7, 17, 21, 30

Activity	November
Animals (Neuter or spay)	no ideal dates
Animals (Sell or buy)	3, 27, 28
Automobile (Buy)	10, 18, 26
Brewing	12, 13, 22
Build (Start foundation)	no ideal dates
Business (Conducting for self and others)	3, 13, 19, 28
Business (Start new)	27
Can Fruits and Vegetables	12, 13, 22, 23
Can Preserves	12, 13, 22, 23
Concrete (Pour)	15, 16
Construction (Begin new)	9, 13, 14, 19, 27, 28
Consultants (Begin work with)	3, 4, 9, 13, 14, 19, 23, 24, 27, 28
Contracts (Bid on)	3, 4, 24, 27, 28
Cultivate	16–18
Decorating	1, 2, 28, 29
Demolition	14, 15
Electronics (Buy)	19, 28
Entertain Guests	14, 19
Floor Covering (Laying new)	9–11, 14–21
Habits (Break)	no ideal dates
Hair (Cut to increase growth)	3, 7, 24–26, 30
Hair (Cut to decrease growth)	9, 10, 14, 23
Harvest (Grain for storage)	9–11, 14, 15
Harvest (Root crops)	10, 11, 14–16
Investments (New)	3, 13
Loan (Ask for)	7
Massage (Relaxing)	14, 19, 28
Mow Lawn (Decrease growth)	9–22
Mow Lawn (Increase growth)	1–5, 7, 24–30
Mushrooms (Pick)	7–9
Negotiate (Business for the elderly)	10, 20, 24
Prune for Better Fruit	22, 23
Prune to Promote Healing	no ideal dates
Wean Children	1, 2, 24–29
Wood Floors (Installing)	no ideal dates
Write Letters or Contracts	3, 13, 18, 24, 26, 30

Activity	December
Animals (Neuter or spay)	21, 22
Animals (Sell or buy)	3, 6, 25, 28
Automobile (Buy)	8, 15, 24
Brewing	9, 10, 11, 19
Build (Start foundation)	no ideal dates
Business (Conducting for self and others)	2, 13, 18, 27
Business (Start new)	6
Can Fruits and Vegetables	9–11, 19
Can Preserves	9–11, 19
Concrete (Pour)	12, 13
Construction (Begin new)	2, 6, 11, 13, 18, 21, 25
Consultants (Begin work with)	1, 3, 6, 11, 15, 20, 21, 24, 25, 28, 29
Contracts (Bid on)	1, 3, 6, 24, 25, 28, 29
Cultivate	16
Decorating	7, 25, 26
Demolition	11–14, 21, 22
Electronics (Buy)	no ideal dates
Entertain Guests	no ideal dates
Floor Covering (Laying new)	8, 12–18
Habits (Break)	no ideal dates
Hair (Cut to increase growth)	4–7, 23, 24, 28, 31
Hair (Cut to decrease growth)	8, 9, 11, 21, 22
Harvest (Grain for storage)	11–14
Harvest (Root crops)	8, 11–13, 21, 22
Investments (New)	2, 13
Loan (Ask for)	4–6, 31
Massage (Relaxing)	no ideal dates
Mow Lawn (Decrease growth)	8–22
Mow Lawn (Increase growth)	1–6, 24–31
Mushrooms (Pick)	6–8
Negotiate (Business for the elderly)	3, 22, 30
Prune for Better Fruit	19–22
Prune to Promote Healing	23
Wean Children	21–26
Wood Floors (Installing)	23
Write Letters or Contracts	10, 15, 24, 28

Choose the Best Time for Your Activities

When rules for elections refer to "favorable" and "unfavorable" aspects to your Sun or other planets, please refer to the Favorable and Unfavorable Days Tables and Lunar Aspectarian for more information. You'll find instructions beginning on page 129 and the tables beginning on page 136.

The material in this section came from several sources including: *The New A to Z Horoscope Maker and Delineator* by Llewellyn George (Llewellyn, 1999), *Moon Sign Book* (Llewellyn, 1945), and *Electional Astrology* by Vivian Robson (Slingshot Publishing, 2000). Robson's book was originally published in 1937.

Advertise (Internet)

The Moon should be conjunct, sextile, or trine Mercury or Uranus and in the sign of Gemini, Capricorn, or Aquarius.

Advertise (Print)

Write ads on a day favorable to your Sun. The Moon should be conjunct, sextile, or trine Mercury or Venus. Avoid hard aspects to Mars and Saturn. Ad campaigns produce the best results when the Moon is well aspected in Gemini (to enhance communication) or Capricorn (to build business).

Animals

Take home new pets when the day is favorable to your Sun, or when the Moon is trine, sextile, or conjunct Mercury, Jupiter or Venus, or in the sign of Virgo or Pisces. However, avoid days when the Moon is either square or opposing the Sun, Mars, Saturn, Uranus, Neptune, or Pluto. When selecting a pet, have the Moon well aspected by the planet that rules the animal. Cats are ruled by the Sun, dogs by Mercury, birds by Venus, horses by Jupiter, and fish by Neptune. Buy large animals when the Moon is in Sagittarius or Pisces and making favorable aspects to Jupiter or Mercury. Buy animals smaller than sheep when the Moon is in Virgo with favorable aspects to Mercury or Venus.

Animals (Breed)

Animals are easiest to handle when the Moon is in Taurus, Cancer, Libra, or Pisces, but try to avoid the Full Moon. To encourage healthy births, animals should be mated so births occur when the Moon is increasing in Taurus, Cancer, Pisces, or Libra. Those born during a semi-fruitful sign (Taurus and Capricorn) will produce leaner meat. Libra yields beautiful animals for showing and racing.

Animals (Neuter or Spay)

Have livestock and pets neutered or spayed when the Moon is in Sagittarius, Capricorn, or Pisces, after it has passed through Scorpio, the sign that rules reproductive organs. Avoid the week before and after the Full Moon.

Animals (Sell or Buy)

In either buying or selling, it is important to keep the Moon and Mercury free from any aspect to Mars. Aspects to Mars will create discord and increase the likelihood of wrangling over price and quality. The Moon should be passing from the first quarter to full and sextile or trine Venus or Jupiter. When buying racehorses, let the Moon be in an air sign. The Moon should be in air signs when you buy birds. If the birds are to be pets, let the Moon be in good aspect to Venus.

Animals (Train)

Train pets when the Moon is in Virgo or trine to Mercury.

Animals (Train Dogs to Hunt)

Let the Moon be in Aries in conjunction with Mars, which makes them courageous and quick to learn. But let Jupiter also be in aspect to preserve them from danger in hunting.

Automobiles

When buying an automobile, select a time when the Moon is conjunct, sextile, or trine to Mercury, Saturn, or Uranus and in the sign of Gemini or Capricorn. Avoid times when Mercury is in retrograde motion.

Baking Cakes

Your cakes will have a lighter texture if you see that the Moon is in Gemini, Libra, or Aquarius and in good aspect to Venus or Mercury. If you are decorating a cake or confections are being made, have the Moon placed in Libra.

Beauty Treatments (Massage, etc.)

See that the Moon is in Taurus, Cancer, Leo, Libra, or Aquarius and in favorable aspect to Venus. In the case of plastic surgery, aspects to Mars should be avoided, and the Moon should not be in the sign ruling the part to be operated on.

Borrow (Money or Goods)

See that the Moon is not placed between 15 degrees Libra and 15 degrees Scorpio. Let the Moon be waning and in Leo, Scorpio (16 to 30 degrees), Sagittarius, or Pisces. Venus should be in good aspect to the Moon, and the Moon should not be square, opposing, or conjunct either Saturn or Mars.

Brewing

Start brewing during the third or fourth quarter, when the Moon is in Cancer, Scorpio, or Pisces.

Build (Start Foundation)

Turning the first sod for the foundation marks the beginning of the building. For best results, excavate the site when the Moon is in the first quarter of a fixed sign and making favorable aspects to Saturn.

Business (Start New)

When starting a business, have the Moon be in Taurus, Virgo, or Capricorn and increasing. The Moon should be sextile or trine Jupiter or Saturn, but avoid oppositions or squares. The planet ruling the business should be well aspected too.

Buy Goods

Buy during the third quarter, when the Moon is in Taurus for quality or in a mutable sign (Gemini, Sagittarius, Virgo, or Pisces) for savings. Good aspects to Venus or the Sun are desirable. If you are buying for yourself, it is good if the day is favorable for your Sun sign. You may also apply rules for buying specific items.

Canning

Can fruits and vegetables when the Moon is in either the third or fourth quarter and in the water sign Cancer or Pisces. Preserves and jellies use the same quarters and the signs Cancer, Pisces, or Taurus.

Clothing

Buy clothing on a day that is favorable for your Sun sign and when Venus or Mercury is well aspected. Avoid aspects to Mars and Saturn. Buy your clothing when the Moon is in Taurus if you want to remain satisfied. Do not buy clothing or jewelry when the Moon is in Scorpio or Aries. See that the Moon is sextile or trine the Sun during the first or second quarters.

Collections

Try to make collections on days when your natal Sun is well aspected. Avoid days when the Moon is opposing or square Mars or Saturn. If possible, the Moon should be in a cardinal sign (Aries, Cancer, Libra, or Capricorn). It is more difficult to collect when the Moon is in Taurus or Scorpio.

Concrete

Pour concrete when the Moon is in the third quarter of the fixed sign Taurus, Leo, or Aquarius.

Construction (Begin New)

The Moon should be sextile or trine Jupiter. According to Hermes, no building should be begun when the Moon is in Scorpio or Pisces. The best time to begin building is when the Moon is in Aquarius.

Consultants (Work with)

The Moon should be conjunct, sextile, or trine Mercury or Jupiter.

Contracts (Bid On)

The Moon should be in Gemini or Capricorn and either the Moon or Mercury should be conjunct, sextile, or trine Jupiter.

Copyrights/Patents

The Moon should be conjunct, trine, or sextile either Mercury or Jupiter.

Coronations and Installations

Let the Moon be in Leo and in favorable aspect to Venus, Jupiter, or Mercury. The Moon should be applying to these planets.

Cultivate

Cultivate when the Moon is in a barren sign and waning, ideally the fourth quarter in Aries, Gemini, Leo, Virgo, or Aquarius. The third quarter in the sign of Sagittarius will also work.

Cut Timber

Timber cut during the waning Moon does not become worm-eaten; it will season well and not warp, decay, or snap during burning. Cut when the Moon is in Taurus, Gemini, Virgo, or Capricorn—especially in August. Avoid the water signs. Look for favorable aspects to Mars.

Decorating or Home Repairs

Have the Moon waxing and in the sign of Libra, Gemini, or Aquarius. Avoid squares or oppositions to either Mars or Saturn. Venus in good aspect to Mars or Saturn is beneficial.

Demolition

Let the waning Moon be in Leo, Sagittarius, or Aries.

Dental and Dentists

Visit the dentist when the Moon is in Virgo, or pick a day marked favorable for your Sun sign. Mars should be marked sextile, conjunct, or trine; avoid squares or oppositions to Saturn, Uranus, or Jupiter.

Teeth are best removed when the Moon is in Gemini, Virgo, Sagittarius, or Pisces and during the first or second quarter. Avoid the Full Moon! The day should be favorable for your lunar cycle, and Mars and Saturn should be marked conjunct, trine, or sextile. Fillings should be done in the third or fourth quarters in the sign of Taurus, Leo, Scorpio, or Pisces. The same applies for dentures.

Dressmaking

William Lilly wrote in 1676: "Make no new clothes, or first put them on when the Moon is in Scorpio or afflicted by Mars, for they will be apt to be torn and quickly worn out." Design, repair, and sew clothes in the first and second quarters of Taurus, Leo, or Libra on a day marked favorable for your Sun sign. Venus, Jupiter, and Mercury should be favorably aspected, but avoid hard aspects to Mars or Saturn.

Egg-Setting (see p. 161)

Eggs should be set so chicks will hatch during fruitful signs. To set eggs, subtract the number of days given for incubation or gestation from the fruitful dates. Chickens incubate in twenty-one days, turkeys and geese in twenty-eight days.

A freshly laid egg loses quality rapidly if it is not handled properly. Use plenty of clean litter in the nests to reduce the number of dirty or cracked eggs. Gather eggs daily in mild weather and at least two times daily in hot or cold weather. The eggs should be placed in a cooler immediately after gathering and stored at 50 to 55°F. Do not store eggs with foods or products that give off pungent odors since eggs may absorb the odors.

Eggs saved for hatching purposes should not be washed. Only clean and slightly soiled eggs should be saved for hatching. Dirty eggs should not be incubated. Eggs should be stored in a cool place with the large ends up. It is not advisable to store the eggs longer than one week before setting them in an incubator.

Electricity and Gas (Install)

The Moon should be in a fire sign, and there should be no squares, oppositions, or conjunctions with Uranus (ruler of electricity),

Neptune (ruler of gas), Saturn, or Mars. Hard aspects to Mars can cause fires.

Electronics (Buying)

Choose a day when the Moon is in an air sign (Gemini, Libra, Aquarius) and well aspected by Mercury and/or Uranus when buying electronics.

Electronics (Repair)

The Moon should be sextile or trine Mars or Uranus and in a fixed sign (Taurus, Leo, Scorpio, Aquarius).

Entertain Friends

Let the Moon be in Leo or Libra and making good aspects to Venus. Avoid squares or oppositions to either Mars or Saturn by the Moon or Venus.

Eyes and Eyeglasses

Have your eyes tested and glasses fitted on a day marked favorable for your Sun sign, and on a day that falls during your favorable lunar cycle. Mars should not be in aspect with the Moon. The same applies for any treatment of the eyes, which should also be started during the Moon's first or second quarter.

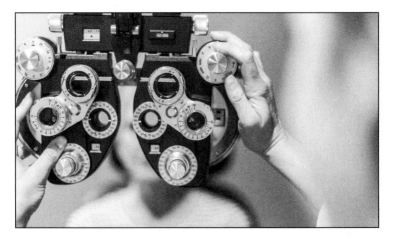

Fence Posts

Set posts when the Moon is in the third or fourth quarter of the fixed sign Taurus or Leo.

Fertilize and Compost

Fertilize when the Moon is in a fruitful sign (Cancer, Scorpio, Pisces). Organic fertilizers are best when the Moon is waning. Use chemical fertilizers when the Moon is waxing. Start compost when the Moon is in the fourth quarter in a water sign.

Find Hidden Treasure

Let the Moon be in good aspect to Jupiter or Venus. If you erect a horoscope for this election, place the Moon in the Fourth House.

Find Lost Articles

Search for lost articles during the first quarter and when your Sun sign is marked favorable. Also check to see that the planet ruling the lost item is trine, sextile, or conjunct the Moon. The Moon rules household utensils; Mercury rules letters and books; and Venus rules clothing, jewelry, and money.

Fishing

During the summer months, the best time of the day to fish is from sunrise to three hours after and from two hours before sunset until one hour after. Fish do not bite in cooler months until the air is warm, from noon to three pm. Warm, cloudy days are good. The most favorable winds are from the south and southwest. Easterly winds are unfavorable. The best days of the month for fishing are when the Moon changes quarters, especially if the change occurs on a day when the Moon is in a water sign (Cancer, Scorpio, Pisces). The best period in any month is the day after the Full Moon.

Friendship

The need for friendship is greater when the Moon is in Aquarius or when Uranus aspects the Moon. Friendship prospers when Venus or Uranus is trine, sextile, or conjunct the Moon. The Moon in Gemini facilitates the chance meeting of acquaintances and friends.

Grafting or Budding

Grafting is the process of introducing new varieties of fruit on less desirable trees. For this process you should use the increasing phase of the Moon in fruitful signs such as Cancer, Scorpio, or Pisces. Capricorn may be used, too. Cut your grafts while trees are dormant, from December to March. Keep them in a cool, dark place, not too dry or too damp. Do the grafting before the sap starts to flow and while the Moon is waxing, preferably while it is in Cancer, Scorpio, or Pisces. The type of plant should determine both cutting and planting times.

Habit (Breaking)

To end an undesirable habit, and this applies to ending everything from a bad relationship to smoking, start on a day when the Moon is in the fourth quarter and in the barren sign of Gemini, Leo, or Aquarius. Aries, Virgo, and Capricorn may be suitable as well, depending on the habit you want to be rid of. Make sure that your lunar cycle is favorable. Avoid lunar aspects to Mars or Jupiter. However, favorable aspects to Pluto are helpful.

Haircuts

Cut hair when the Moon is in Gemini, Sagittarius, Pisces, Taurus, or Capricorn, but not in Virgo. Look for favorable aspects to Venus. For faster growth, cut hair when the Moon is increasing in Cancer or Pisces. To make hair grow thicker, cut when the Moon is full in the signs of Taurus, Cancer, or Leo. If you want your hair to grow more slowly, have the Moon be decreasing in Aries, Gemini, or Virgo, and have the Moon square or opposing Saturn.

Permanents, straightening, and hair coloring will take well if the Moon is in Taurus or Leo and trine or sextile Venus. Avoid hair treatments if Mars is marked as square or in opposition, especially if heat is to be used. For permanents, a trine to Jupiter is helpful. The Moon also should be in the first quarter. Check the lunar cycle for a favorable day in relation to your Sun sign.

Harvest Crops

Harvest root crops when the Moon is in a dry sign (Aries, Leo, Sagittarius, Gemini, Aquarius) and waning. Harvest grain for storage just after the Full Moon, avoiding Cancer, Scorpio, or Pisces. Harvest in the third and fourth quarters in dry signs. Dry crops in the third quarter in fire signs.

Health

A diagnosis is more likely to be successful when the Moon is in Aries, Cancer, Libra, or Capricorn and less so when in Gemini, Sagittarius, Pisces, or Virgo. Begin a recuperation program or enter a hospital when the Moon is in a cardinal or fixed sign and the day is favorable to your Sun sign. For surgery, see "Surgical Procedures." Buy medicines when the Moon is in Virgo or Scorpio.

Home (Buy New)

If you desire a permanent home, buy when the New Moon is in a fixed sign—Taurus or Leo, for example. Each sign will affect your decision in a different way. A house bought when the Moon is in Taurus is likely to be more practical and have a country look—right down to the split-rail fence. A house purchased when the Moon is in Leo will more likely be a real showplace.

If you're buying for speculation and a quick turnover, be certain that the Moon is in a cardinal sign (Aries, Cancer, Libra, Capricorn). Avoid buying when the Moon is in a fixed sign (Leo, Scorpio, Aquarius, Taurus).

Home (Make Repairs)

In all repairs, avoid squares, oppositions, or conjunctions to the planet ruling the place or thing to be repaired. For example,

bathrooms are ruled by Scorpio and Cancer. You would not want to start a project in those rooms when the Moon or Pluto is receiving hard aspects. The front entrance, hall, dining room, and porch are ruled by the Sun So you would want to avoid times when Saturn or Mars are square, opposing, or conjunct the Sun. Also, let the Moon be waxing.

Home (Sell)

Make a strong effort to list your property for sale when the Sun is marked favorable in your sign and in good aspect to Jupiter. Avoid adverse aspects to as many planets as possible.

Home Furnishings (Buy New)

Saturn days (Saturday) are good for buying, and Jupiter days (Thursday) are good for selling. Items bought on days when Saturn is well aspected tend to wear longer and purchases tend to be more conservative.

Job (Start New)

Jupiter and Venus should be sextile, trine, or conjunct the Moon. A day when your Sun is receiving favorable aspects is preferred.

Legal Matters

Good Moon-Jupiter aspects improve the outcome in legal decisions. To gain damages through a lawsuit, begin the process during the increasing Moon. To avoid paying damages, a court date during the decreasing Moon is desirable. Good Moon-Sun aspects strengthen your chance of success. A well-aspected Moon in Cancer or Leo, making good aspects to the Sun, brings the best results in custody cases. In divorce cases, a favorable Moon-Venus aspect is best.

Loan (Ask For)

A first and second quarter phase favors the lender, the third and fourth quarters favor the borrower. Good aspects of Jupiter and Venus to the Moon are favorable to both, as is having the Moon in Leo or Taurus.

Machinery, Appliances, or Tools (Buy)

Tools, machinery, and other implements should be bought on days when your lunar cycle is favorable and when Mars and Uranus are trine, sextile, or conjunct the Moon. Any quarter of the Moon is suitable. When buying gas or electrical appliances, the Moon should be in Aquarius.

Make a Will

Let the Moon be in a fixed sign (Taurus, Leo, Scorpio, or Aquarius) to ensure permanence. If the Moon is in a cardinal sign (Aries, Cancer, Libra, or Capricorn), the will could be altered. Let the Moon be waxing—increasing in light—and in good aspect to Saturn, Venus, or Mercury. In case the will is made in an emergency during illness and the Moon is slow in motion, void-of-course, combust, or under the Sun's beams, the testator will die and the will remain unaltered. There is some danger that it will be lost or stolen, however.

Marriage

The best time for marriage to take place is when the Moon is increasing, but not yet full. Good signs for the Moon to be in are Taurus, Cancer, Leo, or Libra.

The Moon in Taurus produces the most steadfast marriages, but if the partners later want to separate, they may have a difficult time. Make sure that the Moon is well aspected, especially to Venus or Jupiter. Avoid aspects to Mars, Uranus, or Pluto and the signs Aries, Gemini, Virgo, Scorpio, or Aquarius.

The values of the signs are as follows:

- Aries is not favored for marriage
- Taurus from 0 to 19 degrees is good, the remaining degrees are less favorable
- Cancer is unfavorable unless you are marrying a widow
- Leo is favored, but it may cause one party to deceive the other as to his or her money or possessions
- Virgo is not favored except when marrying a widow
- Libra is good for engagements but not for marriage
- Scorpio from 0 to 15 degrees is good, but the last 15 degrees are entirely unfortunate. The woman may be fickle, envious, and quarrelsome
- Sagittarius is neutral
- Capricorn, from 0 to 10 degrees, is difficult for marriage; however, the remaining degrees are favorable, especially when marrying a widow
- Aquarius is not favored
- Pisces is favored, although marriage under this sign can incline a woman to chatter a lot

These effects are strongest when the Moon is in the sign. If the Moon and Venus are in a cardinal sign, happiness between the couple may not continue long.

On no account should the Moon apply to Saturn or Mars, even by good aspect.

Medical Treatment for the Eyes

Let the Moon be increasing in light and motion and making favorable aspects to Venus or Jupiter and be unaspected by Mars. Keep the Moon out of Taurus, Capricorn, or Virgo. If an aspect between the Moon and Mars is unavoidable, let it be separating.

Medical Treatment for the Head

If possible, have Mars and Saturn free of hard aspects. Let the Moon be in Aries or Taurus, decreasing in light, in conjunction or aspect with Venus or Jupiter and free of hard aspects. The Sun should not be in any aspect to the Moon.

Medical Treatment for the Nose

Let the Moon be in Cancer, Leo, or Virgo and not aspecting Mars or Saturn and also not in conjunction with a retrograde or weak planet.

Mining

Saturn rules mining. Begin work when Saturn is marked conjunct, trine, or sextile. Mine for gold when the Sun is marked conjunct, trine, or sextile. Mercury rules quicksilver, Venus rules copper, Jupiter rules tin, Saturn rules lead and coal, Uranus rules radioactive elements, Neptune rules oil, the Moon rules water. Mine for these items when the ruling planet is marked conjunct, trine, or sextile.

Move to New Home

If you have a choice, and sometimes you don't, make sure that Mars is not aspecting the Moon. Move on a day favorable to your Sun sign or when the Moon is conjunct, sextile, or trine the Sun.

Mow Lawn

Mow in the first and second quarters (waxing phase) to increase growth and lushness, and in the third and fourth quarters (waning phase) to decrease growth.

Negotiate

When you are choosing a time to negotiate, consider what the meeting is about and what you want to have happen. If it is agreement or compromise between two parties that you desire, have the Moon be in the sign of Libra. When you are making contracts, it is best to have the Moon in the same element. For example, if your concern is communication, then elect a time when the Moon is in an air sign. If, on the other hand, your concern is about possessions, an earth sign would be more appropriate. Fixed signs are unfavorable, with the exception of Leo; so are cardinal signs, except for Capricorn. If you are negotiating the end of something, use the rules that apply to ending habits.

Occupational Training

When you begin training, see that your lunar cycle is favorable that day and that the planet ruling your occupation is marked conjunct or trine.

Paint

Paint buildings during the waning Libra or Aquarius Moon. If the weather is hot, paint when the Moon is in Taurus. If the weather is cold, paint when the Moon is in Leo. Schedule the painting to start in the fourth quarter as the wood is drier and paint will penetrate wood better. Avoid painting around the New Moon, though, as the wood is likely to be damp, making the paint subject to scalding when hot weather hits it. If the temperature is below 70°F, it is not advisable to paint while the Moon is in Cancer, Scorpio, or Pisces as the paint is apt to creep, check, or run.

Party (Host or Attend)

A party timed so the Moon is in Gemini, Leo, Libra, or Sagittarius, with good aspects to Venus and Jupiter, will be fun and well attended. There should be no aspects between the Moon and Mars or Saturn.

Pawn

Do not pawn any article when Jupiter is receiving a square or opposition from Saturn or Mars or when Jupiter is within 17 degrees of the Sun, for you will have little chance to redeem the items.

Pick Mushrooms

Mushrooms, one of the most promising traditional medicines in the world, should be gathered at the Full Moon.

Plant

Root crops, like carrots and potatoes, are best if planted in the sign Taurus or Capricorn. Beans, peas, tomatoes, peppers, and other fruit-bearing plants are best if planted in a sign that supports seed growth. Leaf plants, like lettuce, broccoli, or cauliflower, are best planted when the Moon is in a water sign.

It is recommended that you transplant during a decreasing Moon, when forces are streaming into the lower part of the plant. This helps root growth.

Promotion (Ask For)

Choose a day favorable to your Sun sign. Mercury should be marked conjunct, trine, or sextile. Avoid days when Mars or Saturn is aspected.

Prune

Prune during the third and fourth quarter of a Scorpio Moon to retard growth and to promote better fruit. Prune when the Moon is in cardinal Capricorn to promote healing.

Reconcile with People

If the reconciliation is with a woman, let Venus be strong and well aspected. If elders or superiors are involved, see that Saturn is receiving good aspects; if the reconciliation is between young people or between an older and younger person, see that Mercury is well aspected.

Romance

There is less control of when a romance starts, but romances begun under an increasing Moon are more likely to be permanent or satisfying, while those begun during the decreasing Moon tend to transform the participants. The tone of the relationship can be guessed from the sign the Moon is in. Romances begun with the Moon in Aries may be impulsive. Those begun in Capricorn will take greater effort to bring to a desirable conclusion, but they may be very rewarding. Good aspects between the Moon and Venus will have a positive influence on the relationship. Avoid unfavorable aspects to Mars, Uranus, and Pluto. A decreasing Moon, particularly the fourth quarter, facilitates ending a relationship and causes the least pain.

Roof a Building

Begin roofing a building during the third or fourth quarter, when the Moon is in Aries or Aquarius. Shingles laid during the New Moon have a tendency to curl at the edges.

Sauerkraut

The best-tasting sauerkraut is made just after the Full Moon in the fruitful signs of Cancer, Scorpio, or Pisces.

Select a Child's Sex

Count from the last day of menstruation to the first day of the next cycle and divide the interval between the two dates in half. Pregnancy in the first half produces females, but copulation should take place with the Moon in a feminine sign. Pregnancy in the latter half, up to three days before the beginning of menstruation, produces males, but copulation should take place with the Moon in a masculine sign. The three-day period before the next period again produces females.

Sell or Canvass

Begin these activities during a day favorable to your Sun sign. Otherwise, sell on days when Jupiter, Mercury, or Mars is trine, sextile, or conjunct the Moon. Avoid days when Saturn is square or opposing the Moon, for that always hinders business and causes discord. If the Moon is passing from the first quarter to full, it is best to have the Moon swift in motion and in good aspect with Venus and/or Jupiter.

Sign Papers

Sign contracts or agreements when the Moon is increasing in a fruitful sign and on a day when the Moon is making favorable aspects to Mercury. Avoid days when Mars, Saturn, or Neptune are square or opposite the Moon.

Spray and Weed

Spray pests and weeds during the fourth quarter when the Moon is in the barren sign Leo or Aquarius and making favorable aspects to Pluto. Weed during a waning Moon in a barren sign.

Staff (Fire)

Have the Moon in the third or fourth quarter, but not full. The Moon should not be square any planets.

Staff (Hire)

The Moon should be in the first or second quarter, and preferably in the sign of Gemini or Virgo. The Moon should be conjunct, trine, or sextile Mercury or Jupiter.

Stocks (Buy)

The Moon should be in Taurus or Capricorn, and there should be a sextile or trine to Jupiter or Saturn.

Surgical Procedures

Blood flow, like ocean tides, appears to be related to Moon phases. To reduce hemorrhage after a surgery, schedule it within one week before or after a New Moon. Schedule surgery to occur during the increase of the Moon if possible, as wounds heal better and vitality is greater than during the decrease of the Moon. Avoid surgery within one week before or after the Full Moon. Select a date when the Moon is past the sign governing the part of the body involved in the operation. For example, abdominal operations should be done when the Moon is in Sagittarius, Capricorn, or Aquarius. The further removed the Moon sign is from the sign ruling the afflicted part of the body, the better.

For successful operations, avoid times when the Moon is applying to any aspect of Mars. (This tends to promote inflammation and complications.) See the Lunar Aspectarian on odd pages 137–159 to find days with negative Mars aspects and positive

Venus and Jupiter aspects. Never operate with the Moon in the same sign as a person's Sun sign or Ascendant. Let the Moon be in a fixed sign and avoid square or opposing aspects. The Moon should not be void-of-course. Cosmetic surgery should be done in the increase of the Moon, when the Moon is not square or in opposition to Mars. Avoid days when the Moon is square or opposing Saturn or the Sun

Travel (Air)

Start long trips when the Moon is making favorable aspects to the Sun For enjoyment, aspects to Jupiter are preferable; for visiting, look for favorable aspects to Mercury. To prevent accidents, avoid squares or oppositions to Mars, Saturn, Uranus, or Pluto. Choose a day when the Moon is in Sagittarius or Gemini and well aspected to Mercury, Jupiter, or Uranus. Avoid adverse aspects of Mars, Saturn, or Uranus.

Visit

On setting out to visit a person, let the Moon be in aspect with any retrograde planet, for this ensures that the person you're visiting will be at home. If you desire to stay a long time in a place, let the Moon be in good aspect to Saturn. If you desire to leave the place quickly, let the Moon be in a cardinal sign.

Wean Children

To wean a child successfully, do so when the Moon is in Sagittarius, Capricorn, Aquarius, or Pisces—signs that do not rule vital human organs. By observing this astrological rule, much trouble for parents and child may be avoided.

Weight (Reduce)

If you want to lose weight, the best time to get started is when the Moon is in the third or fourth quarter and in the barren sign of Virgo. Review the section on How to Use the Moon Tables and

Lunar Aspectarian beginning on page 136 to help you select a date that is favorable to begin your weight-loss program.

Wine and Drink Other Than Beer

Start brewing when the Moon is in Pisces or Taurus. Sextiles or trines to Venus are favorable, but avoid aspects to Mars or Saturn.

Write

Write for pleasure or publication when the Moon is in Gemini. Mercury should be making favorable aspects to Uranus and Neptune.

How to Use the Moon Tables and Lunar Aspectarian

Timing activities is one of the most important things you can do to ensure success. In many Eastern countries, timing by the planets is so important that practically no event takes place without first setting up a chart for it. Weddings have occurred in the middle of the night because the influences were at the best then. You may not want to take it that far, but you can still make use of the influences of the Moon whenever possible. It's easy and it works!

Llewellyn's Moon Sign Book has information to help you plan just about any activity: weddings, fishing, making purchases, cutting your hair, traveling, and more. We provide the guidelines you need to pick the best day out of the several from which you have to choose. The Moon Tables are the *Moon Sign Book's* primary method for choosing dates. Following are instructions, examples, and directions on how to read the Moon Tables. More advanced information on using the tables containing the Lunar Aspectarian and favorable and unfavorable days (found on odd-numbered pages opposite the Moon Tables), Moon void-of-course and retrograde information to choose the dates best for you is also included.

The Five Basic Steps

Step 1: Directions for Choosing Dates
Look up the directions for choosing dates for the activity that you wish to begin, then go to step 2.

Step 2: Check the Moon Tables
You'll find two tables for each month of the year beginning on page 136. The Moon Tables (on the left-hand pages) include the day, date, and sign the Moon is in; the element and nature of the sign; the Moon's phase; and when it changes sign or phase. If there is a time listed after a date, that time is the time when the Moon moves into that zodiac sign. Until then, the Moon is considered to be in the sign for the previous day.

The abbreviation Full signifies Full Moon and New signifies New Moon. The times listed with dates indicate when the Moon changes sign. The times listed after the phase indicate when the Moon changes phase.

Turn to the month you would like to begin your activity. You will be using the Moon's sign and phase information most often when you begin choosing your own dates. Use the Time Zone Map on page 164 and the Time Zone Conversions table on page 165 to convert time to your own time zone.

When you find dates that meet the criteria for the correct Moon phase and sign for your activity, you may have completed the process. For certain simple activities, such as getting a haircut, the phase and sign information is all that is needed. If the directions for your activity include information on certain lunar aspects, however, you should consult the Lunar Aspectarian. An example of this would be if the directions told you not to perform a certain activity when the Moon is square (Q) Jupiter.

Step 3: Check the Lunar Aspectarian

On the pages opposite the Moon Tables you will find tables containing the Lunar Aspectarian and Favorable and Unfavorable Days. The Lunar Aspectarian gives the aspects (or angles) of the Moon to other planets. Some aspects are favorable, while others are not. To use the Lunar Aspectarian, find the planet that the directions list as favorable for your activity, and run down the column to the date desired. For example, you should avoid aspects to Mars if you are planning surgery. So you would look for Mars across the top and then run down that column looking for days where there are no aspects to Mars (as signified by empty boxes). If you want to find a **favorable** aspect (sextile (X) or trine (T)) to Mercury, run your finger down the column under Mercury until you find an X or T. **Adverse** aspects to planets are squares (Q) or oppositions (O). A conjunction (C) is sometimes beneficial, sometimes not, depending on the activity or planets involved.

Step 4: Favorable and Unfavorable Days

The tables listing favorable and unfavorable days are helpful when you want to choose your personal best dates because your Sun sign is taken into consideration. The twelve Sun signs are listed on the right side of the tables. Once you have determined which days meet your criteria for phase, sign, and aspects, you can determine whether or not those days are positive for you by checking the favorable and unfavorable days for your Sun sign.

To find out if a day is positive for you, find your Sun sign and then look down the column. If it is marked F, it is very favorable. The Moon is in the same sign as your Sun on a favorable day. If it is marked f, it is slightly favorable; U is very unfavorable; and u means slightly unfavorable. A day marked very unfavorable (U) indicates that the Moon is in the sign opposing your Sun

Once you have selected good dates for the activity you are about to begin, you can go straight to "Using What You've Learned," beginning on the next page. To learn how to fine-tune your selections even further, read on.

Step 5: Void-of-Course Moon and Retrogrades

This last step is perhaps the most advanced portion of the procedure. It is generally considered poor timing to make decisions, sign important papers, or start special activities during a Moon void-of-course period or during a Mercury retrograde. Once you have chosen the best date for your activity based on steps one through four, you can check the Void-of-Course tables, beginning on page 76, to find out if any of the dates you have chosen have void periods.

The Moon is said to be void-of-course after it has made its last aspect to a planet within a particular sign, but before it has moved into the next sign. Put simply, the Moon is "resting" during the void-of-course period, so activities initiated at this time generally don't come to fruition. You will notice that there are many void periods during the year, and it is nearly impossible to avoid all of them. Some people choose to ignore these altogether and do not take them into consideration when planning activities.

Next, you can check the Retrograde Planets tables on page 160 to see what planets are retrograde during your chosen date(s).

A planet is said to be retrograde when it appears to move backward in the sky as viewed from Earth. Generally, the farther a planet is away from the Sun, the longer it can stay retrograde. Some planets will retrograde for several months at a time. Avoiding retrogrades is not as important in lunar planning as avoiding the Moon void-of-course, with the exception of the planet Mercury.

Mercury rules thought and communication, so it is advisable not to sign important papers, initiate important business or legal work, or make crucial decisions during these times. As with the Moon void-of-course, it is difficult to avoid all planetary retrogrades when beginning events, and you may choose to ignore this step of the process. Following are some examples using some or all of the steps outlined above.

Using What You've Learned

Let's say it's a new year and you want to have your hair cut. It's thin and you would like it to look fuller, so you find the directions for hair care and you see that for thicker hair you should cut hair while the Moon is Full and in the sign of Taurus, Cancer, or Leo. You should avoid the Moon in Aries, Gemini, or Virgo. Look at the January Moon Table on page 136. You see that the Full Moon is on January 17 at 6:48 pm. The Moon is in Leo from January 17 and moves into Virgo on January 20 at 9:02 am, so January 17–19 meet both the phase and sign criteria.

Let's move on to a more difficult example using the sign and phase of the Moon. You want to buy a permanent home. After checking the instructions for purchasing a house: "Home (Buy New)" on page 117, you see that you should buy a home when the Moon is in Taurus, Cancer, or Leo. You need to get a loan, so you should also look under "Loan (Ask For)" on page 119. Here it says that the third and fourth quarters favor the borrower (you). You are going to buy the house in October, so go to page 154. The Moon is in the third quarter Oct 9–16 and fourth quarter October 17–24. The Moon is in Leo on Oct 18 until Oct 20 at 12:25 pm; in Taurus from 5:04 pm Oct 10 until Oct 13 at 1:08 am; in Cancer from 12:11 pm Oct 15 to 12:45 am Oct 18 and in Leo from Oct 18 at 12:45 am until Oct 20 at 12:25 pm. The best days for obtaining a loan would be October 9–16 and 17–24.

Just match up the best sign and phase (quarter) to come up with the best date. With all activities, be sure to check the favorable and unfavorable days for your Sun sign in the table adjoining the Lunar Aspectarian. If there is a choice between several dates, pick the one most favorable for you. Because buying a home is an important business decision, you may also wish to see if the Moon is void or if Mercury is retrograde during these dates.

Now let's look at an example that uses signs, phases, and aspects. Our example is starting new home construction. We will use the month of February. Look under "Build (Start Foundation)" on page 110 and you'll see that the Moon should be in the first quarter of a fixed sign—Leo, Taurus, Aquarius, or Scorpio. You should select a time when the Moon is not making unfavorable aspects to Saturn. (Conjunctions are usually considered unfavorable if they are to Mars, Saturn, or Neptune.) Look in the February Moon Table on page 138. You will see that the Moon is in the first quarter Feb 1–7 and in Aquarius from 4:43 am Jan 31 until 12:46 am Feb 1 and it is in Taurus from 5:52 pm on Feb 6 until 5:27 am on Feb 9. Now, look to the February Lunar Aspectarian. We see that there are no unfavorable squares to Saturn the 2–7; therefore, Feb 2–7 would be the best dates to start a foundation.

A Note About Time and Time Zones

All tables in the Moon Sign Book use Eastern Time. You must calculate the difference between your time zone and the Eastern Time Zone. Please refer to the Time Zone Conversions chart on page 165 for help with time conversions. The sign the Moon is in at midnight is the sign shown in the Aspectarian and Favorable and Unfavorable Days tables.

How Does the Time Matter?

Due to the three-hour time difference between the East and West Coasts of the United States, those of you living on the East Coast may be, for example, under the influence of a Virgo

Moon, while those of you living on the West Coast will still have a Leo Moon influence.

We follow a commonly held belief among astrologers: whatever sign the Moon is in at the start of a day—12:00 am Eastern Time— is considered the dominant influence of the day. That sign is indicated in the Moon Tables. If the date you select for an activity shows the Moon changing signs, you can decide how important the sign change may be for your specific election and adjust your election date and time accordingly.

Use Common Sense

Some activities depend on outside factors. Obviously, you can't go out and plant when there is a foot of snow on the ground. You should adjust to the conditions at hand. If the weather was bad during the first quarter, when it was best to plant crops, do it during the second quarter while the Moon is in a fruitful sign. If the Moon is not in a fruitful sign during the first or second quarter, choose a day when it is in a semi-fruitful sign. The best advice is to choose either the sign or phase that is most favorable, when the two don't coincide.

To Summarize

First, look up the activity under the proper heading, then look for the information given in the tables. Choose the best date considering the number of positive factors in effect. If most of the dates are favorable, there is no problem choosing the one that will fit your schedule. However, if there aren't any really good dates, pick the ones with the least number of negative influences. Please keep in mind that the information found here applies in the broadest sense to the events you want to plan or are considering. To be the most effective, when you use electional astrology, you should also consider your own birth chart in relation to a chart drawn for the time or times you have under consideration. The best advice we can offer you is: read the entire introduction to each section.

January Moon Table

Date	Sign	Element	Nature	Phase
1 Sat 6:02 pm	Capricorn	Earth	Semi-fruitful	4th
2 Sun	Capricorn	Earth	Semi-fruitful	New 1:33 pm
3 Mon 5:44 pm	Aquarius	Air	Barren	1st
4 Tue	Aquarius	Air	Barren	1st
5 Wed 7:17 pm	Pisces	Water	Fruitful	1st
6 Thu	Pisces	Water	Fruitful	1st
7 Fri	Pisces	Water	Fruitful	1st
8 Sat 12:26 am	Aries	Fire	Barren	1st
9 Sun	Aries	Fire	Barren	2nd 1:11 pm
10 Mon 9:47 am	Taurus	Earth	Semi-fruitful	2nd
11 Tue	Taurus	Earth	Semi-fruitful	2nd
12 Wed 10:08 pm	Gemini	Air	Barren	2nd
13 Thu	Gemini	Air	Barren	2nd
14 Fri	Gemini	Air	Barren	2nd
15 Sat 11:11 am	Cancer	Water	Fruitful	2nd
16 Sun	Cancer	Water	Fruitful	2nd
17 Mon 11:03 pm	Leo	Fire	Barren	Full 6:48 pm
18 Tue	Leo	Fire	Barren	3rd
19 Wed	Leo	Fire	Barren	3rd
20 Thu 9:02 am	Virgo	Earth	Barren	3rd
21 Fri	Virgo	Earth	Barren	3rd
22 Sat 5:03 pm	Libra	Air	Semi-fruitful	3rd
23 Sun	Libra	Air	Semi-fruitful	3rd
24 Mon 10:57 pm	Scorpio	Water	Fruitful	3rd
25 Tue	Scorpio	Water	Fruitful	4th 8:41 am
26 Wed	Scorpio	Water	Fruitful	4th
27 Thu 2:34 am	Sagittarius	Fire	Barren	4th
28 Fri	Sagittarius	Fire	Barren	4th
29 Sat 4:09 am	Capricorn	Earth	Semi-fruitful	4th
30 Sun	Capricorn	Earth	Semi-fruitful	4th
31 Mon 4:43 am	Aquarius	Air	Barren	4th

January Aspectarian/Favorable & Unfavorable Days

Date	Sun	Mercury	Venus	Mars	Jupiter	Saturn	Uranus	Neptune	Pluto
1					X			Q	
2	C						T		
3		C	C					X	C
4				X		C	Q		
5						C			
6							X		
7	X		X	Q				C	X
8		X							
9	Q		Q	T		X			
10					X				Q
11		Q	T				Q	C	
12	T							X	T
13		T			Q				
14			O			T		Q	
15						T			
16			O				X		
17	O							T	O
18		O					Q		
19							O		
20				T	O				
21			T				T		
22	T	T		Q				O	T
23			Q			T			
24				X					Q
25	Q	Q	X		T		O		
26						Q		T	X
27	X	X			Q				
28						X		Q	
29			C	C	X		T		
30		C						X	C
31						Q			

Date	Aries	Taurus	Gemini	Cancer	Leo	Virgo	Libra	Scorpio	Sagittarius	Capricorn	Aquarius	Pisces
1	f		U		f	u	f		F		f	u
2	u	f		U		f	u	f		F		f
3	u	f		U		f	u	f		F		f
4	f	u	f	U			f	u	f		F	
5	f	u	f	U			f	u	f		F	
6		f	u	f	U			f	u	f		F
7		f	u	f	U			f	u	f		F
8	F		f	u	f		U		f	u	f	
9	F		f	u	f		U		f	u	f	
10	F		f	u	f		U		f	u	f	
11		F		f	u	f		U		f	u	f
12		F		f	u	f		U		f	u	f
13	f		F		f	u	f		U		f	u
14	f		F		f	u	f		U		f	u
15	f		F		f	u	f		U		f	u
16	u	f		F		f	u	f		U		f
17	u	f		F		f	u	f		U		f
18	f	u	f		F		f	u	f		U	
19	f	u	f		F		f	u	f		U	
20	f	u	f		F		f	u	f		U	
21		f	u	f		F		f	u	f		U
22		f	u	f		F		f	u	f		U
23	U		f	u	f		F		f	u	f	
24	U		f	u	f		F		f	u	f	
25		U		f	u	f		F		f	u	f
26		U		f	u	f		F		f	u	f
27	f		U		f	u	f		F		f	u
28	f		U		f	u	f		F		f	u
29	f		U		f	u	f		F		f	u
30	u	f		U		f	u	f		F		f
31	u	f		U		f	u	f		F		f

February Moon Table

Date	Sign	Element	Nature	Phase
1 Tue	Aquarius	Air	Barren	New 12:46 am
2 Wed 6:00 am	Pisces	Water	Fruitful	1st
3 Thu	Pisces	Water	Fruitful	1st
4 Fri 9:57 am	Aries	Fire	Barren	1st
5 Sat	Aries	Fire	Barren	1st
6 Sun 5:52 pm	Taurus	Earth	Semi-fruitful	1st
7 Mon	Taurus	Earth	Semi-fruitful	1st
8 Tue	Taurus	Earth	Semi-fruitful	2nd 8:50 am
9 Wed 5:27 am	Gemini	Air	Barren	2nd
10 Thu	Gemini	Air	Barren	2nd
11 Fri 6:27 pm	Cancer	Water	Fruitful	2nd
12 Sat	Cancer	Water	Fruitful	2nd
13 Sun	Cancer	Water	Fruitful	2nd
14 Mon 6:17 am	Leo	Fire	Barren	2nd
15 Tue	Leo	Fire	Barren	2nd
16 Wed 3:42 pm	Virgo	Earth	Barren	Full 11:56 am
17 Thu	Virgo	Earth	Barren	3rd
18 Fri 10:51 pm	Libra	Air	Semi-fruitful	3rd
19 Sat	Libra	Air	Semi-fruitful	3rd
20 Sun	Libra	Air	Semi-fruitful	3rd
21 Mon 4:19 am	Scorpio	Water	Fruitful	3rd
22 Tue	Scorpio	Water	Fruitful	3rd
23 Wed 8:29 am	Sagittarius	Fire	Barren	4th 5:32 pm
24 Thu	Sagittarius	Fire	Barren	4th
25 Fri 11:27 am	Capricorn	Earth	Semi-fruitful	4th
26 Sat	Capricorn	Earth	Semi-fruitful	4th
27 Sun 1:36 pm	Aquarius	Air	Barren	4th
28 Mon	Aquarius	Air	Barren	4th

February Aspectarian/Favorable & Unfavorable Days

Date	Sun	Mercury	Venus	Mars	Jupiter	Saturn	Uranus	Neptune	Pluto
1	C					C			
2				X	C				
3		X	X				X	C	
4									X
5	X		Q	Q		X			
6		Q							Q
7			T	T	X		C		
8	Q	T				Q		X	T
9									
10					Q	T			
11	T							Q	
12			O	T			X		
13			O					T	
14		O							O
15						O	Q		
16	O								
17				O			T		
18			T	T				O	T
19		T							
20			Q	Q		T			
21	T	Q							Q
22			X	X	T	Q	O	T	
23	Q								X
24		X			Q	X		Q	
25									
26	X				X		T		
27			C	C				X	C
28		C				C	Q		

Date	Aries	Taurus	Gemini	Cancer	Leo	Virgo	Libra	Scorpio	Sagittarius	Capricorn	Aquarius	Pisces
1	f	u	f		U		f	u	f		F	
2	f	u	f		U		f	u	f		F	
3		f	u	f		U		f	u	f		F
4		f	u	f		U		f	u	f		F
5	F		f	u	f		U		f	u	f	
6	F		f	u	f		U		f	u	f	u
7		F		f	u	f		U		f	u	f
8		F		f	u	f		U		f	u	f
9		F		f	u	f		U		f	u	f
10	f		F		f	u	f		U		f	u
11	f		F		f	u	f		U		f	u
12	u	f		F		f	u	f		U		f
13	u	f		F		f	u	f		U		f
14	u	f		F		f	u	f		U		f
15	f	u	f		F		f	u	f		U	
16	f	u	f		F		f	u	f		U	
17		f	u	f		F		f	u	f		U
18		f	u	f		F		f	u	f		U
19	U		f	u	f		F		f	u	f	
20	U		f	u	f		F		f	u	f	
21	U		f	u	f		F		f	u	f	
22		U		f	u	f		F		f	u	f
23		U		f	u	f		F		f	u	f
24	f		U		f	u	f		F		f	u
25	f		U		f	u	f		F		f	u
26	u	f		U		f	u	f		F		f
27	u	f		U		f	u	f		F		f
28	f	u	f		U		f	u	f		F	

March Moon Table

Date	Sign	Element	Nature	Phase
1 Tue 3:53 pm	Pisces	Water	Fruitful	4th
2 Wed	Pisces	Water	Fruitful	New 12:35 pm
3 Thu 7:52 pm	Aries	Fire	Barren	1st
4 Fri	Aries	Fire	Barren	1st
5 Sat	Aries	Fire	Barren	1st
6 Sun 3:00 am	Taurus	Earth	Semi-fruitful	1st
7 Mon	Taurus	Earth	Semi-fruitful	1st
8 Tue 1:40 pm	Gemini	Air	Barren	1st
9 Wed	Gemini	Air	Barren	1st
10 Thu	Gemini	Air	Barren	2nd 5:45 am
11 Fri 2:24 am	Cancer	Water	Fruitful	2nd
12 Sat	Cancer	Water	Fruitful	2nd
13 Sun 3:32 pm	Leo	Fire	Barren	2nd
14 Mon	Leo	Fire	Barren	2nd
15 Tue	Leo	Fire	Barren	2nd
16 Wed 12:59 am	Virgo	Earth	Barren	2nd
17 Thu	Virgo	Earth	Barren	2nd
18 Fri 7:26 am	Libra	Air	Semi-fruitful	Full 3:18 am
19 Sat	Libra	Air	Semi-fruitful	3rd
20 Sun 11:45 am	Scorpio	Water	Fruitful	3rd
21 Mon	Scorpio	Water	Fruitful	3rd
22 Tue 2:59 pm	Sagittarius	Fire	Barren	3rd
23 Wed	Sagittarius	Fire	Barren	3rd
24 Thu 5:54 pm	Capricorn	Earth	Semi-fruitful	3rd
25 Fri	Capricorn	Earth	Semi-fruitful	4th 1:37 am
26 Sat 8:55 pm	Aquarius	Air	Barren	4th
27 Sun	Aquarius	Air	Barren	4th
28 Mon	Aquarius	Air	Barren	4th
29 Tue 12:32 am	Pisces	Water	Fruitful	4th
30 Wed	Pisces	Water	Fruitful	4th
31 Thu 5:30 am	Aries	Fire	Barren	4th

March Aspectarian/Favorable & Unfavorable Days

Date	Sun	Mercury	Venus	Mars	Jupiter	Saturn	Uranus	Neptune	Pluto
1									
2	C					C	X		
3			X	X				C	X
4									
5		X				X			Q
6			Q	Q					
7	X				X	Q	C	X	
8		Q	T	T					T
9					Q				
10	Q					T		Q	
11		T							
12	T					T	X		
13								T	O
14			O	O				Q	
15							O		
16		O					T		
17				O				O	
18	O								T
19			T	T		T			
20									Q
21		T	Q	Q	T	Q	O		
22	T							T	X
23			X	X	Q				
24		Q				X		Q	
25	Q					T			
26		X			X			X	C
27	X					Q			
28			C	C	C				
29						X			
30				C				C	
31		C							X

Date	Aries	Taurus	Gemini	Cancer	Leo	Virgo	Libra	Scorpio	Sagittarius	Capricorn	Aquarius	Pisces
1	f	u	f		U		f	u	f		F	
2		f	u	f		U		f	u	f		F
3		f	u	f		U		f	u	f		F
4	F		f	u	f		U		f	u	f	
5	F		f	u	f		U		f	u	f	
6	F		f	u	f		U		f	u	f	
7		F		f	u	f		U		f	u	f
8		F		f	u	f		U		f	u	f
9	f		F		f	u	f		U		f	u
10	f		F		f	u	f		U		f	u
11	u	f		F		f	u	f		U		f
12	u	f		F		f	u	f		U		f
13	u	f		F		f	u	f		U		f
14	f	u	f		F		f	u	f		U	
15	f	u	f		F		f	u	f		U	
16		f	u	f		F		f	u	f		U
17		f	u	f		F		f	u	f		U
18		f	u	f		F		f	u	f		U
19	U		f	u	f		F		f	u	f	
20	U		f	u	f		F		f	u	f	
21		U		f	u	f		F		f	u	f
22		U		f	u	f		F		f	u	f
23	f		U		f	u	f		F		f	u
24	f		U		f	u	f		F		f	u
25	u	f		U		f	u	f		F		f
26	u	f		U		f	u	f		F		f
27	f	u	f		U		f	u	f		F	
28	f	u	f		U		f	u	f		F	
29		f	u	f		U		f	u	f		F
30		f	u	f		U		f	u	f		F
31		f	u	f		U		f	u	f		F

April Moon Table

Date	Sign	Element	Nature	Phase
1 Fri	Aries	Fire	Barren	New 2:24 am
2 Sat 12:50 pm	Taurus	Earth	Semi-fruitful	1st
3 Sun	Taurus	Earth	Semi-fruitful	1st
4 Mon 11:04 pm	Gemini	Air	Barren	1st
5 Tue	Gemini	Air	Barren	1st
6 Wed	Gemini	Air	Barren	1st
7 Thu 11:30 am	Cancer	Water	Fruitful	1st
8 Fri	Cancer	Water	Fruitful	1st
9 Sat	Cancer	Water	Fruitful	2nd 2:48 am
10 Sun 12:00 am	Leo	Fire	Barren	2nd
11 Mon	Leo	Fire	Barren	2nd
12 Tue 10:07 am	Virgo	Earth	Barren	2nd
13 Wed	Virgo	Earth	Barren	2nd
14 Thu 4:46 pm	Libra	Air	Semi-fruitful	2nd
15 Fri	Libra	Air	Semi-fruitful	2nd
16 Sat 8:23 pm	Scorpio	Water	Fruitful	Full 2:55 pm
17 Sun	Scorpio	Water	Fruitful	3rd
18 Mon 10:16 pm	Sagittarius	Fire	Barren	3rd
19 Tue	Sagittarius	Fire	Barren	3rd
20 Wed 11:52 pm	Capricorn	Earth	Semi-fruitful	3rd
21 Thu	Capricorn	Earth	Semi-fruitful	3rd
22 Fri	Capricorn	Earth	Semi-fruitful	3rd
23 Sat 2:17 am	Aquarius	Air	Barren	4th 7:56 am
24 Sun	Aquarius	Air	Barren	4th
25 Mon 6:15 am	Pisces	Water	Fruitful	4th
26 Tue	Pisces	Water	Fruitful	4th
27 Wed 12:10 pm	Aries	Fire	Barren	4th
28 Thu	Aries	Fire	Barren	4th
29 Fri 8:19 pm	Taurus	Earth	Semi-fruitful	4th
30 Sat	Taurus	Earth	Semi-fruitful	New 4:28 pm

April Aspectarian/Favorable & Unfavorable Days

Date	Sun	Mercury	Venus	Mars	Jupiter	Saturn	Uranus	Neptune	Pluto
1	T					X			
2			T	O	X			Q	
3		Q					T		
4	Q		Q					X	
5		X							C
6	X		X	T		C	Q		
7					C				
8							X		
9			Q					C	X
10									
11	C	C				X			
12			C	X	X				Q
13						Q	C		
14					Q			X	T
15									
16						T	Q		
17	X	X	X	C	T				
18							X		
19								T	O
20	Q	Q	Q				Q		
21					O				
22	T	T		X	O				
23			T				T	O	
24			Q						T
25					T				
26	O			T	T				Q
27		O	O			Q	O	T	
28			Q						X
29				X		Q			
30				O	X				

Date	Aries	Taurus	Gemini	Cancer	Leo	Virgo	Libra	Scorpio	Sagittarius	Capricorn	Aquarius	Pisces
1	F		f	u	f		U		f	u	f	
2	F		f	u	f		U		f	u	f	u
3		F		f	u	f		U		f	u	f
4		F		f	u	f		U		f	u	f
5	f		F		f	u	f		U		f	u
6	f		F		f	u	f		U		f	u
7	f		F		f	u	f		U		f	u
8	u	f		F		f	u	f		U		f
9	u	f		F		f	u	f		U		f
10	f	u	f		F		f	u	f		U	
11	f	u	f		F		f	u	f		U	
12	f	u	f		F		f	u	f		U	
13		f	u	f		F		f	u	f		U
14		f	u	f		F		f	u	f		U
15	U		f	u	f		F		f	u	f	
16	U		f	u	f		F		f	u	f	
17		U		f	u	f		F		f	u	f
18		U		f	u	f		F		f	u	f
19	f		U		f	u	f		F		f	u
20	f		U		f	u	f		F		f	u
21	u	f		U		f	u	f		F		f
22	u	f		U		f	u	f		F		f
23	f	u	f		U		f	u	f		F	
24	f	u	f		U		f	u	f		F	
25	f	u	f		U		f	u	f		F	
26		f	u	f		U		f	u	f		F
27		f	u	f		U		f	u	f		F
28	F		f	u	f		U		f	u	f	
29	F		f	u	f		U		f	u	f	
30		F		f	u	f		U		f	u	f

May Moon Table

Date	Sign	Element	Nature	Phase
1 Sun	Taurus	Earth	Semi-fruitful	1st
2 Mon 6:47 am	Gemini	Air	Barren	1st
3 Tue	Gemini	Air	Barren	1st
4 Wed 7:05 pm	Cancer	Water	Fruitful	1st
5 Thu	Cancer	Water	Fruitful	1st
6 Fri	Cancer	Water	Fruitful	1st
7 Sat 7:50 am	Leo	Fire	Barren	1st
8 Sun	Leo	Fire	Barren	2nd 8:21 pm
9 Mon 6:53 pm	Virgo	Earth	Barren	2nd
10 Tue	Virgo	Earth	Barren	2nd
11 Wed	Virgo	Earth	Barren	2nd
12 Thu 2:34 am	Libra	Air	Semi-fruitful	2nd
13 Fri	Libra	Air	Semi-fruitful	2nd
14 Sat 6:34 am	Scorpio	Water	Fruitful	2nd
15 Sun	Scorpio	Water	Fruitful	2nd
16 Mon 7:50 am	Sagittarius	Fire	Barren	Full 12:14 am
17 Tue	Sagittarius	Fire	Barren	3rd
18 Wed 8:02 am	Capricorn	Earth	Semi-fruitful	3rd
19 Thu	Capricorn	Earth	Semi-fruitful	3rd
20 Fri 8:53 am	Aquarius	Air	Barren	3rd
21 Sat	Aquarius	Air	Barren	3rd
22 Sun 11:49 am	Pisces	Water	Fruitful	4th 2:43 pm
23 Mon	Pisces	Water	Fruitful	4th
24 Tue 5:39 pm	Aries	Fire	Barren	4th
25 Wed	Aries	Fire	Barren	4th
26 Thu	Aries	Fire	Barren	4th
27 Fri 2:22 am	Taurus	Earth	Semi-fruitful	4th
28 Sat	Taurus	Earth	Semi-fruitful	4th
29 Sun 1:23 pm	Gemini	Air	Barren	4th
30 Mon	Gemini	Air	Barren	New 7:30 am
31 Tue	Gemini	Air	Barren	1st

May Aspectarian/Favorable & Unfavorable Days

Date	Sun	Mercury	Venus	Mars	Jupiter	Saturn	Uranus	Neptune	Pluto
1						Q	C	X	
2		C	X		X				T
3				Q					
4					Q	T		Q	
5			Q						
6	X			T				X	T
7		X	T		T				O
8	Q							Q	
9							O		
10		Q						T	
11	T			O				O	
12		T	O		O				T
13						T			
14									Q
15				T		Q	O	T	
16	O	O			T				X
17			T	Q		X		Q	
18					Q				
19			Q					T	
20	T	T		X	X			X	C
21			X				Q		
22	Q	Q				C			
23							X		
24		X		C	C			C	X
25	X								
26			C			X			Q
27									
28							C		
29		C		X	X	Q		X	T
30	C								
31						T		Q	

Date	Aries	Taurus	Gemini	Cancer	Leo	Virgo	Libra	Scorpio	Sagittarius	Capricorn	Aquarius	Pisces
1		F		f	u	f		U		f	u	f
2		F		f	u	f		U		f	u	f
3	f		F		f	u	f		U		f	u
4	f		F		f	u	f		U		f	u
5	u	f		F		f	u	f		U		f
6	u	f		F		f	u	f		U		f
7	u	f		F		f	u	f		U		f
8	f	u	f		F		f	u	f		U	
9	f	u	f		F		f	u	f		U	
10		f	u	f		F		f	u	f		U
11		f	u	f		F		f	u	f		U
12	U		f	u	f		F		f	u	f	
13	U		f	u	f		F		f	u	f	
14	U		f	u	f		F		f	u	f	
15		U		f	u	f		F		f	u	f
16		U		f	u	f		F		f	u	f
17	f		U		f	u	f		F		f	u
18	f		U		f	u	f		F		f	u
19	u	f		U		f	u	f		F		f
20	u	f		U		f	u	f		F		f
21	f	u	f		U		f	u	f		F	
22	f	u	f		U		f	u	f		F	
23		f	u	f		U		f	u	f		F
24		f	u	f		U		f	u	f		F
25	F		f	u	f		U		f	u	f	
26	F		f	u	f		U		f	u	f	
27		F		f	u	f		U		f	u	f
28		F		f	u	f		U		f	u	f
29		F		f	u	f		U		f	u	f
30	f		F		f	u	f		U		f	u
31	f		F		f	u	f		U		f	u

June Moon Table

Date	Sign	Element	Nature	Phase
1 Wed 1:49 am	Cancer	Water	Fruitful	1st
2 Thu	Cancer	Water	Fruitful	1st
3 Fri 2:38 pm	Leo	Fire	Barren	1st
4 Sat	Leo	Fire	Barren	1st
5 Sun	Leo	Fire	Barren	1st
6 Mon 2:22 am	Virgo	Earth	Barren	1st
7 Tue	Virgo	Earth	Barren	2nd 10:48 am
8 Wed 11:23 am	Libra	Air	Semi-fruitful	2nd
9 Thu	Libra	Air	Semi-fruitful	2nd
10 Fri 4:41 pm	Scorpio	Water	Fruitful	2nd
11 Sat	Scorpio	Water	Fruitful	2nd
12 Sun 6:31 pm	Sagittarius	Fire	Barren	2nd
13 Mon	Sagittarius	Fire	Barren	2nd
14 Tue 6:14 pm	Capricorn	Earth	Semi-fruitful	Full 7:52 am
15 Wed	Capricorn	Earth	Semi-fruitful	3rd
16 Thu 5:44 pm	Aquarius	Air	Barren	3rd
17 Fri	Aquarius	Air	Barren	3rd
18 Sat 7:01 pm	Pisces	Water	Fruitful	3rd
19 Sun	Pisces	Water	Fruitful	3rd
20 Mon 11:37 pm	Aries	Fire	Barren	4th 11:11 pm
21 Tue	Aries	Fire	Barren	4th
22 Wed	Aries	Fire	Barren	4th
23 Thu 7:58 am	Taurus	Earth	Semi-fruitful	4th
24 Fri	Taurus	Earth	Semi-fruitful	4th
25 Sat 7:13 pm	Gemini	Air	Barren	4th
26 Sun	Gemini	Air	Barren	4th
27 Mon	Gemini	Air	Barren	4th
28 Tue 7:53 am	Cancer	Water	Fruitful	New 10:52 pm
29 Wed	Cancer	Water	Fruitful	1st
30 Thu 8:40 pm	Leo	Fire	Barren	1st

June Aspectarian/Favorable & Unfavorable Days

Date	Sun	Mercury	Venus	Mars	Jupiter	Saturn	Uranus	Neptune	Pluto
1			X	Q	Q				
2								X	
3		X			T			T	O
4	X		Q	T			Q		
5		Q				O			
6									
7	Q		T				T		
8		T			O			O	T
9	T				O				
10							T		Q
11			O				O		
12		O					Q	T	X
13				T	T				
14	O					X		Q	
15				Q	Q		T		
16		T	T					X	C
17				X	X		Q		
18	T		Q			C			
19		Q							
20	Q		X				X	C	X
21		X			C				
22				C		X			
23	X								Q
24						C			
25							Q	X	T
26		C		X					
27		C		X	T		Q		
28	C					Q			
29								X	
30				Q				T	O

Date	Aries	Taurus	Gemini	Cancer	Leo	Virgo	Libra	Scorpio	Sagittarius	Capricorn	Aquarius	Pisces
1	u	f		F		f	u	f		U		f
2	u	f		F		f	u	f		U		f
3	u	f		F		f	u	f		U		f
4	f	u	f		F		f	u	f		U	
5	f	u	f		F		f	u	f		U	
6		f	u	f		F		f	u	f		U
7		f	u	f		F		f	u	f		U
8		f	u	f		F		f	u	f		U
9	U		f	u	f		F		f	u	f	
10	U		f	u	f		F		f	u	f	
11		U		f	u	f		F		f	u	f
12		U		f	u	f		F		f	u	f
13	f		U		f	u	f		F		f	u
14	f		U		f	u	f		F		f	u
15	u	f		U		f	u	f		F		f
16	u	f		U		f	u	f		F		f
17	f	u	f		U		f	u	f		F	
18	f	u	f		U		f	u	f		F	U
19		f	u	f		U		f	u	f		F
20		f	u	f		U		f	u	f		F
21	F		f	u	f		U		f	u	f	
22	F		f	u	f		U		f	u	f	
23	F		f	u	f		U		f	u	f	
24		F		f	u	f		U		f	u	f
25		F		f	u	f		U		f	u	f
26	f		F		f	u	f		U		f	u
27	f		F		f	u	f		U		f	u
28	f		F		f	u	f		U		f	u
29	u	f		F		f	u	f		U		f
30	u	f		F		f	u	f		U		f

July Moon Table

Date	Sign	Element	Nature	Phase
1 Fri	Leo	Fire	Barren	1st
2 Sat	Leo	Fire	Barren	1st
3 Sun 8:31 am	Virgo	Earth	Barren	1st
4 Mon	Virgo	Earth	Barren	1st
5 Tue 6:25 pm	Libra	Air	Semi-fruitful	1st
6 Wed	Libra	Air	Semi-fruitful	2nd 10:14 pm
7 Thu	Libra	Air	Semi-fruitful	2nd
8 Fri 1:15 am	Scorpio	Water	Fruitful	2nd
9 Sat	Scorpio	Water	Fruitful	2nd
10 Sun 4:34 am	Sagittarius	Fire	Barren	2nd
11 Mon	Sagittarius	Fire	Barren	2nd
12 Tue 5:01 am	Capricorn	Earth	Semi-fruitful	2nd
13 Wed	Capricorn	Earth	Semi-fruitful	Full 2:38 pm
14 Thu 4:13 am	Aquarius	Air	Barren	3rd
15 Fri	Aquarius	Air	Barren	3rd
16 Sat 4:18 am	Pisces	Water	Fruitful	3rd
17 Sun	Pisces	Water	Fruitful	3rd
18 Mon 7:17 am	Aries	Fire	Barren	3rd
19 Tue	Aries	Fire	Barren	3rd
20 Wed 2:23 pm	Taurus	Earth	Semi-fruitful	4th 10:19 am
21 Thu	Taurus	Earth	Semi-fruitful	4th
22 Fri	Taurus	Earth	Semi-fruitful	4th
23 Sat 1:11 am	Gemini	Air	Barren	4th
24 Sun	Gemini	Air	Barren	4th
25 Mon 1:54 pm	Cancer	Water	Fruitful	4th
26 Tue	Cancer	Water	Fruitful	4th
27 Wed	Cancer	Water	Fruitful	4th
28 Thu 2:36 am	Leo	Fire	Barren	New 1:55 pm
29 Fri	Leo	Fire	Barren	1st
30 Sat 2:11 pm	Virgo	Earth	Barren	1st
31 Sun	Virgo	Earth	Barren	1st

July Aspectarian/Favorable & Unfavorable Days

Date	Sun	Mercury	Venus	Mars	Jupiter	Saturn	Uranus	Neptune	Pluto
1			X		T				
2						O	Q		
3		X		T					
4	X		Q					T	
5		Q						O	T
6	Q				O				
7			T			T			Q
8		T		O					
9	T					Q	O	T	
10					T				X
11			O			X		Q	
12				T	Q				
13	O	O						T	X
14				Q	X				C
15						C	Q		
16			T	X					
17	T							X	C
18		T	Q		C				X
19									
20	Q	Q	X			X			Q
21				C					
22						Q	C	X	T
23	X	X			X				
24									
25						T		Q	
26			C	X	Q				
27							X	T	O
28	C				T				
29		C		Q			Q		
30						O			
31			X						

Date	Aries	Taurus	Gemini	Cancer	Leo	Virgo	Libra	Scorpio	Sagittarius	Capricorn	Aquarius	Pisces
1	f	u	f		F		f	u	f		U	
2	f	u	f		F		f	u	f		U	
3	f	u	f		F		f	u	f		U	
4		f	u	f		F		f	u	f		U
5		f	u	f		F		f	u	f		U
6	U		f	u	f		F		f	u	f	
7	U		f	u	f		F		f	u	f	
8		U		f	u	f		F		f	u	f
9		U		f	u	f		F		f	u	f
10		U		f	u	f		F		f	u	f
11	f		U		f	u	f		F		f	u
12	f		U		f	u	f		F		f	u
13	u	f		U		f	u	f		F		f
14	u	f		U		f	u	f		F		f
15	f	u	f		U		f	u	f		F	
16	f	u	f		U		f	u	f		F	
17		f	u	f		U		f	u	f		F
18		f	u	f		U		f	u	f		F
19	F		f	u	f		U		f	u	f	
20	F		f	u	f		U		f	u	f	
21		F		f	u	f		U		f	u	f
22		F		f	u	f		U		f	u	f
23	f		F		f	u	f		U		f	u
24	f		F		f	u	f		U		f	u
25	f		F		f	u	f		U		f	u
26	u	f		F		f	u	f		U		f
27	u	f		F		f	u	f		U		f
28	f	u	f		F		f	u	f		U	
29	f	u	f		F		f	u	f		U	
30	f	u	f		F		f	u	f		U	u
31		f	u	f		F		f	u	f		U

August Moon Table

Date	Sign	Element	Nature	Phase
1 Mon	Virgo	Earth	Barren	1st
2 Tue 12:06 am	Libra	Air	Semi-fruitful	1st
3 Wed	Libra	Air	Semi-fruitful	1st
4 Thu 7:47 am	Scorpio	Water	Fruitful	1st
5 Fri	Scorpio	Water	Fruitful	2nd 7:07 am
6 Sat 12:39 pm	Sagittarius	Fire	Barren	2nd
7 Sun	Sagittarius	Fire	Barren	2nd
8 Mon 2:39 pm	Capricorn	Earth	Semi-fruitful	2nd
9 Tue	Capricorn	Earth	Semi-fruitful	2nd
10 Wed 2:45 pm	Aquarius	Air	Barren	2nd
11 Thu	Aquarius	Air	Barren	Full 9:36 pm
12 Fri 2:44 pm	Pisces	Water	Fruitful	3rd
13 Sat	Pisces	Water	Fruitful	3rd
14 Sun 4:43 pm	Aries	Fire	Barren	3rd
15 Mon	Aries	Fire	Barren	3rd
16 Tue 10:22 pm	Taurus	Earth	Semi-fruitful	3rd
17 Wed	Taurus	Earth	Semi-fruitful	3rd
18 Thu	Taurus	Earth	Semi-fruitful	3rd
19 Fri 8:06 am	Gemini	Air	Barren	4th 12:36 am
20 Sat	Gemini	Air	Barren	4th
21 Sun 8:29 pm	Cancer	Water	Fruitful	4th
22 Mon	Cancer	Water	Fruitful	4th
23 Tue	Cancer	Water	Fruitful	4th
24 Wed 9:09 am	Leo	Fire	Barren	4th
25 Thu	Leo	Fire	Barren	4th
26 Fri 8:25 pm	Virgo	Earth	Barren	4th
27 Sat	Virgo	Earth	Barren	New 4:17 am
28 Sun	Virgo	Earth	Barren	1st
29 Mon 5:45 am	Libra	Air	Semi-fruitful	1st
30 Tue	Libra	Air	Semi-fruitful	1st
31 Wed 1:11 pm	Scorpio	Water	Fruitful	1st

August Aspectarian/Favorable & Unfavorable Days

Date	Sun	Mercury	Venus	Mars	Jupiter	Saturn	Uranus	Neptune	Pluto
1				T			T	O	T
2	X				O				
3		Q				T			
4		X							Q
5	Q		O			Q	O		
6		Q	T					T	X
7	T				T				
8						X	Q		
9		T			Q		T		
10			O	T				X	C
11	O				X		Q		
12				Q		C			
13		O					X		
14			T	X				C	X
15						C			
16	T						X		Q
17			Q						
18		T				Q	C	X	
19	Q			C	X				T
20			X						
21	X	Q				T		Q	
22					Q				
23							X	T	
24		X		X					O
25			C		T		Q		
26						O			
27	C			Q					
28							T	O	T
29		C		T	O				
30						T			
31			X						Q

Date	Aries	Taurus	Gemini	Cancer	Leo	Virgo	Libra	Scorpio	Sagittarius	Capricorn	Aquarius	Pisces
1		f	u	f		F		f	u	f		U
2	U		f	u	f		F		f	u	f	
3	U		f	u	f		F		f	u	f	
4	U		f	u	f		F		f	u	f	
5		U		f	u	f		F		f	u	f
6		U		f	u	f		F		f	u	f
7	f		U		f	u	f		F		f	u
8	f		U		f	u	f		F		f	u
9	u	f		U		f	u	f		F		f
10	u	f		U		f	u	f		F		f
11	f	u	f		U		f	u	f		F	
12	f	u	f		U		f	u	f		F	
13		f	u	f		U		f	u	f		F
14		f	u	f		U		f	u	f		F
15	F		f	u	f		U		f	u	f	
16	F		f	u	f		U		f	u	f	
17		F		f	u	f		U		f	u	f
18		F		f	u	f		U		f	u	f
19		F		f	u	f		U		f	u	f
20	f		F		f	u	f		U		f	u
21	f		F		f	u	f		U		f	u
22	u	f		F		f	u	f		U		f
23	u	f		F		f	u	f		U		f
24	u	f		F		f	u	f		U		f
25	f	u	f		F		f	u	f		U	
26	f	u	f		F		f	u	f		U	
27		f	u	f		F		f	u	f		U
28		f	u	f		F		f	u	f		U
29		f	u	f		F		f	u	f		U
30	U		f	u	f		F		f	u	f	
31	U		f	u	f		F		f	u	f	

September Moon Table

Date	Sign	Element	Nature	Phase
1 Thu	Scorpio	Water	Fruitful	1st
2 Fri 6:39 pm	Sagittarius	Fire	Barren	1st
3 Sat	Sagittarius	Fire	Barren	2nd 2:08 pm
4 Sun 10:03 pm	Capricorn	Earth	Semi-fruitful	2nd
5 Mon	Capricorn	Earth	Semi-fruitful	2nd
6 Tue 11:41 pm	Aquarius	Air	Barren	2nd
7 Wed	Aquarius	Air	Barren	2nd
8 Thu	Aquarius	Air	Barren	2nd
9 Fri 12:42 am	Pisces	Water	Fruitful	2nd
10 Sat	Pisces	Water	Fruitful	Full 5:59 am
11 Sun 2:47 am	Aries	Fire	Barren	3rd
12 Mon	Aries	Fire	Barren	3rd
13 Tue 7:39 am	Taurus	Earth	Semi-fruitful	3rd
14 Wed	Taurus	Earth	Semi-fruitful	3rd
15 Thu 4:16 pm	Gemini	Air	Barren	3rd
16 Fri	Gemini	Air	Barren	3rd
17 Sat	Gemini	Air	Barren	4th 5:52 pm
18 Sun 3:59 am	Cancer	Water	Fruitful	4th
19 Mon	Cancer	Water	Fruitful	4th
20 Tue 4:38 pm	Leo	Fire	Barren	4th
21 Wed	Leo	Fire	Barren	4th
22 Thu	Leo	Fire	Barren	4th
23 Fri 3:53 am	Virgo	Earth	Barren	4th
24 Sat	Virgo	Earth	Barren	4th
25 Sun 12:43 pm	Libra	Air	Semi-fruitful	New 5:55 pm
26 Mon	Libra	Air	Semi-fruitful	1st
27 Tue 7:15 pm	Scorpio	Water	Fruitful	1st
28 Wed	Scorpio	Water	Fruitful	1st
29 Thu	Scorpio	Water	Fruitful	1st
30 Fri 12:03 am	Sagittarius	Fire	Barren	1st

September Aspectarian/Favorable & Unfavorable Days

Date	Sun	Mercury	Venus	Mars	Jupiter	Saturn	Uranus	Neptune	Pluto
1	X						O		
2			Q			Q	T	X	
3	Q	X			O	T			
4			T			X		Q	
5	T	Q			Q				
6							T	X	C
7		T		T	X				
8						C	Q		
9			O	Q					
10	O						X	C	X
11		O		X	C				
12						X			
13									Q
14			T			Q	C		
15	T							X	T
16		T	Q	C	X				
17	Q					T		Q	
18		Q			Q				
19			X			X			
20	X	X						T	O
21					T				
22			X			O	Q		
23									
24				Q			T		
25	C	C	C		O			O	T
26			T			T			
27									Q
28									
29		X				Q	O	T	X
30	X		X		T				

Date	Aries	Taurus	Gemini	Cancer	Leo	Virgo	Libra	Scorpio	Sagittarius	Capricorn	Aquarius	Pisces
1	U		f	u	f		F		f	u		f
2	U		f	u	f		F		f	u		f
3		U		f	u	f		F		f	u	
4		U		f	u	f		F		f	u	
5	f		U		f	u	f		F		f	u
6	f		U		f	u	f		F		f	u
7	u	f		U		f	u	f		F		f
8	u	f		U		f	u	f		F		f
9	f	u	f		U		f	u	f		F	
10		f	u	f		U		f	u	f		F
11	F		f	u	f		U		f	u		f
12	F		f	u	f		U		f	u		f
13	F		f	u	f		U		f	u		f
14		F		f	u	f		U		f	u	f
15		F		f	u	f		U		f	u	f
16	f		F		f	u	f		U		f	u
17	f		F		f	u	f		U		f	u
18	f		F		f	u	f		U		f	u
19	u	f		F		f	u	f		U		f
20	u	f		F		f	u	f		U		f
21	f	u	f		F		f	u	f		U	
22	f	u	f		F		f	u	f		U	
23	f	u	f		F		f	u	f		U	
24		f	u	f		F		f	u	f		U
25		f	u	f		F		f	u	f		U
26	U		f	u	f		F		f	u		f
27	U		f	u	f		F		f	u		f
28		U		f	u	f		F		f	u	f
29		U		f	u	f		F		f	u	f
30	f		U		f	u	f		F		f	u

153

October Moon Table

Date	Sign	Element	Nature	Phase
1 Sat	Sagittarius	Fire	Barren	1st
2 Sun 3:38 am	Capricorn	Earth	Semi-fruitful	2nd 8:14 pm
3 Mon	Capricorn	Earth	Semi-fruitful	2nd
4 Tue 6:20 am	Aquarius	Air	Barren	2nd
5 Wed	Aquarius	Air	Barren	2nd
6 Thu 8:47 am	Pisces	Water	Fruitful	2nd
7 Fri	Pisces	Water	Fruitful	2nd
8 Sat 11:57 am	Aries	Fire	Barren	2nd
9 Sun	Aries	Fire	Barren	Full 4:55 pm
10 Mon 5:04 pm	Taurus	Earth	Semi-fruitful	3rd
11 Tue	Taurus	Earth	Semi-fruitful	3rd
12 Wed	Taurus	Earth	Semi-fruitful	3rd
13 Thu 1:08 am	Gemini	Air	Barren	3rd
14 Fri	Gemini	Air	Barren	3rd
15 Sat 12:11 pm	Cancer	Water	Fruitful	3rd
16 Sun	Cancer	Water	Fruitful	3rd
17 Mon	Cancer	Water	Fruitful	4th 1:15 pm
18 Tue 12:45 am	Leo	Fire	Barren	4th
10 Wed	Leo	Fire	Barren	4th
20 Thu 12:25 pm	Virgo	Earth	Barren	4th
21 Fri	Virgo	Earth	Barren	4th
22 Sat 9:24 pm	Libra	Air	Semi-fruitful	4th
23 Sun	Libra	Air	Semi-fruitful	4th
24 Mon	Libra	Air	Semi-fruitful	4th
25 Tue 3:18 am	Scorpio	Water	Fruitful	New 6:49 am
26 Wed	Scorpio	Water	Fruitful	1st
27 Thu 6:55 am	Sagittarius	Fire	Barren	1st
28 Fri	Sagittarius	Fire	Barren	1st
29 Sat 9:21 am	Capricorn	Earth	Semi-fruitful	1st
30 Sun	Capricorn	Earth	Semi-fruitful	1st
31 Mon 11:43 am	Aquarius	Air	Barren	1st

October Aspectarian/Favorable & Unfavorable Days

Date	Sun	Mercury	Venus	Mars	Jupiter	Saturn	Uranus	Neptune	Pluto
1		Q		O		X		Q	
2	Q		Q		Q				
3		T					T	X	C
4			T		X				
5	T			T		C	Q		
6									
7			Q				X		
8		O			C			C	X
9	O		O			X			
10				X					Q
11									
12						Q	C	X	T
13		T			X				
14	T		T			T		Q	
15				C		Q			
16		Q							
17	Q		Q				X	T	O
18					T				
19		X				O	Q		
20	X		X	X					
21							T		
22			Q	O			O	T	
23									
24		C		T		T			Q
25	C		C						
26						Q	O	T	
27					T				X
28						X		Q	
29	X	X	X	O	Q				
30								T	X
31		Q			X				C

Date	Aries	Taurus	Gemini	Cancer	Leo	Virgo	Libra	Scorpio	Sagittarius	Capricorn	Aquarius	Pisces
1	f		U		f	u	f		F		f	u
2	f		U		f	u	f		F		f	u
3	u	f		U		f	u	f		F		f
4	u	f		U		f	u	f		F		f
5	f	u	f		U		f	u	f		F	
6	f	u	f		U		f	u	f		F	
7		f	u	f		U		f	u	f		F
8		f	u	f		U		f	u	f		F
9	F		f	u	f		U		f	u	f	
10	F		f	u	f		U		f	u	f	
11		F		f	u	f		U		f	u	f
12		F		f	u	f		U		f	u	f
13	f		F		f	u	f		U		f	u
14	f		F		f	u	f		U		f	u
15	f		F		f	u	f		U		f	u
16	u	f		F		f	u	f		U		f
17	u	f		F		f	u	f		U		f
18	f	u	f		F		f	u	f		U	
19	f	u	f		F		f	u	f		U	
20	f	u	f		F		f	u	f		U	
21		f	u	f		F		f	u	f		U
22		f	u	f		F		f	u	f		U
23	U		f	u	f		F		f	u	f	
24	U		f	u	f		F		f	u	f	
25	U		f	u	f		F		f	u	f	
26		U		f	u	f		F		f	u	f
27		U		f	u	f		F		f	u	f
28	f		U		f	u	f		F		f	u
29	f		U		f	u	f		F		f	u
30	u	f		U		f	u	f		F		f
31	u	f		U		f	u	f		F		f

November Moon Table

Date	Sign	Element	Nature	Phase
1 Tue	Aquarius	Air	Barren	2nd 2:37 am
2 Wed 2:46 pm	Pisces	Water	Fruitful	2nd
3 Thu	Pisces	Water	Fruitful	2nd
4 Fri 7:07 pm	Aries	Fire	Barren	2nd
5 Sat	Aries	Fire	Barren	2nd
6 Sun	Aries	Fire	Barren	2nd
7 Mon 12:15 am	Taurus	Earth	Semi-fruitful	2nd
8 Tue	Taurus	Earth	Semi-fruitful	Full 6:02 am
9 Wed 8:37 am	Gemini	Air	Barren	3rd
10 Thu	Gemini	Air	Barren	3rd
11 Fri 7:22 pm	Cancer	Water	Fruitful	3rd
12 Sat	Cancer	Water	Fruitful	3rd
13 Sun	Cancer	Water	Fruitful	3rd
14 Mon 7:48 am	Leo	Fire	Barren	3rd
15 Tue	Leo	Fire	Barren	3rd
16 Wed 8:04 pm	Virgo	Earth	Barren	4th 8:27 am
17 Thu	Virgo	Earth	Barren	4th
18 Fri	Virgo	Earth	Barren	4th
19 Sat 5:50 am	Libra	Air	Semi-fruitful	4th
20 Sun	Libra	Air	Semi-fruitful	4th
21 Mon 12:16 pm	Scorpio	Water	Fruitful	4th
22 Tue	Scorpio	Water	Fruitful	4th
23 Wed 3:16 pm	Sagittarius	Fire	Barren	New 5:57 pm
24 Thu	Sagittarius	Fire	Barren	1st
25 Fri 4:18 pm	Capricorn	Earth	Semi-fruitful	1st
26 Sat	Capricorn	Earth	Semi-fruitful	1st
27 Sun 5:07 pm	Aquarius	Air	Barren	1st
28 Mon	Aquarius	Air	Barren	1st
29 Tue 7:15 pm	Pisces	Water	Fruitful	1st
30 Wed	Pisces	Water	Fruitful	2nd 9:37 am

November Aspectarian/Favorable & Unfavorable Days

Date	Sun	Mercury	Venus	Mars	Jupiter	Saturn	Uranus	Neptune	Pluto
1	Q		Q			C	Q		
2				T					
3	T	T	T				X		
4				Q	C			C	X
5									
6				X		X			Q
7									
8	O	O	O			Q	C	X	
9					X				T
10						T			
11				C	Q			Q	
12									
13	T	T					X	T	
14			T		T				O
15					O	Q			
16	Q	Q	Q	X					
17									
18				Q			T	O	T
19	X	X	X		O				
20				T		T			
21									Q
22						Q	O		
23	C				T			T	X
24		C	C			X			
25				O	Q			Q	
26							T		
27					X			X	C
28	X	X	X				Q		
29				T		C			
30	Q						X		

Date	Aries	Taurus	Gemini	Cancer	Leo	Virgo	Libra	Scorpio	Sagittarius	Capricorn	Aquarius	Pisces
1	f	u	f		U		f	u	f		F	
2	f	u	f		U		f	u	f		F	
3		f	u	f		U		f	u	f		F
4		f	u	f		U		f	u	f		F
5	F		f	u	f		U		f	u	f	
6	F		f	u	f		U		f	u	f	
7		F		f	u	f		U		f	u	f
8		F		f	u	f		U		f	u	f
9		F		f	u	f		U		f	u	f
10	f		F		f	u	f		U		f	u
11	f		F		f	u	f		U		f	u
12	u	f		F		f	u	f		U		f
13	u	f		F		f	u	f		U		f
14	u	f		F		f	u	f		U		f
15	f	u	f		F		f	u	f		U	
16	f	u	f		F		f	u	f		U	
17		f	u	f		F		f	u	f		U
18		f	u	f		F		f	u	f		U
19		f	u	f		F		f	u	f		U
20	U		f	u	f		F		f	u	f	
21	U		f	u	f		F		f	u	f	
22		U		f	u	f		F		f	u	f
23		U		f	u	f		F		f	u	f
24	f		U		f	u	f		F		f	u
25	f		U		f	u	f		F		f	u
26	u	f		U		f	u	f		F		f
27	u	f		U		f	u	f		F		f
28	f	u	f		U		f	u	f		F	
29	f	u	f		U		f	u	f		F	
30		f	u	f		U		f	u	f		F

December Moon Table

Date	Sign	Element	Nature	Phase
1 Thu 11:41 pm	Aries	Fire	Barren	2nd
2 Fri	Aries	Fire	Barren	2nd
3 Sat	Aries	Fire	Barren	2nd
4 Sun 6:38 am	Taurus	Earth	Semi-fruitful	2nd
5 Mon	Taurus	Earth	Semi-fruitful	2nd
6 Tue 3:49 pm	Gemini	Air	Barren	2nd
7 Wed	Gemini	Air	Barren	Full 11:08 pm
8 Thu	Gemini	Air	Barren	3rd
9 Fri 2:49 am	Cancer	Water	Fruitful	3rd
10 Sat	Cancer	Water	Fruitful	3rd
11 Sun 3:09 pm	Leo	Fire	Barren	3rd
12 Mon	Leo	Fire	Barren	3rd
13 Tue	Leo	Fire	Barren	3rd
14 Wed 3:45 am	Virgo	Earth	Barren	3rd
15 Thu	Virgo	Earth	Barren	3rd
16 Fri 2:49 pm	Libra	Air	Semi-fruitful	4th 3:56 am
17 Sat	Libra	Air	Semi-fruitful	4th
18 Sun 10:31 pm	Scorpio	Water	Fruitful	4th
19 Mon	Scorpio	Water	Fruitful	4th
20 Tue	Scorpio	Water	Fruitful	4th
21 Wed 2:12 am	Sagittarius	Fire	Barren	4th
22 Thu	Sagittarius	Fire	Barren	4th
23 Fri 2:49 am	Capricorn	Earth	Semi-fruitful	New 5:17 am
24 Sat	Capricorn	Earth	Semi-fruitful	1st
25 Sun 2:14 am	Aquarius	Air	Barren	1st
26 Mon	Aquarius	Air	Barren	1st
27 Tue 2:34 am	Pisces	Water	Fruitful	1st
28 Wed	Pisces	Water	Fruitful	1st
29 Thu 5:36 am	Aries	Fire	Barren	2nd 8:21 pm
30 Fri	Aries	Fire	Barren	2nd
31 Sat 12:08 pm	Taurus	Earth	Semi-fruitful	2nd

December Aspectarian/Favorable & Unfavorable Days

Date	Sun	Mercury	Venus	Mars	Jupiter	Saturn	Uranus	Neptune	Pluto
1		Q	Q	Q	C			C	X
2	T								
3		T	T	X		X			
4									Q
5						Q	C		
6					X			X	T
7	O			C					
8						T		Q	
9		O	O	Q					
10							X		
11						T		T	O
12				X				Q	
13	T					O			
14			T						
15		T		Q			T		
16	Q				O			O	T
17		Q	Q	T					
18	X					T			Q
19			X						
20		X				Q	O	T	X
21			O	T					
22						X		Q	
23	C				Q				
24		C	C				T	X	C
25				T	X				
26						C	Q		
27	X			Q					
28		X	X				X	C	
29	Q			X	C				X
30						X			
31		Q	Q						Q

Date	Aries	Taurus	Gemini	Cancer	Leo	Virgo	Libra	Scorpio	Sagittarius	Capricorn	Aquarius	Pisces
1		f		u	f		U		f	u	f		F
2	F		f	u	f		U		f	u	f	
3	F		f	u	f		U		f	u	f	
4	F		f	u	f		U		f	u	f	
5		F		f	u	f		U		f	u	f
6		F		f	u	f		U		f	u	f
7	f		F		f	u	f		U		f	u
8	f		F		f	u	f		U		f	u
9	u	f		F		f	u	f		U		f
10	u	f		F		f	u	f		U		f
11	u	f		F		f	u	f		U		f
12	f	u	f		F		f	u	f		U	
13	f	u	f		F		f	u	f		U	
14	f	u	f		F		f	u	f		U	
15		f	u	f		F		f	u	f		U
16		f	u	f		F		f	u	f		U
17	U		f	u	f		F		f	u	f	
18	U		f	u	f		F		f	u	f	
19		U		f	u	f		F		f	u	f
20		U		f	u	f		F		f	u	f
21	f		U		f	u	f		F		f	u
22	f		U		f	u	f		F		f	u
23	u	f		U		f	u	f		F		f
24	u	f		U		f	u	f		F		f
25	f	u	f		U		f	u	f		F	
26	f	u	f		U		f	u	f		F	
27		f	u	f		U		f	u	f		F
28		f	u	f		U		f	u	f		F
29		f	u	f		U		f	u	f		F
30	F		f	u	f		U		f	u	f	
31	F		f	u	f		U		f	u	f	u

2022 Retrograde Planets

Planet	Begin	Eastern	Pacific	End	Eastern	Pacific
Uranus	8/19/21	9:40 pm	**6:40 pm**	1/18	10:27 am	**7:27 am**
Venus	12/19/21	5:36 am	**2:36 am**	1/29	3:46 am	**12:46 am**
Mercury	1/14	6:41 am	**3:41 am**	2/3	11:13 pm	**8:13 pm**
Pluto	4/29	2:38 pm	**11:38 am**	10/8	5:56 pm	**2:56 pm**
Mercury	5/10	7:47 am	**4:47 am**	6/3	4:00 am	**1:00 am**
Saturn	6/4	5:47 pm	**2:47 pm**	10/22		**9:07 pm**
Saturn	6/4	5:47 pm	**2:47 pm**	10/23	12:07 am	
Neptune	6/28	3:55 am	**12:55 am**	12/3	7:15 pm	**4:15 pm**
Jupiter	7/28	4:37 pm	**1:37 pm**	11/23	6:02 pm	**3:02 pm**
Uranus	8/24	9:54 am	**6:54 am**	1/22/23	5:59 pm	**2:59 pm**
Mercury	9/9	11:38 pm	**8:38 pm**	10/2	5:07 am	**2:07 am**
Mars	10/30	9:26 am	**6:26 am**	1/12/23	3:56 pm	**12:56 pm**
Mercury	12/29	4:32 am	**1:32 am**	1/18/23	8:12 am	**5:12 am**

Eastern Time in plain type, **Pacific Time in bold type**

160

Egg-Setting Dates

To Have Eggs by this Date	Sign	Qtr.	Date to Set Eggs
Jan 5, 7:17 pm–Jan 8, 12:26 am	Pisces	1st	Dec 15, 2021
Jan 10, 9:47 am–Jan 12, 10:08 pm	Taurus	2nd	Dec 20, 2021
Jan 15, 11:11 am–Jan 17, 6:48 pm	Cancer	2nd	Dec 25, 2021
Feb 2, 6:00 am–Feb 4, 9:57 am	Pisces	1st	Jan 12, 2022
Feb 6, 5:52 pm–Feb 9, 5:27 am	Taurus	1st	Jan 16
Feb 11, 6:27 pm–Feb 14, 6:17 am	Cancer	2nd	Jan 21
Mar 2, 12:35 pm–Mar 3, 7:52 pm	Pisces	1st	Feb 09
Mar 6, 3:00 am–Mar 8, 1:40 pm	Taurus	1st	Feb 13
Mar 11, 2:24 am–Mar 13, 3:32 pm	Cancer	2nd	Feb 18
Apr 2, 12:50 pm–Apr 4, 11:04 pm	Taurus	1st	Mar 12
Apr 7, 11:30 am–Apr 10, 12:00 am	Cancer	1st	Mar 17
Apr 14, 4:46 pm–Apr 16, 2:55 pm	Libra	2nd	Mar 24
Apr 30, 4:28 pm–May 2, 6:47 am	Taurus	1st	Apr 09
May 4, 7:05 pm–May 7, 7:50 am	Cancer	1st	Apr 13
May 12, 2:34 am–May 14, 6:34 am	Libra	2nd	Apr 21
Jun 1, 1:49 am–Jun 3, 2:38 pm	Cancer	1st	May 11
Jun 8, 11:23 am–Jun 10, 4:41 pm	Libra	2nd	May 18
Jun 28, 10:52 pm–Jun 30, 8:40 pm	Cancer	1st	Jun 07
Jul 5, 6:25 pm–Jul 8, 1:15 am	Libra	1st	Jun 14
Aug 2, 12:06 am–Aug 4, 7:47 am	Libra	1st	Jul 12
Aug 29, 5:45 am–Aug 31, 1:11 pm	Libra	1st	Aug 08
Sep 9, 12:42 am–Sep 10, 5:59 am	Pisces	2nd	Aug 19
Sep 25, 5:55 pm–Sep 27, 7:15 pm	Libra	1st	Sep 04
Oct 6, 8:47 am–Oct 8, 11:57 am	Pisces	2nd	Sep 15
Nov 2, 2:46 pm–Nov 4, 7:07 pm	Pisces	2nd	Oct 12
Nov 7, 12:15 am–Nov 8, 6:02 am	Taurus	2nd	Oct 17
Nov 29, 7:15 pm–Dec 1, 11:41 pm	Pisces	1st	Nov 08
Dec 4, 6:38 am–Dec 6, 3:49 pm	Taurus	2nd	Nov 13
Dec 27, 2:34 am–Dec 29, 5:36 am	Pisces	1st	Dec 06

Dates to Hunt and Fish

Date	Quarter	Sign
Jan 5, 7:17 pm–Jan 8, 12:26 am	1st	Pisces
Jan 15, 11:11 am–Jan 17, 11:03 pm	2nd	Cancer
Jan 24, 10:57 pm–Jan 27, 2:34 am	3rd	Scorpio
Feb 2, 6:00 am–Feb 4, 9:57 am	1st	Pisces
Feb 11, 6:27 pm–Feb 14, 6:17 pm	2nd	Cancer
Feb 21, 4:19 am–Feb 23, 8:29 am	3rd	Scorpio
Feb 23, 8:29 am–Feb 25, 11:27 am	3rd	Sagittarius
Mar 1, 3:53 pm–Mar 3, 7:52 pm	4th	Pisces
Mar 11, 2:24 am–Mar 13, 3:32 pm	2nd	Cancer
Mar 20, 11:45 am–Mar 22, 2:59 pm	3rd	Scorpio
Mar 22, 2:59 pm–Mar 24, 5:54 pm	3rd	Sagittarius
Mar 29, 12:32 am–Mar 31, 5:30 am	4th	Pisces
Apr 7, 11:30 am–Apr 10, 12:00 am	1st	Cancer
Apr 16, 8:23 pm–Apr 18, 10:16 pm	3rd	Scorpio
Apr 18, 10:16 pm–Apr 20, 11:52 pm	3rd	Sagittarius
Apr 25, 6:15 am–Apr 27, 12:10 pm	4th	Pisces
May 4, 7:05 pm–May 7, 7:50 am	1st	Cancer
May 14, 6:34 am–May 16, 7:50 am	2nd	Scorpio
May 16, 7:50 am–May 18, 8:02 am	3rd	Sagittarius
May 22, 11:49 am–May 24, 5:39 pm	3rd	Pisces
Jun 1, 1:49 am–Jun 3, 2:38 pm	1st	Cancer
Jun 10, 4:41 pm–Jun 12, 6:31 pm	2nd	Scorpio
Jun 12, 6:31 pm–Jun 14, 6:14 pm	2nd	Sagittarius
Jun 18, 7:01 pm–Jun 20, 11:37 pm	3rd	Pisces
Jun 28, 7:53 am–Jun 30, 8:40 pm	4th	Cancer
Jul 8, 1:15 am–Jul 10, 4:34 am	2nd	Scorpio
Jul 10, 4:34 am–Jul 12, 5:01 am	2nd	Sagittarius
Jul 16, 4:18 am–Jul 18, 7:17 am	3rd	Pisces
Jul 18, 7:17 am–Jul 20, 2:23 pm	3rd	Aries
Jul 25, 1:54 pm–Jul 28, 2:36 am	4th	Cancer
Aug 4, 7:47 am–Aug 6, 12:39 pm	1st	Scorpio
Aug 6, 12:39 pm–Aug 8, 2:39 pm	2nd	Sagittarius
Aug 12, 2:44 pm–Aug 14, 4:43 pm	3rd	Pisces
Aug 14, 4:43 pm–Aug 16, 10:22 pm	3rd	Aries
Aug 21, 8:29 pm–Aug 24, 9:09 am	4th	Cancer
Aug 31, 1:11 pm–Sep 2, 6:39 pm	1st	Scorpio
Sep 9, 12:42 am–Sep 11, 2:47 am	2nd	Pisces
Sep 11, 2:47 am–Sep 13, 7:39 am	3rd	Aries
Sep 18, 3:59 am–Sep 20, 4:38 pm	4th	Cancer
Sep 27, 7:15 pm–Sep 30, 12:03 am	1st	Scorpio
Oct 6, 8:47 am–Oct 8, 11:57 am	2nd	Pisces
Oct 8, 11:57 am–Oct 10, 5:04 pm	2nd	Aries
Oct 15, 12:11 pm–Oct 18, 12:45 am	3rd	Cancer
Oct 25, 3:18 am–Oct 27, 6:55 am	4th	Scorpio
Nov 2, 2:46 pm–Nov 4, 7:07 pm	2nd	Pisces
Nov 4, 7:07 pm–Nov 7, 12:15 am	2nd	Aries
Nov 11, 7:22 pm–Nov 14, 7:48 am	3rd	Cancer
Nov 21, 12:16 pm–Nov 23, 3:16 pm	4th	Scorpio
Nov 29, 7:15 pm–Dec 1, 11:41 pm	1st	Pisces
Dec 1, 11:41 pm–Dec 4, 6:38 am	2nd	Aries
Dec 9, 2:49 am–Dec 11, 3:09 pm	3rd	Cancer
Dec 18, 10:31 pm–Dec 21, 2:12 am	4th	Scorpio
Dec 27, 2:34 am–Dec 29, 5:36 am	1st	Pisces
Dec 28, 4:16 pm–Dec 30, 6:08 pm	4th	Scorpio

Dates to Destroy Weeds and Pests

Date	Sign	Qtr.
Jan 17, 11:03 pm–Jan 20, 9:02 am	Leo	3rd
Jan 20, 9:02 am–Jan 22, 5:03 pm	Virgo	3rd
Jan 27, 2:34 am–Jan 29, 4:09 am	Sagittarius	4th
Jan 31, 4:43 am–Feb 1, 12:46 am	Aquarius	4th
Feb 16, 11:56 am–Feb 16, 3:42 pm	Leo	3rd
Feb 16, 3:42 pm–Feb 18, 10:51 pm	Virgo	3rd
Feb 23, 8:29 am–Feb 23, 5:32 pm	Sagittarius	3rd
Feb 23, 5:32 pm–Feb 25, 11:27 am	Sagittarius	4th
Feb 27, 1:36 pm–Mar 1, 3:53 pm	Aquarius	4th
Mar 18, 3:18 am–Mar 18, 7:26 am	Sagittarius	3rd
Mar 22, 2:59 pm–Mar 24, 5:54 pm	Sagittarius	3rd
Mar 26, 8:55 pm–Mar 29, 12:32 am	Aquarius	4th
Mar 31, 5:30 am–Apr 1, 2:24 am	Aries	4th
Apr 18, 10:16 pm–Apr 20, 11:52 pm	Sagittarius	3rd
Apr 23, 2:17 am–Apr 23, 7:56 am	Aquarius	3rd
Apr 23, 7:56 am–Apr 25, 6:15 am	Aquarius	4th
Apr 27, 12:10 pm–Apr 29, 8:19 pm	Aries	4th
May 16, 7:50 am–May 18, 8:02 am	Sagittarius	3rd
May 20, 8:53 am–May 22, 11:49 am	Aquarius	3rd
May 24, 5:39 pm–May 27, 2:22 am	Aries	4th
May 29, 1:23 pm–May 30, 7:30 am	Gemini	4th
Jun 14, 7:52 am–Jun 14, 6:14 pm	Sagittarius	3rd
Jun 16, 5:44 pm–Jun 18, 7:01 pm	Aquarius	3rd
Jun 20, 11:37 pm–Jun 23, 7:58 am	Aries	4th
Jun 25, 7:13 pm–Jun 28, 7:53 am	Gemini	4th
Jul 14, 4:13 am–Jul 16, 4:18 am	Aquarius	3rd
Jul 18, 7:17 am–Jul 20, 10:19 am	Aries	3rd
Jul 20, 10:19 am–Jul 20, 2:23 pm	Aries	4th
Jul 23, 1:11 am–Jul 25, 1:54 pm	Gemini	4th
Jul 28, 2:36 am–Jul 28, 1:55 pm	Leo	4th
Aug 11, 9:36 pm–Aug 12, 2:44 pm	Aquarius	3rd
Aug 14, 4:43 pm–Aug 16, 10:22 pm	Aries	3rd
Aug 19, 8:06 am–Aug 21, 8:29 pm	Gemini	4th
Aug 24, 9:09 am–Aug 26, 8:25 pm	Leo	4th
Aug 26, 8:25 pm–Aug 27, 4:17 am	Virgo	4th
Sep 11, 2:47 am–Sep 13, 7:39 am	Aries	3rd
Sep 15, 4:16 pm–Sep 17, 5:52 pm	Gemini	3rd
Sep 17, 5:52 pm–Sep 18, 3:59 am	Gemini	4th
Sep 20, 4:38 pm–Sep 23, 3:53 am	Leo	4th
Sep 23, 3:53 am–Sep 25, 12:43 pm	Virgo	4th
Oct 9, 4:55 pm–Oct 10, 5:04 pm	Aries	3rd
Oct 13, 1:08 am–Oct 15, 12:11 pm	Gemini	3rd
Oct 18, 12:45 am–Oct 20, 12:25 pm	Leo	4th
Oct 20, 12:25 pm–Oct 22, 9:24 pm	Virgo	4th
Nov 9, 8:37 am–Nov 11, 7:22 pm	Gemini	3rd
Nov 14, 7:48 am–Nov 16, 8:27 am	Leo	3rd
Nov 16, 8:27 am–Nov 16, 8:04 pm	Leo	4th
Nov 16, 8:04 pm–Nov 19, 5:58 am	Virgo	4th
Nov 23, 3:16 pm–Nov 23, 5:57 pm	Sagittarius	4th
Dec 7, 11:08 pm–Dec 9, 2:49 am	Gemini	3rd
Dec 11, 3:09 pm–Dec 14, 3:45 am	Leo	3rd
Dec 14, 3:45 am–Dec 16, 3:56 am	Virgo	3rd
Dec 16, 3:56 am–Dec 16, 2:49 pm	Virgo	4th
Dec 21, 2:12 am–Dec 23, 2:49 am	Sagittarius	4th

Time Zone Map

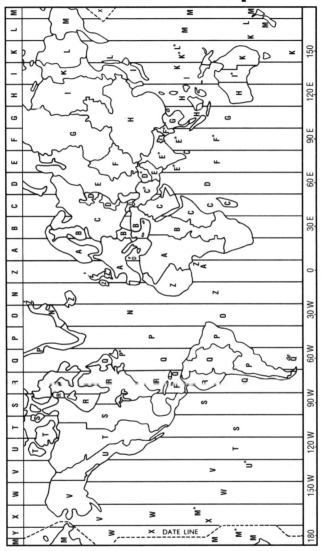

Time Zone Conversions

(R) EST—Used in book
(S) CST—Subtract 1 hour
(T) MST—Subtract 2 hours
(U) PST—Subtract 3 hours
(V) Subtract 4 hours
(V*) Subtract 4½ hours
(U*) Subtract 3½ hours
(W) Subtract 5 hours
(X) Subtract 6 hours
(Y) Subtract 7 hours
(Q) Add 1 hour
(P) Add 2 hours
(P*) Add 2½ hours
(O) Add 3 hours
(N) Add 4 hours
(Z) Add 5 hours
(A) Add 6 hours
(B) Add 7 hours
(C) Add 8 hours
(C*) Add 8½ hours

(D) Add 9 hours
(D*) Add 9½ hours
(E) Add 10 hours
(E*) Add 10½ hours
(F) Add 11 hours
(F*) Add 11½ hours
(G) Add 12 hours
(H) Add 13 hours
(I) Add 14 hours
(I*) Add 14½ hours
(K) Add 15 hours
(K*) Add 15½ hours
(L) Add 16 hours
(L*) Add 16½ hours
(M) Add 17 hours
(M*) Add 18 hours
(P*) Add 2½ hours

Important!

All times given in the *Moon Sign Book* are set in Eastern Time. The conversions shown here are for standard times only. Use the time zone conversions map and table to calculate the difference in your time zone. You must make the adjustment for your time zone and adjust for Daylight Saving Time where applicable.

Weather, Economic & Lunar Forecasts

An Introduction to Long-Range Weather Forecasting

Vincent Decker

Long-range weather forecasting based on planetary cycles, also known as astrometeorology, has been a field of study for centuries. The basic premise underlying the field is that the main heavenly bodies of our solar system exercise an influence over weather conditions on Earth.

Planets

The heat of summer and the chill of winter can be traced back to the Sun's apparent movement north and south of our terrestrial equator. The Moon, while mostly known for its effect on the oceans' tides, in astrometeorology also affects air tides in its circuit around the Earth and serves as a triggering influence on solar and planetary configurations as they form. Under Mercury's domain, we find high pressure or fair weather as well as gentle breezes to hurricane-force winds. Venus is known for gentle showers, moderate temperatures, and snowfall or freezing rain in winter. Mars, the red planet, brings hot summers, mild winters, dry conditions, and fierce storms. Jupiter's trademark is a temperate and invigorating atmosphere under benign configurations. The traditional malefic Saturn engenders cold, damp conditions, and when aggravated by certain configurations, low-pressure systems. Like Mercury, the power of Uranus brings high-barometer and erratic wind velocities. Neptune is the pluvial planet par excellence capable of torrential downpours, flooding conditions, and warming trends. Pluto is held by some to be a warm influence while for others it is considered cold. In the forecasts included here, Pluto is considered a cold influence.

Aspects and Influences

The foregoing effects of the Sun, Moon, and planets are modified depending on the aspect that each one makes in relation to the other heavenly bodies. The traditional astrological aspects are employed: the conjunction, sextile, square, trine, opposition, and parallel of declination. Fair weather aspects are the sextile and trine. Disturbed weather is induced by the square and opposition. The kind of weather produced by the conjunction and parallel of declination vary depending on if the celestial bodies involved are of similar or contrary natures.

The signs of the zodiac in which the members of the solar system reside at any given moment also affect the manifestation of weather conditions. Heat and dryness are associated with the fire signs Aries, Leo, and Sagittarius. The water signs of Cancer, Scorpio, and Pisces enhance precipitation. Air signs such as Gemini,

Libra, and Aquarius relate to lower temperatures and wind, while the earth signs Taurus, Virgo, and Capricorn are generally wet and cold.

Forecasting

Although the aspects involved in the planetary configurations determine the time that weather processes will be at work (do keep in mind to allow a day or two leeway in all forecasting), it is by the use of key charts that the geographical locations of weather systems are ascertained. When a planet in a key chart is angular, that is to say it is on the cusp of the first, fourth, seventh, or tenth house, the influence associated with that planet will be strongest at that locale. The monthly alignments of the Sun and Moon such as New Moon, Full Moon, and Quarter Moons are examples of key charts. Other important charts include the cardinal solar ingresses and solar and lunar eclipses to name a few. Through setting up these key charts, noting the angular planets, the signs they tenant, and their aspects, as well as the kind of weather typical at the location in question, the long-range weather forecaster makes a judgement as to the type of weather to be expected. By faithfully comparing the forecasts with the actual ensuing weather, the forecaster has an opportunity to improve on method and results.

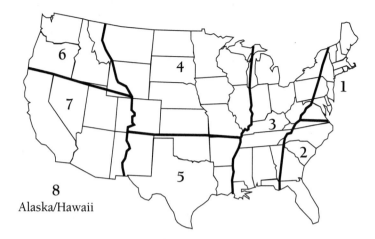

Weather Forecast for 2022

Vincent Decker

Winter

Eastern portions of Zone 1 will tend toward cold and windy weather with below average precipitation. Western areas will generally experience more moderate temperatures and fair conditions but will also contend with bouts of windy and colder weather and seasonal to below-average precipitation. Zone 2 falls into this latter category.

Zone 3 tends toward more mild temperatures and dry conditions. As the season progresses, cold and damp influences take hold over western areas, lowering temperatures and increasing precipitation and some windy conditions.

Below-average temperatures are indicated for western sections of Zones 4 and 5 resulting in cold waves and frosts. Winds are generally from the northwest, fresh to strong, and precipitation below average. The central sections should prove to experience boisterous weather as low-pressure systems traverse the plains in eastward transit. Eastern areas see below-average temperatures and increased precipitation.

Eastern portions of Zones 6 and 7 see below-average temperatures, increased wind velocities, cold waves, and frosts. Western portions experience periods of southerly winds elevating temperatures and exciting precipitation. As the season progresses, a drier, milder influence envelops the area.

Alaska will generally see prevailing southerly winds and milder temperatures interspersed with cold and stormy conditions. Hawaii experiences seasonal to above-average temperatures and a generally pleasant atmosphere interspersed with showers and thunderstorms.

New Moon January 2–9

Zone 1: Southerly airflows bring milder temperatures, humidity, and precipitation. **Zone 2:** Mild, humid air infiltrates over the region with a low-pressure system in and around Georgia. **Zone 3:** Northeast section starts off stormy. Warm, moist air drawn up over southwestern sections clashes with colder air over the southern Mississippi Valley, generating storms. The period ends with low-pressure systems affecting the Great Lakes and Georgia areas. **Zone 4:** Colder air pushes through the northwest region, bringing storm potential to the northern plains. The period sees stormy conditions for the Great Lakes region while temperatures begin to moderate. **Zone 5:** Unsettled west, mild temperatures east and central, then turning colder after the fourth with increasing cloudiness and rain east. **Zone 6:** Offshore front or low brings declining temperatures and windy conditions from west to east. Temperatures moderate after the fifth. Around the eighth, another offshore front brings rain. **Zone 7:** Declining temperatures and windy conditions. Temperatures moderate after the fifth. Around the eighth, an offshore front brings rain. **Zone 8:** Declining temperatures and stormy conditions over Alaska. After the fifth, temperatures moderate. Hawaii experiences increasing temperatures leading to precipitation, then after the fifth, calm. By the ninth, increasing cloudiness with a chance of rain west.

2nd Quarter Moon January 9–17

Zone 1: Winter storm likely over the northeast and New England. Windy conditions for the remainder of the period. **Zone 2:** Period begins stormy and ends with cold air, generating a low-pressure system over the Georgia area. **Zone 3:** Storms traverse the region. By the twelfth, low pressure affects the Great Lakes. An influx of cold air starting on the sixteenth. **Zone 4:** Briefly fair northwest. Cold air pushes southward over central regions, generating wind and low pressure. Strong storm potential around the fourteenth. By the seventeenth, storm system affects the western Great Lakes. **Zone 5:** Cloudy and cold east. Windy with rain potential. Around the fifteenth, stormy over western regions. **Zone 6:** Cold and windy east. Storm front pushes through from offshore. Windy conditions kick up around the fourteenth. Storm fronts continue through the area. **Zone 7:** Cooler and windy east. Storm front pushes through the area. Available moisture continues to fuel precipitation. **Zone 8:** Stormy over western Alaska, pushing toward central zone. Chance of rain over Hawaii. Thunderstorm development likely after the fourteenth.

Full Moon January 17–25

Zone 1: Strong high pressure brings abnormally low temperatures and windy conditions with a chance of thunderstorms toward the end of the period. **Zone 2:** Strong high pressure brings abnormally low temperatures and windy conditions with a chance of thunderstorms toward the end of the period. **Zone 3:** Cold air pushes southward through the region, bringing a chance of showers. Cold and windy northeast. High likelihood of thunderstorms toward the end of the period. **Zone 4:** An influx of cold air over the region lowers temperatures, possibly generating showers.

By the twenty-third, a greater propensity toward increased wind velocities and storminess, especially over the central region. **Zone 5:** A cold front pushes into the region, increasing the likelihood of showers. By the twenty-third, wind velocities and storminess increase. **Zone 6:** Cold air over the eastern region and available moisture set the stage for atmospheric disturbance. Western areas milder. By the twenty-fourth, a Pacific Northwest front delivers rain and snow. **Zone 7:** Colder east. Milder west. By the twenty-fourth, storm potential increases. **Zone 8:** Alaska: Falling temperatures and increased wind velocities. By the twenty-fourth, storm potential increases from west to east. Hawaii: Expect a period of thunderstorm formation.

4th Quarter Moon January 25–February 1

Zone 1: A stormy pattern gears up around the twenty-eighth. By the thirtieth, a new influx of cold air embraces the region. **Zone 2:** Cold and cloudy. By the thirtieth, low-pressure centers over southern portions. **Zone 3:** Cold and cloudy west. Potential low-pressure area over the Great Lakes. Mild, humid air drawn up over Gulf states. By the end of the period, contrary air masses collide, producing thunderstorms. **Zone 4:** The region continues its cold, windy, and stormy trend. The most intense of these on the thirtieth and thirty-first. **Zone 5:** Generally stormy throughout the region. The most intense of these on the thirtieth and thirty-first. **Zone 6:** The period begins fair then turns stormy around the thirtieth as cold air clashes with humid air east. **Zone 7:** Fair conditions west, then toward the end of the period storm potential east as cold air infiltrates. **Zone 8:** Alaska: Cold air infiltrates the region. Storm potential increases. By the thirtieth, gusty winds, lower temperatures, stormy. Hawaii: Chance of rain the twenty-seventh through the twenty-eighth. Stronger storms build the twenty-ninth through the thirty-first.

New Moon February 1–8

Zone 1: Unsettled around the first. Expect mild conditions from the second through the fourth, then thunderstorm potential increases. **Zone 2:** Lower temperatures, cloudy with a chance of rain. Windy at times. **Zone 3:** Period begins cold and unsettled over the Great Lakes. Cold air by the fourth pushes toward the Gulf Coast, bringing thunderstorm potential. **Zone 4:** Cold and unsettled east. North turning windy after the third. Storms eject from the Rockies into the plains through the sixth. **Zone 5:** Cold and unsettled east. Stormy west between the fourth and sixth. **Zone 6:** Mild and fair. Around the fifth, becoming unsettled. Pacific Northwest front around the sixth bringing storms and cold air. **Zone 7:** Fair and mild. Around the fifth, becoming unsettled. Front enters northern area. Period ends cold east. **Zone 8:** Alaska: Fair west. Around the fifth, unsettled east. By the seventh, cold air infiltrates. Hawaii: Unsettled, then around the third, temperatures and humidity increase, bringing shower potential.

2nd Quarter Moon February 8–16

Zone 1: Wintery weather over northeast. Mild and breezy New England then becoming cloudy with a chance of showers. By the fourteenth, stormy coastal New England. **Zone 2:** Wintery weather over coastal Carolinas. Coastal areas stormy through the fourteenth. **Zone 3:** Declining temperatures, windy, cloudy, and rainy. **Zone 4:** Cold fronts over the northern plains will trigger stormy, windy conditions during this period. **Zone 5:** Unsettled from west to east as the period begins. Another unsettled period from the thirteenth through the fifteenth. **Zone 6:** Offshore system brings windy conditions around the eighth. A stormy and windy period. Strong intensity around the twelfth. Another Pacific Northwest front around the fourteenth. **Zone 7:** Storm conditions push inland on the eighth and ninth. A windy and stormy period with maximum intensity between the twelfth and fifteenth. **Zone 8:** Alaska: Western area starts mild with showers, then fair. Windy along northern coast and east. Generally unsettled weather across the region. Hawaii: Southerly winds bring moisture and rain, especially around the eleventh.

Full Moon February 16–23

Zone 1: Chance of storms then breezy and fair conditions. Around the twentieth, milder with a chance of showers. **Zone 2:** Rising temperatures, some breeze, fair conditions. Around the twentieth, chance of showers. **Zone 3:** Rising temperatures and fair conditions east. Around the twentieth, mild conditions. The twenty-second brings a cold front and showers to western portions. **Zone 4:** Rising temperatures, breezy with possible showers over northwestern zone, which moves east, then fair conditions around the twenty-second. Around the twenty-first, unsettled central and northeast. Cloudy with a chance of rain along western plains around the twenty-second. Then around the twenty-third, rising temperatures over northern areas may provoke thunderstorms. **Zone 5:** West Texas storms on the sixteenth. Unsettled over New Mexico on the twentieth. Unsettled central on the twenty-first. Cloudy with a chance of rain over Colorado, New Mexico, and Texas around the twenty-second. Around the twenty-third, rising temperatures over western and central areas may provoke thunderstorms. **Zone 6:** Rising temperatures, breezy, possible showers over eastern zone around the seventeenth. Chance of rain over Pacific Northwest, then fair by the eighteenth. Unsettled over central and east around the twentieth, then fair and breezy. **Zone 7:** Rising temperatures, breezy with possible showers over eastern zone around the seventeenth. Unsettled over eastern portions around the twenty-first. Fair over Nevada and California around the twenty-second. Then by the twenty-third, rising temperatures over eastern areas may provoke thunderstorms. **Zone 8:** Alaska: Fair and breezy over northwestern portions. Chance of precipitation on the eighteenth. Continuing fair over western areas from the twenty-first through

the twenty-second, but cold air enters north. South becomes stormy. Hawaii: Chance of thunderstorms early. Southerly airflow and a chance of rain around the eighteenth, then fair conditions.

4th Quarter Moon February 23–March 2

Zone 1: Period begins with low pressure and gusty winds. Another storm system affects the area around the twenty-seventh. **Zone 2:** Around the twenty-fourth, showers and thunderstorms across the area. Another round on the twenty-seventh. **Zone 3:** Mild temperatures, possible shower, then windy around the twenty-fifth. By the twenty-seventh, a more energetic storm system with major intensity along the Gulf Coast. Cold front bringing showers traverses the zone toward the end of the period. **Zone 4:** Eastern (around Missouri) and northwest portions start stormy. Central area thunderstorms around the twenty-seventh. Special intensity over Dakotas and around Missouri. On the twenty-eighth, a storm system over western plains and the Front Range. **Zone 5:** Cold front triggering storms east. Western and eastern portions end stormy—special intensity over Louisiana. **Zone 6:** Coast mild with chance of showers early. Low pressure and windy conditions east. Cold front enters coast around the twenty-eighth. **Zone 7:** Mild west with a chance of showers. Cold, windy, and stormy east. **Zone 8:** Alaska: Windy and stormy north and central. Calm with rising temperatures south. Storm potential west after the twenty-fifth. Strong front and thunderstorms southwest to northeast around the twenty-eighth. Hawaii: Showers around the twenty-fourth. Otherwise, generally fair.

2nd Quarter Moon and New Moon March 2–10
Zone 1: The first through the second is predominantly fair. The third through the fourth is stormy. The fifth through the seventh is mostly fair. The eighth through the ninth is unsettled. **Zone 2:** Starting cloudy, cold with precipitation, then pleasant. **Zone 3:** Period mostly cloudy with precipitation. Low pressure affects the Great Lakes around the seventh. Becoming fair northeast toward the end. **Zone 4:** Western portions cold, windy, precipitation. Various storm systems central and east. Low-pressure Great Lakes around the seventh. **Zone 5:** Mostly stormy west. The third through the sixth sees increasing cloudiness, cold, and precipitation central. Ends cold and showery east. **Zone 6:** Cold and fair east then later cold, windy, stormy. Storm fronts enter west on third through the seventh. Then fair. **Zone 7:** Eastern portions cold and fair, then turning cold, windy, stormy. Storm fronts enter third through the seventh. **Zone 8:** Alaska: Mostly fair west. The third is stormy in the central area. East is windy by the fourth. By the sixth, storm front approaches north coast, becoming generally stormy throughout zone. Hawaii: Starts fair. By the third, increasing temperatures, humidity, showers, then fair.

2nd Quarter Moon March 10–18
Zone 1: Rising temperatures with a chance of heavy rain. Increasing winds. Around the sixteenth, cold front triggers showers.

Ending cold and windy. **Zone 2:** Influx of warm, moist air with possible fog or heavy rain. Around the sixteenth there will be cloudy, low-pressure, windy conditions. **Zone 3:** Windy conditions early. The thirteenth has the potential for fog or rain. Then cold front brings clouds and chance of rain. Windy again by the seventeenth. **Zone 4:** Northwest cold front triggers thunderstorms from the thirteenth through the fifteenth. Central and eastern portions cloudy, cold with low pressure. Northwest becomes cold and gusty. **Zone 5:** Front brings opportunity for showers to west and central portions early. Period ends with central and eastern sections cloudy, cold with low pressure. **Zone 6:** Northwest front brings a chance of precipitation. By the fourteenth, colder over eastern portions with chance of showers, then fair, cold, and gusty. **Zone 7:** West is dry, seasonal temperatures. Eastern portions cold with chance of thunderstorms then becoming fair, cold, and gusty. **Zone 8:** Alaska: Rising temperatures and humidity lead to possible heavy precipitation over central areas. Northwest begins and ends with storm potential. By the fourteenth, cold front may trigger precipitation. Period ends with increasing temperatures over central areas. Hawaii: Rising temperatures leading to humidity and chance of moderate to heavy showers.

Spring

Zone 1 is generally cold and windy with springtime storms periodically. As the season progresses, warmth and humidity increase only to see temperatures plummet again in mid-May with cool windy weather—the theme until the end of the season.

Zones 2 and 3 generally experience temperatures somewhat below average and precipitation above the norm. Western portions of Zone 3 show higher concentrations of these characteristics. By May, Zone 2 shifts gears and sees an increase in temperatures, humidity, and precipitation.

Zones 4 and 5 exhibit below-average temperatures over their western sections. The central and eastern portions record above-average temperatures, which begin to subside in May with somewhat cooler and windy weather.

Zones 6 and 7 see below-average temperatures with increased wind velocities and mostly high pressure resulting generally in below-average precipitation. By mid-May, coastal areas see a warming influence with higher humidity resulting in more precipitation.

Variable weather conditions for the season with lower-than-normal temperatures in May and June are shown for Alaska. Generally, moderate temperatures and average precipitation for Hawaii.

Full Moon March 18–25
Zone 1: Cold and rainy, then briefly fair around the twenty-first. Afterward, gusty storms. **Zone 2:** Fair, then a passing cold front on the twenty-first, and again around the twenty-third brings chance of showers. **Zone 3:** Western portions of zone stormier. Northeastern zone starts fair. Cold front over northeast around the twenty-first. Next front around the twenty-third generally brings chance of showers to the forecast area. **Zone 4:** Western portions start with storm potential. Central section cold and fair. Around the twentieth, some strong storms over central areas, which then move east. **Zone 5:** Western portions begin cool and fair. Cool and rainy east. Central becoming stormy after the twentieth. **Zone 6:** Eastern zone begins cold with chance of precipitation. Cold front potentially generates showers through zone from the twentieth through the twenty-fourth. **Zone 7:** Cold front around the twentieth brings lower temperatures and chance of precipitation. Stronger storms the twenty-second through the twenty-fourth. **Zone 8:** Alaska: Cold, precipitation on the north coast with strong storm around the twenty-second pushing southward. East is fair. Period ends with chance of precipitation

along south coast. Hawaii: Mostly fair. Toward the end of the period, there is increasing clouds with chance of precipitation.

4th Quarter Moon March 25–April 1

Zone 1: Period begins cool, fair, windy. Thunderstorms over central and eastern zones around the twenty-eighth. Period ends with an increase in humidity and chance of showers. **Zone 2:** Windy conditions around the twenty-ninth. **Zone 3:** Western zone starts with chance of showers, increasing in intensity from the twenty-seventh on. Northeast zone thunderstorms around the twenty-eighth. **Zone 4:** Northwestern area starts cool, fair, windy. Central area starts and ends stormy. Eastern zone sees a cold front and increasing storminess ending with rising temperatures, humidity, and possible heavy precipitation. **Zone 5:** West starts and ends windy and stormy. Cold front in the central area around the twenty-seventh brings chance of showers. Storm potential intensifies over eastern areas around the twenty-eighth. Ends with rising temperatures, possible fog. **Zone 6:** Eastern sections begin cool and fair. West Coast front around the twenty-seventh bringing showers. Zone ends with rising temperatures, humidity, and possible heavy precipitation and West Coast front. **Zone 7:** Eastern areas begin cool, fair, and windy. Low pressure over Arizona around the twenty-seventh. West Coast front brings precipitation around the twenty-eighth. Period ends with rising temperatures, humidity, possible heavy precipitation, and West Coast front. **Zone 8:** Alaska: Eastern portions' stormy conditions intensifying around the twenty-eighth. Western sections fair. By the twenty-seventh, chance of storminess increases west and central. Western area ends with rising temperatures, increased chance of rain, possible fog. Hawaii: Windy, possible showers early. Thunderstorm potential around the twenty-eighth. Period ends with increasing chance of showers.

New Moon April 1–9

Zone 1: Increasing temperatures, humidity, wind, and chance of rain. Strong storms around the fourth. New England ends fair and breezy and there are thunderstorms in the northeast. **Zone 2:** Strong storms by the fourth and sixth. By the eighth, southerly winds, slight increase in humidity, chance of rain. **Zone 3:** Potentially destructive storms and squally weather through the sixth. The seventh becoming breezy and fair. On the eighth, the northeast section has a chance of rain. **Zone 4:** Potentially destructive storms and squally weather. The seventh becoming breezy and fair. Eastern section sees a chance of rain on the eighth. **Zone 5:** Potentially dangerous storms from west to east, then breezy and fair around the seventh. **Zone 6:** Cold front pushes eastward, bringing a chance of showers by the third and strong storms by the fourth. The eighth sees increasing humidity and rain east. **Zone 7:** Cold front, possible showers by the third and strong storms by the fourth. The eighth sees increasing humidity and rain east. **Zone 8:** Alaska: Strong cold front generates potentially destructive storms from north to south. The seventh becomes breezy, ending with a chance of heavy precipitation east. Hawaii: Increasing temperatures, humidity, and chance of rain, especially around the third.

2nd Quarter Moon April 9–16

Zone 1: Thunderstorms over the northeast. Rising temperatures and humidity. Potential heavy rain over New England around the fourteenth. **Zone 2:** A windy start. Increasing humidity and the chance for heavy downpours. Ending with lower temperatures and windy conditions. **Zone 3:** Windy conditions and chance of heavy rain northeast. West and central zone cool and cloudy. Then potential heavy rain west as front enters zone. After the fourteenth, potential heavy rain west. **Zone 4:** Frontal systems trigger storms and windy conditions. **Zone 5:** Scattered thunderstorms and windy conditions. **Zone 6:** Coastal thunderstorms. Chance of heavy downpours over eastern zone. **Zone 7:** Scattered thunderstorms throughout the zone. Chance of heavy downpours over eastern sections, ending with lower temperatures and windy conditions. **Zone 8:** Alaska: Scattered thunderstorms throughout the zone. The central area sees energetic storms around the tenth. The twelfth through the fourteenth, precipitation, possibly heavy, in far eastern and western sections. Generally windy conditions around the fifteenth. Hawaii: Increasing humidity and shower probability. The fourteenth sees potentially heavy rain.

Full Moon April 16–23

Zone 1: Mostly fair, except by the eighteenth a chance of thunderstorms. **Zone 2:** Rising temperatures, then a cold front with a chance of thunderstorms by the nineteenth. Afterward, a chance of showers. **Zone 3:** Low-pressure northwest zone. Becoming cold, windy by the eighteenth. Northeast section unsettled. Around the twenty-second, western areas cloudy, Great Lakes low pressure, colder. **Zone 4:** Potentially dangerous thunderstorms roam the plains from the seventeenth through the nineteenth. By the twenty-second, the east is cloudy, low pressure, colder. Cold front in Montana with possible thunderstorms. **Zone 5:** Potentially dangerous thunderstorms begin the period through the nineteenth. **Zone 6:** Cold and windy. Chance of thunderstorms east. Twenty-second sees possible thunderstorms. **Zone 7:** Cold and windy. Chance of thunderstorms central and east. Twenty-second sees possible thunderstorms. **Zone 8:** Alaska: West begins cool with a chance of precipitation and ends cool, fair. Central has higher temperatures; chance of precipitation around the eighteenth. East is warmer, fair. Hawaii: Period begins mostly fair. Shower potential between the eighteenth and twentieth then increasing temperatures.

4th Quarter Moon April 23–30

Zone 1: Strong storms in and around Delmarva. Cool, cloudy over northeast. Increasing temperatures over New England, potential thunderstorms. **Zone 2:** Cool, cloudy, chance of showers. Period ends fair. **Zone 3:** Low pressure over Kentucky area. Lower ranges of temperatures, cloudy with chance of rain. Cold air mass pushes south. Period ends with low pressure over central area. **Zone 4:** Period begins with lower temperatures and showers. Potential low pressure over Wisconsin. Around the twenty-seventh, potential for heavy rain west. Strong cold front after the twenty-ninth over western portions. Period ends stormy with cold front over central and eastern areas. **Zone 5:** Period begins with lower temperatures and showers. Fair conditions central around the twenty-seventh. Eastern portions rainy. By the thirtieth, storms increase central. **Zone 6:** Cooler, windy, possible storms. Around the twenty-seventh, potential heavy rain in the Pacific Northwest and eastern zone. Strong cold front after the twenty-ninth over eastern portions. **Zone 7:** Cooler, windy, possible storms. Around the twenty-seventh, potential heavy rain in the Pacific Northwest and eastern zone. Strong cold front after the twenty-ninth over eastern portions and coastal California. **Zone 8:** Alaska: Increasing temperatures west. Central area cooler with chance of precipitation, then fair. Chance of heavier rain east. Hawaii: Rising temperatures with a chance of showers, becoming fair, ending with a chance of thunderstorms.

New Moon April 30–May 8

Zone 1: Generally warm and fair. Windy around the first. Shower potential around the fourth and eighth. **Zone 2:** Generally fair. Unsettled conditions south by the third and fourth, remaining fair north. **Zone 3:** Frontal activity brings chance of showers. Cool and fair by the fourth but chance of showers for northeast zone. **Zone 4:** Central area has a potential thunderstorm moving eastward. Fair conditions west progress toward central areas.

Eastern zone ends warmer. **Zone 5:** West and central areas see a potential thunderstorm moving eastward. By the sixth, the east is fair. The eighth brings shower potential east. **Zone 6:** Generally lower ranges of temperatures, high pressure, and breezy to windy conditions. Warming toward the end. Eastern area cool and fair. **Zone 7:** Eastern portions fair, warming toward the end. West and central have generally lower ranges of temperatures, high pressure, and breezy to windy conditions. Warming toward the end. Potential Santa Ana winds on May first. **Zone 8:** Alaska: Warmer west; stormy, breezy. Central is windy, stormy. East is fair then has thunderstorm potential. Hawaii: Begins windy. Generally warm and fair. Shower potential and breezy around the third. Thunderstorm potential on the eighth.

2nd Quarter Moon May 8–16

Zone 1: Mostly cloudy, lower temperatures, showers especially along the coast. Briefly fair around the twelfth. **Zone 2:** Storm center over Florida Panhandle. Lower temperatures, high pressure north. Chance of rain over central zone. Period ends with a chance of showers along coast. **Zone 3:** Generally lower temperatures, cloudy, rainy, increasing winds south. **Zone 4:** West is cooler with periods of rain. Central has increasing wind velocities, stormy. East is cold, rainy on the eleventh. **Zone 5:** West is windy and variable. Ends with clouds, rain. East has increasing winds, unsettled. **Zone 6:** East is cooler, unsettled. West and central have lower temperatures, some wind, high pressure, chance of rain. **Zone 7:** East has lower temperatures, some wind, high pressure, ending with storm potential. West has increasing temperatures, humidity, rain. **Zone 8:** Alaska: Central area begins and ends with storm potential; warm in between. East is generally mild with a chance of precipitation. West has a lower temperature, windy, then warmer. Hawaii: Begins with thunderstorm potential, then fair. Ends warmer with a chance of showers.

Full Moon May 16–22

Zone 1: Generally lower ranges of temperatures, stormy. Central area has strong thunderstorm potential from the nineteenth through the twenty-second. **Zone 2:** Rising temperatures, potential for abundant rain. Strong thunderstorms in the northeast of the zone from the nineteenth through the twenty-second. **Zone 3:** High pressure over Great Lakes. Generally cooler. Northeast zone sees strong thunderstorms the nineteenth through the twenty-second. **Zone 4:** Generally cooler, stormy. Wind and storm potential from the nineteenth through the twenty-second. **Zone 5:** Cooler temperatures, stormy. Wind event likely the nineteenth through the twenty-second with chance of storms. **Zone 6:** West coastal areas are stormy and windy. East is cool, fair, with thunderstorm potential near end of period. **Zone 7:** East has lower ranges of temperatures and is windy with thunderstorm potential. West has increasing temperatures and humidity with chance of showers. **Zone 8:** Alaska: Central area stormy. Increasing wind velocities east. West has strong storm potential the nineteenth through the twenty-second. Hawaii: Generally lower ranges of temperatures and shower potential interspersed with clearing.

4th Quarter Moon May 22–30

Zone 1: Cold front, possible showers central. New England fair, breezy with a chance of thunderstorms by period's end. **Zone 2:** Cold front, cloudy, possible showers. Temperatures then increase, bringing possible showers. Period ends with increasing warmth, leading to atmospheric disturbance. **Zone 3:** Cooler, chance of showers and some wind interspersed with fair periods. **Zone 4:** West starts fair and breezy, then cloudy, showers, windy. Central is generally fair then increase in temperatures brings atmospheric disturbance. East cold fronts bring windy storms. **Zone 5:** Southwest zone starts windy. Zone generally fair, breezy. Increase in temperatures bring atmospheric disturbance, showers, and wind.

Zone 6: West has storms interspersed with fair periods. East is breezy, cool, fair. Stormy, windy from the twenty-sixth on. **Zone 7:** West is fair then a northcoast storm moves inland. East is breezy, cool, fair. Stormy, windy from the twenty-sixth on. **Zone 8:** Alaska: West is fair; chance of thunderstorms by twenty-ninth. Central is showery. East is fair, breezy, becoming warmer with thunderstorms. Hawaii: Showers early then fair, breezy. Chance of thunderstorms by twenty-ninth.

New Moon May 30–June 7

Zone 1: Period begins fair over central area while New England has a chance of thunderstorms. Cooler, windy with shower potential over zone after the fourth. **Zone 2:** Northeast zone begins with thunderstorms, then mild. Southern zone mostly cool, cloudy conditions with shower potential. **Zone 3:** Lower ranges of temperatures. Predominantly cloudy and damp weather, especially after the fifth. **Zone 4:** West has a chance of showers, increased wind velocities, lower ranges of temperatures. Central is warmer, thunderstorms, becoming windy. East becomes cloudy and rainy with thunderstorm potential. **Zone 5:** Warmer with a chance of showers and thunderstorms. Becoming windy with lower temperatures. **Zone 6:** Lower temperatures throughout period with fair conditions at first. Shower potential increases but period ends fair. **Zone 7:** Lower temperatures throughout period with fair conditions at first. Shower potential increases but period ends fair. **Zone 8:** Alaska: West has thunderstorm potential early, unsettled conditions. East has chance of thunderstorms then becomes windy. Hawaii: Higher temperatures with chance of showers, then becoming fair.

2nd Quarter June 7–14

Zone 1: A period of lower temperatures with a good chance of showers and some clearing. Windy toward the end. **Zone 2:** Chance of showers south and north. South ends warm and fair, chance of rain north. **Zone 3:** North and northeast zone begin unsettled. Zone experiences cooler temperatures with chance of showers. **Zone 4:** West is generally cool with periods of showers and clearing. Period ends warmer with a chance of storms. Central is cool, fair; possible storms around the fourteenth. East has showers around the eighth. Cold, rainy, windy by the eleventh. **Zone 5:** West has low pressure then generally cool and fair. By the twelfth, showers. Increasing warmth and storms by the fourteenth. Central is cool, fair with a chance of storms. East sees showers early then becomes cold, rainy, windy. **Zone 6:** Zone generally cooler with shower potential. West cold front enters coast by the tenth, lower temperatures, wind, rain. Coastal disturbance by the fourteenth. East has scattered precipitation; cooler and windy. **Zone 7:** Zone generally cooler with shower potential. West cold front enters coast by the tenth, lower temperatures, wind, rain. Coastal disturbance by the fourteenth. East has scattered precipitation; cooler and windy. **Zone 8:** Alaska: Generally stormy central and east. Hawaii: Unsettled. From the eleventh on, cooler, chance of rain, windy.

Full Moon June 14–20

Zone 1: Southern zone begins cool, northern portions fair, then turning stormy. Central zone ends cool, windy, with a chance of rain then fair. **Zone 2:** Southern portions begin cool and fair and end cool and rainy. Northern zone has scattered storms. **Zone 3:** Conditions oscillate between fair and rainy while temperatures remain below average. Strongest storms on the eighteenth through the nineteenth. **Zone 4:** West is cooler with scattered showers. Period ends stormy. Central is cooler with scattered showers. Period ends fair. East is cooler with a chance of rain, then fair. **Zone 5:** West is cooler with scattered showers. Period ends stormy. Central is cooler with scattered showers. Period ends fair. East is cooler with a chance of rain, then fair. **Zone 6:** Zone sees lower ranges of temperatures with a chance of showers and wind, then warmer and fair. **Zone 7:** Zone sees lower ranges of temperatures with a chance of showers the sixteenth through the eighteenth, then warmer and fair. **Zone 8:** Alaska: West is cool and windy with shower potential. Period ends fair. Central scattered storms. East begins and ends with a chance of showers. Hawaii: Increasing temperatures and chance of rain, then warm and fair.

4th Quarter June 20–28

Zone 1: Fair with scattered showers. **Zone 2:** Generally fair with cooler temperatures and a chance of rain. **Zone 3:** Generally fair with cooler temperatures and a chance of rain. **Zone 4:** West has cooler temperatures, fair with a chance of showers. Central and east are fair with rising temperatures, a chance of thunderstorms, then fair. **Zone 5:** West is cool, windy with a chance of showers. Central has high pressure, rising temperatures leading to thunderstorms. East has variable temperatures and chance of rain. **Zone 6:** West is mostly warm and dry inland. Coastal front brings chance of precipitation. Period ends cloudy and windy. East, cooler temperatures predominate, chance of showers, wind. **Zone 7:** West is mostly warm and dry inland. Possible fire danger. Front brings chance of precipitation. Period ends cloudy and windy. East, cooler temperatures predominate, chance of showers, wind. **Zone 8:** Alaska: West is generally cool and fair then ends windy. Central is cool and fair. Stormy period east. Hawaii is predominately fair with cooler temperatures.

Summer

Changeable weather is shown for Zone 1 as periods of fair conditions alternate with showers and storms. Cool and breezy periods are displaced by warmer and more humid conditions and vice versa. Zone 2 and northeastern portions of Zone 3 show a proclivity toward cool and damp conditions, local showers and, at times, more intense rains. The rest of Zone 3 is subject to breezy, cool conditions and general showers with somewhat warmer and drier conditions in September.

The western portions of Zones 4 and 5 experience much cooler conditions, sometimes suddenly so, and occasionally windy and squally weather. Central areas see times of fine weather, warmer with precipitation ranging from showery to more intense rains; somewhat warmer and drier in August. Eastern regions of Zone 4 are breezy and variable.

Eastern areas of Zones 6 and 7 are cooler with times of sudden dips in temperatures. Windy and squally weather is indicated. Western portions are hot and dry at times with thunderstorm activity. Humidity increases during August.

Western areas of Alaska are subject to breezy, cool conditions, and general showers that spread eastward over central and eastern portions. July is generally warmer with rising humidity across the zone. By September, warmer and drier conditions prevail. Hawaii is generally breezy, somewhat cooler with showers. Temperatures and humidity increase during July, and September is somewhat hotter and drier.

New Moon June 28–July 6

Zone 1: Fair, becoming cooler and windy with a chance of showers and thunderstorms. **Zone 2:** Potential tropical activity off southeast shore. Florida Panhandle sees strong storms or tropical system around the first, then warm, showers. Elsewhere, a chance of showers but mostly cool and fair. **Zone 3:** Rising temperatures, scattered thunderstorms northwest, cold front northeast with a chance of showers. Southeast warmer with chance of showers. Becoming dry and windy over Great Lakes. **Zone 4:** West has a chance of showers and thunderstorms; becoming dry and windy. Central is mostly fair, scattered thunderstorms, becoming windy. East is mostly fair with thunderstorm potential. **Zone 5:** West is warm, thunderstorm potential around the first (New Mexico and eastward), then scattered showers. Becoming dry and windy west.

East is dry and fair, chance of thunderstorms. **Zone 6:** West has strong storm potential around the thirtieth then dry and windy. East is cooler, western storm pushes east, then dry and windy. **Zone 7:** West and southwest zone anomalous heat and atmospheric disturbances, strong storm potential around the thirtieth, then dry and windy. East is cooler, western storm pushes east, then dry and windy. **Zone 8:** Alaska: West is generally fair; chance of rain then dry and windy. East has increasing humidity and rain potential. Hawaii: Mostly fair. Chance of showers. Possible tropical wave east of islands.

2nd Quarter Moon July 6–13

Zone 1: Front triggering storms, then fair and cool conditions. **Zone 2:** Coastal areas have storms. Warm and showery weather becoming cool and fair. **Zone 3:** Northeast warm and showery, becoming cool and fair weather. South and central areas mostly below average temperatures, becoming breezy. **Zone 4:** West has a chance of showers then fair, cool, breezy. Central is fair and cool. East has showers then lower temperatures. **Zone 5:** Seventh has chance of showers west and east, then generally fair and cool. **Zone 6:** Warm and dry conditions give way to thunderstorms. Period ends cooler. **Zone 7:** Warm and dry conditions give way to thunderstorms. Period ends cooler. **Zone 8:** Alaska: West is cool and fair, becoming breezy. Central and eastern sections see increasing temperatures and showers. East ends cool and fair. Hawaii: Generally fair with shower potential.

Full Moon July 13–20

Zone 1: Increasing temperatures and humidity over New England brings periods of rain. Possible tropical moisture over the northeast around the sixteenth, then cooler with occasional rain. **Zone 2:** Chance of rain, then possible tropical moisture over northern zone around the sixteenth. Elsewhere, dry with cooler temperatures. **Zone 3:** Generally cooler weather. Western sections mostly fair, scattered storms that push eastward. **Zone 4:** Western areas start off cool and fair, increasing thunderstorm potential. Central area lower temperatures, windy, increasing storm potential. **Zone 5:** Western areas see average temperatures, fair. Storm potential increases. Central area lower temperatures, windy, increasing storm potential. **Zone 6:** West is fair, scattered showers; becoming windy, increasing thunderstorms. East has scattered thunderstorms. **Zone 7:** West during this period begins cool and fair. Windy conditions pick up, with thunderstorms likely. Eastern areas see scattered thunderstorms. **Zone 8:** Alaska: Western areas are cooler with a chance of showers and wind is potentially strong. Eastern zone has heavy rain potential. Hawaii: Cooler and cloudy with a chance of rain, then becoming fair.

4th Quarter Moon July 20–28

Zone 1: Increasing temperatures with a chance of rain and some windy conditions or gusty thunderstorms. **Zone 2:** Increasing cloudiness with a chance of rain and gusty thunderstorms. **Zone 3:** Eastern portions increasing cloudiness with a chance of rain. Western areas warm, breezy, then thunderstorms and sharp winds. **Zone 4:** Western areas see cooler temperatures with rain and some windy conditions. Eastern areas warm, breezy, then thunderstorms and sharp winds. **Zone 5:** Western areas experience cooler temperatures with rain and at times windy conditions, then warming. Eastern areas warm, breezy, then thunderstorms and sharp winds. **Zone 6:** West has chance of showers, rising temperatures, windy. East has cold front, possible showers; becoming stormier and windier. **Zone 7:** West has chance of showers, rising temperatures, windy. East has cold front, possible showers; becoming stormier and windier. **Zone 8:** Alaska: West has increasing wind velocities, gusty storms. East is becoming windy. Increasing temperatures, chance of gusty storms. Hawaii: Generally warmer, southerly winds with higher chance of rain. Becoming mostly fair but breezy.

New Moon July 28–August 5

Zone 1: Stormy and windy conditions. Period ends fair. **Zone 2:** Storm potential increases throughout the period, especially over eastern Gulf Coast area, possibly a tropical system. Period ends cooler, clear, windy. **Zone 3:** Generally, a period of thunderstorms and gusty winds. Possibly a tropical system threatens the Gulf Coast area. Period ends cooler, clear, windy. **Zone 4:** West has mostly lower temperatures, stormy, windy. Central fair conditions give way to showers then clear, cooler, windy. Eastern storm potential gives way to fair conditions. Afterward, clear, cooler, windy. **Zone 5:** West is mostly windy with storm potential. East is fair then a chance of rain. Period ends clear, cooler, windy. **Zone 6:** West is breezy; strong storms around the thirtieth. Afterward, clearing with a chance of showers. Increased wind velocities east and storm potential. **Zone 7:** West is breezy; strong storms around the thirtieth. Afterward, clearing with a chance of showers. Increased wind velocities east and storm potential. **Zone 8:** Alaska: West is generally stormy and windy. Central has increasing temperatures, fair. Rising temperatures east, possible rain. Hawaii: Increasing temperatures, predominantly fair, chance of rain.

2nd Quarter Moon August 5–11

Zone 1: Potentially intense storms with gusty winds, possibly tropical in nature. Temperatures may dip, rebound, and skies clear. **Zone 2:** Generally, a stormy period with special intensity along coastal North Carolina and Virginia, which may be tropical in nature. **Zone 3:** East has declining temperatures, potential for intense storms. Low pressure over eastern Great Lakes. West has rising temperatures. Period ends with sharp cold front, windy, stormy weather. **Zone 4:** Rising temperatures, intense storms, high winds from west to east the seventh through the ninth. Strong low pressure over the high northern plains. Period ends warm and fair. **Zone 5:** Rising temperatures, intense storms with high winds from west to east the seventh through the ninth. Period ends warm and fair. **Zone 6:** Cold front and showers west then increasing temperatures and fair conditions. Storm potential increases over eastern portions with windy conditions and lower temperatures. **Zone 7:** Scattered showers west then rising temperatures, fair conditions. Storm potential increases over eastern portions with windy conditions and lower temperatures. **Zone 8:** Alaska: Rising temperatures west, intense storms, gusty winds. Temperatures then decline. Cold front east, storms early, then warmer, fair. Period ends with strong storms. Hawaii: Temperatures below average. Strong chance of strong thunderstorms, then fair.

Full Moon August 11–19
Zone 1: Rising temperatures and scattered strong storms for the northeast. Mostly fair over New England with a slight chance of thunderstorms. **Zone 2:** Lower ranges of temperatures, scattered showers. **Zone 3:** Lower ranges of temperatures east with rain. Potential warming trend west with some showers. **Zone 4:** Western areas mostly fair, lower ranges of temperatures, some wind. Central and eastern portions mostly fair, then scattered thunderstorms. Period ends fair. **Zone 5:** Western zone cooler, fair with some wind. Central area becoming stormy. Rising temperatures east, scattered thunderstorms. Period ends fair. **Zone 6:** Fair conditions over the northwest, then heightened shower potential. Eastern portions see cooler temperatures with fair conditions. **Zone 7:** Western areas generally fair, then storm potential increases. Eastern portions see cooler temperatures with fair conditions. **Zone 8:** Alaska: Generally fair conditions west. Central and eastern portions see strong storms, then fair central. Hawaii: Potential for strong thunderstorms. Afterward, fair.

4th Quarter Moon August 19–27
Zone 1: Calm with a chance of showers. After the twenty-fourth, potentially windy; stormy weather increases. **Zone 2:** Rising

temperatures, chance of showers increases, then falling temperatures and some wind. **Zone 3:** Rising temperatures east, chance of showers. West and Great Lakes areas are warmer, a chance of showers. Strong cold front brings wet and windy weather, which pushes eastward. **Zone 4:** Increase in temperatures and humidity, showers over central and eastern areas. Strong central and eastern storms around the twenty-seventh. Western portions see falling temperatures, wind, and rain. **Zone 5:** Increased temperatures, humidity, and showers over eastern areas. Western portions see falling temperatures, wind, and rain. **Zone 6:** Rising temperatures and atmospheric disturbance over western zone. Period ends with increased wind velocities or gusty storms. Eastern areas see falling temperatures, wind, and rain. **Zone 7:** West sees rising temperatures and atmospheric disturbance. Period ends cooler with some wind and rain. East sees falling temperatures, wind, and rain. **Zone 8:** Alaska: Cooler and windy east. Western and central zones see rising temperatures; chance of showers and stronger storms. Hawaii: Rising temperatures, possible showers. Potential for strong atmospheric disturbance from the twenty-fourth through the twenty-sixth.

New Moon August 27–September 3

Zone 1: Mid-Atlantic atmospheric disturbance, then cloudy with a chance of storms. New England is dry and windy. **Zone 2:** Generally cloudy, cooler, with a propensity toward rain. **Zone 3:** Western portions are mostly windy with a chance of rain or gusty storms. Central and eastern areas are cooler with rain. **Zone 4:** Western areas begin warmer with a chance of showers and storms, then cooler. Central and eastern portions dry with warming trend and some windy conditions. **Zone 5:** Western areas begin warmer with a chance of showers and storms, then cooler. Central and eastern portions experience a dry and warming trend with some windy conditions. **Zone 6:** Atmospheric disturbance along coast. Scattered showers inland. Eastern portions see lower

temperatures and some showers. **Zone 7:** Atmospheric disturbance along northern coast. Scattered showers inland. Eastern
portions see lower temperatures and some showers. **Zone 8:**
Alaska: Increasing temperatures west; dry, windy, chance of thunderstorms. Increasing chance of showers east. Hawaii: Increasing
wind velocities, possible thunderstorms. Period ends dry and
windy.

2nd Quarter Moon September 3–10

Zone 1: Generally, warmer temperatures, cloudy, and showery.
Wind increases over New England. Strong coastal storms around
the ninth. **Zone 2:** Generally, showery from South Carolina north-
ward. Stronger storms assail coastal areas around the fifth and the
ninth. **Zone 3:** Generally warm and dry. Chance of thunderstorms
pushing eastward. **Zone 4:** Lower temperatures over western zone
with occasional showers. Eastern area stormy and windy. Central
area begins with atmospheric disturbance then fair. **Zone 5:**
Lower temperatures over western zone with occasional showers.

Eastern area stormy and windy. Central begins with atmospheric disturbance, then fair. **Zone 6:** West is fair, then rainfall over coastal areas. Lower temperatures east, possible showers. **Zone 7:** West is fair, then rainfall over north coast. Lower temperatures east, possible showers. **Zone 8:** Alaska: West is warm and dry, ending with cold front and showers. Central is windy with possible thunderstorms. Possible showers east. Hawaii: Warm and dry, becoming windy with potential thunderstorms.

Full Moon September 10–17

Zone 1: Southerly winds, rising temperatures, showers. New England sees heavy rain (may be a tropical system) around the sixteenth. **Zone 2:** Potential for above-normal precipitation for southern zone. Elsewhere, rising temperatures and showers. **Zone 3:** Southern portions showery while north remains fair. Storm potential increases throughout the zone with a possibility of above-average precipitation. **Zone 4:** Western areas cool, fair, and breezy, then shower potential increases. Central area sees atmospheric disturbance. Southerly winds bring a chance of showers over eastern portions. **Zone 5:** Western areas begin cool, fair, and breezy, then shower potential increases. Central area sees atmospheric disturbance. Southerly winds bring a chance of showers over eastern portions. **Zone 6:** West Coast fronts bring increasing storm potential. Eastern area is cool, fair, and breezy. Potential for showers and storms increases. **Zone 7:** West Coast fronts bring increasing storm potential. Eastern area is cool, fair, and breezy. Potential for showers and storms increases. **Zone 8:** Alaska: Western and central areas generally warm with probable showers. Potentially heavy rain around the sixteenth. East is cool, then rising temperatures leading to showers. Hawaii: Generally warm with shower potential. Strong storms, perhaps tropical, around the sixteenth.

4th Quarter Moon September 17–25

Zone 1: New England is windy and stormy. Mid-Atlantic scattered storms. **Zone 2:** Generally warm and dry. Then stormy with above-average precipitation. **Zone 3:** Generally warm and dry. Then stormy with above-average precipitation. After the twenty-third, there are storms with special intensity over the Deep South. **Zone 4:** West and central areas see lower temperatures and fair conditions. Between the twenty-third and twenty-fifth, there is potential for a major storm bringing high wind and heavy precipitation that pushes out of the Rockies and traverses the plains. **Zone 5:** West and central areas see lower temperatures and fair conditions. Between the twenty-third and twenty-fifth, there is potential for a major storm bringing high wind and heavy precipitation that pushes out of the Rockies and traverses the plains. **Zone 6:** Pacific Northwest has heavy rain possible. Strong thunderstorms move onshore around the twenty-third and push eastward. Eastern portions cool and are fair. Major storm develops between the twenty-third and twenty-fifth. **Zone 7:** The west is temperate. Strong thunderstorms move onshore around the twenty-third and push eastward. Eastern portions cool and are fair. Major storm develops between the twenty-third and twenty-fifth. **Zone 8:** Alaska: The west has generally lower temperatures across the zone. Western storms likely. Central and east see increasing chance of showers and stronger storms with heavy precipitation and wind. Hawaii: Increasing temperatures and humidity with a chance of showers, some strong.

Autumn

Zone 1 should expect fair, windy, and colder conditions periodically. Cold waves and winter-like storms are possible as well. Zone 2 sees lower ranges of temperatures and variable weather. Lower temperatures for northeastern portions of Zone 3. Elsewhere, clear and mild periods, increasing cloudiness and showers, as well as windy and fair weather with chances of rain.

Western areas of Zones 4 and 5 are generally breezy to windy with moderate to cooler temperatures. Central and eastern areas run the gamut from clear to cloudy conditions and mild temperatures to stormy, windy weather with lower temperatures.

Eastern portions of Zone 6 and 7 are mild and pleasant with increasing cloudiness, wind, and rain. Western regions see rising temperatures and dry conditions, which later become windy and stormy.

In Zone 8, Alaska is slated for periodic high-pressure systems with windy and colder conditions. Cold and damp precipitation is expected with increased wind velocities and storminess, especially over central portions. Hawaii generally sees below-average temperatures with conditions ranging from fair to stormy.

New Moon September 25–October 2

Zone 1: Potential for heavy precipitation, wind, and thunderstorms throughout zone. **Zone 2:** Northern zone has potential for heavy precipitation, wind, and thunderstorms. Southeast is windy. **Zone 3.** Cooler temperatures and windy conditions. **Zone 4:** An increase in western moisture brings rainy and windy conditions. Windy in central area. Eastern cold front triggers showers, then atmospheric disturbance and windy conditions. **Zone 5:** West, moisture is drawn up over the Rockies bringing rainy and windy conditions. Cold front triggers showers, then atmospheric disturbance, and windy conditions in the east. **Zone 6:** West has cloudy and windy weather with chance of storms. East has rainy and windy conditions. **Zone 7:** West has cloudy and windy weather with chance of storms. Potential wind for southern California. Rainy and windy conditions east. **Zone 8:** Alaska: Western sections windy with showers. Central and eastern areas see mostly rising temperatures, breezy, showers likely. Period ends with strong western storm that moves eastward. Hawaii:

Generally, increasing temperatures, showers, and breezy conditions; possible thunderstorms.

2nd Quarter Moon October 2–9

Zone 1: A series of cold fronts lowers temperatures and possibly triggers some showers. **Zone 2:** A series of possible cold fronts triggers some showers and storms. Temperatures remain lower behind the fronts. **Zone 3:** Storm potential for Great Lakes area and central zone. Northeast zone has lower temperatures, some showers. Strong cold front and precipitation throughout the zone around the fifth through the seventh. **Zone 4:** West is cool, and fair conditions give way to thunderstorms. Central and eastern areas see potential for strong storms. Period ends with rising temperatures and a chance of showers. **Zone 5:** West is cool and fair with a chance of showers. Central and eastern areas see potential for strong storms. Period ends with rising temperatures and a chance of showers. **Zone 6:** Coastal areas are windy and stormy with potential for heavy rains. Eastern portions are cool and fair; chance of thunderstorms increases. Cooler air mass lowers temperatures starting on the eighth. **Zone 7:** Potential for heavy rains over western zone. Eastern portions are cool and fair; chance of thunderstorms increases. Cooler air mass lowers temperatures starting on the eighth. **Zone 8:** Alaska: Western areas see rising temperatures and chance of showers. Central area is generally breezy, then stormy. Southern coast is stormy around the seventh. Eastern area sees strong cold front and storms and ends with rising temps and a chance of showers. Hawaii: Generally cooler with a chance of thunderstorms.

Full Moon October 9–17

Zone 1: Lower temperatures and thunderstorm activity throughout the zone, especially over New England. **Zone 2:** Lower temperatures and thunderstorm activity. A chance of showers for southern regions as the period ends. **Zone 3:** Lower temperatures over western and central areas with a chance of thunderstorms. Northeastern zone sees mostly cooler temperatures with possible thunderstorms. **Zone 4:** Western portions are windy and stormy. Central and eastern areas have cooler temperatures and fair conditions with possible thunderstorms. A warm-up around the seventeenth. **Zone 5:** Western portions are windy and stormy. Central and eastern areas have cooler temperatures and fair conditions with possible thunderstorms. A warm-up around the seventeenth. **Zone 6:** Western potential for heavy rain during the period. Eastern zone is subject to thunderstorms. **Zone 7:** Western potential for heavy rain during the period. Eastern zone is subject to thunderstorms. **Zone 8:** Alaska: West and central areas are colder with thunderstorms that push eastward. The southern coast is stormy, then zone becomes fair, warmer toward the end. Hawaii: Stormy conditions around the twelfth, possibly from a strong low-pressure area, becoming mild by the end of the period.

4th Quarter Moon October 17–25

Zone 1: The zone starts warm and fair then cold fronts generate showers and thunderstorms. Period ends mostly fair. **Zone 2:** The Mid-Atlantic area is subject to cold fronts, generating showers and thunderstorms, then becoming fair. Potential for heavy rainfall over southern portions. **Zone 3:** Showers over Great Lakes area. Eastern area has potential for heavy rain then cold fronts, thunderstorms, ending warmer. Western region is warm and fair, then cloudy with showers. Cooler toward the end. **Zone 4:** Western area is warm, fair, and breezy with a chance of showers. Central area is warm, breezy, and has an increasing shower or storm potential. Eastern area is warm, breezy, fair, giving way to clouds and a chance of rain. **Zone 5:** Western zone is warmer, becoming breezy, chance of showers. Storm system develops by the twentieth. Central area is warm, breezy, with an increasing shower or storm potential. Eastern area is warm, breezy, fair, giving way to clouds and a chance of rain, ending a bit cooler.

Zone 6: Western potential for heavy precipitation. Warm and fair conditions over eastern zone give way to showers. **Zone 7:** Western potential for heavy precipitation. Warm and fair conditions over eastern zone give way to showers. **Zone 8:** Alaska: Western chance of thunderstorms, then cooler. Central area is briefly warm, then colder with precipitation. Eastern chance of thunderstorms and lower temperatures. Period ends stormy. Hawaii: Initially warm and fair. Temperatures decrease with a chance of showers and thunderstorms, then ending mostly fair.

New Moon October 25–November 1

Zone 1: Thunderstorms over Mid-Atlantic, cooler. Cloudy, cooler, and showery for New England. **Zone 2:** Thunderstorms over the Mid-Atlantic region, becoming cloudy, rainy, cooler. Southern zone cloudy with a chance of showers. **Zone 3:** Northeast and Great Lakes have a chance of thunderstorms then cloudy, rainy, cooler. Southwest sees a chance of thunderstorms, then clearing. Central area is cloudy, rainy, cooler. **Zone 4:** West is moderate and breezy, becoming warm and dry; chance of thunderstorms. Central area is fair. East is breezy, fair, with chance of thunderstorms. **Zone 5:** West is moderate and breezy. Central scattered thunderstorms. East is breezy, fair, with chance of thunderstorms. **Zone 6:** West front brings rain. East is warmer, dry, and breezy. Thunderstorms. Possible red flag warnings. **Zone 7:** Western chance of rain. East is warmer, dry, and breezy. Strong thunderstorms over Arizona. Possible red flag warnings. **Zone 8:** Alaska: Cloudy, rainy, cooler west. Low pressure and precipitation for Aleutian Islands. Potential strong western storm by the thirtieth. Central cold front and thunderstorms. Breezy east. Hawaii: Chance of thunderstorms. Becoming cloudy, rainy, cooler. Strong thunderstorm potential around the thirtieth.

2nd Quarter Moon November 1–8

Zone 1: Period begins with a cold front and chance of thunderstorms over zone. Between the fifth and eighth, potential exists for a major winter storm to assail the forecast area with gusty winds, snow or rain, and lower temperatures. **Zone 2:** Period begins with a cold front and chance of thunderstorms over the Mid Atlantic. Between the fifth and eighth, potential exists for a major winter storm to assail the northern forecast area with gusty winds, snow or rain, and lower temperatures. Southern portions may also see windy and stormy conditions. **Zone 3:** Period begins with a cold front and chance of thunderstorms over the Great Lakes and northeast zone. Between the fifth and eighth, potential exists for a major winter storm to assail northeast portions of the forecast area with gusty winds, snow or rain, and lower temperatures. **Zone 4:** Potential for a major winter storm to form that would include lower temperatures, gusty winds, and precipitation is indicated for most of the zone between the third and fifth, which then pushes eastward, possibly across the central Mississippi Valley. Period ends with thunderstorm potential over the

Rockies and eastern plains. **Zone 5:** Potential for the formation of a major winter storm that would include lower temperatures, gusty winds, and precipitation is indicated for some parts of the zone, which will effect the area with differing degrees of intensity between the third and fifth. Period ends with thunderstorm potential over western and central zone. **Zone 6:** Western cold fronts bring showers and wind. Period ends with thunderstorm potential. Eastern thunderstorms likely. **Zone 7:** Western cold front brings showers and wind. Eastern thunderstorms likely. **Zone 8:** Alaska: Chance of thunderstorms. Between the fifth and eighth, winter storm warnings likely for Alaska as the potential exists for a low-pressure area to bring gusty winds, snow, and lower temperatures. Hawaii: Lower temperatures and an increasing chance of thunderstorms.

Full Moon Nov 8–16

Zone 1: Storm conditions, lowest temperatures, gusty winds continue through the eleventh. Afterward, skies clear and temperatures rebound. **Zone 2:** Storm conditions, lowest temperatures, gusty winds continue over northern sections through the eleventh. Afterward, skies clear and temperatures rebound. **Zone 3:** Storm conditions, lowest temperatures, and gusty winds continue over the northeast zone through the eleventh. Afterward, skies clear and temperatures rebound. **Zone 4:** Western thunderstorm potential then pleasant conditions. Central cold fronts and thunderstorm potential. Eastern cold front, chance of thunderstorms, then cool, mostly fair. **Zone 5:** Western thunderstorm potential, then pleasant conditions. Eastern cold front, chance of thunderstorms, then cool, mostly fair. **Zone 6:** Western strong front likely enters with wind and rain, then fair. Eastern storm potential, then pleasant conditions. **Zone 7:** Western strong front likely enters with wind and rain. Chance of showers, then fair. Eastern storm potential, then pleasant conditions. **Zone 8:** Alaska: Storm conditions, lowest temperatures, and gusty winds continue through the eleventh. Afterward, skies clear and temperatures rebound. Hawaii: Lower temperatures and thunderstorms continue; becoming fair with moderating temperatures.

4th Quarter Moon November 16–23

Zone 1: Mostly fair conditions and seasonal temperatures for the zone. Toward the end, some showers over the Mid-Atlantic area push eastward. **Zone 2:** Mostly cool and fair conditions. Southern areas are warmer with thunderstorm potential. At the end of the period, a chance of showers for northern sections. **Zone 3:** Northeast zone is mostly cool, fair, increasing chance of rain toward the end. Central areas see increasing temperatures with a chance of showers or thunderstorms. **Zone 4:** Predominately fair conditions throughout the zone. **Zone 5:** Predominately fair conditions throughout the zone. **Zone 6:** Western front brings atmospheric disturbance, then clearing. Eastern area sees increasing thunderstorm potential. **Zone 7:** Western front brings atmospheric disturbance, then clearing. Scattered thunderstorms east, especially southern portions. **Zone 8:** Alaska: Thunderstorm potential across zone. Otherwise, mostly fair conditions. Hawaii: Mostly fair and cooler with a chance of showers.

New Moon November 23–30

Zone 1: Mid-Atlantic region sees lower temperatures, showers. Period ends with gusty thunderstorms over New England. **Zone 2:** Southern chance of thunderstorms. Central and northern portions lower temperatures, possible thunderstorms. **Zone 3:** Thunderstorm potential high over central area and Great Lakes. Northeast section cold front brings showers or thunderstorms. Period ends with strong thunderstorm potential in the southern portions. **Zone 4:** West is fair. Central is warmer, chance of showers. Eastern cold front, showers. Period ends with possible gusty thunderstorms across the zone. **Zone 5:** Western area has fair weather. Central has southerly winds, chance of showers. Potential gusty

thunderstorms on the twenty-ninth. Eastern cold front, showers.
Zone 6: Stormy period characterized by western fronts bringing
windy and rainy weather that pushes toward eastern portions.
Zone 7: Stormy period characterized by western fronts bringing
windy and rainy weather that pushes toward eastern portions.
Zone 8: Alaska: Northern cold fronts bring precipitation over
southern areas. Gusty thunderstorms east and west. Hawaii:
Southerly winds, possible showers. Occasional cold fronts bring
rain and a chance of thunderstorms.

2nd Quarter Moon November 30–December 7

Zone 1: Windy conditions or gusty thunderstorms that spread
eastward through New England. **Zone 2:** Northern windy conditions or gusty thunderstorms. Cold front, possible showers.
South sees increasing warmth and possible showers. Potential for
heavy rain over Florida-Georgia area. **Zone 3:** Northeast zone sees
windy conditions or gusty thunderstorms. Cold front, possible
showers. Central is warmer with possible showers. Eastern potential for heavy rain. **Zone 4:** Western scattered thunderstorms,
seasonal temperatures. Central is warmer with thunderstorms.
Possible heavy rain. Eastern cold front, possible showers, and
wind. **Zone 5:** Western scattered thunderstorms. Central sees
strong storms over Texas begin the period, then possible heavy
rain over southern and central portions after the fourth. Eastern
cold front, possible showers, and wind. **Zone 6:** Southerly winds
increase temps, humidity, and thunderstorm potential across zone,
triggering heavy rain at times. **Zone 7:** Southerly winds increase
temps, humidity, and thunderstorm potential across zone, triggering heavy rain at times. Southern California and Nevada may be
subject to heavy rain, flash flooding, and wind. **Zone 8:** Alaska:
Thunderstorm potential over southern zone. West is warmer with
possible showers. Period ends stormy. Cold front over central
area. Eastern wind or gusty thunderstorms. Hawaii: Warmer with
possible showers. Cold front brings likelihood for thunderstorms.

Full Moon December 7–16

Zone 1: Mid-Atlantic region is cooler with a chance of precipitation. New England is cloudy with showers. **Zone 2:** Northern regions see potential for sharp winds or gusty storms. Central regions are cooler; chance of precipitation. Southern area is cool, cloudy, possible thunderstorms. **Zone 3:** North zone has potential for sharp winds or gusty storms, then cooler with a chance of precipitation. Central area is windy with a chance of thunderstorms, especially the southwestern zone. **Zone 4:** West sees increasing clouds, temperatures, and chance of rain; breezy. Central is generally cooler with a chance of showers. Eastern area sees lower temperatures, possible showers. Period ends windy with chance of precipitation. **Zone 5:** West sees increasing clouds, temperatures, and chance of rain; breezy. East is generally cooler with possible showers. Thunderstorms over southeastern zone. Period ends windy with chance of precipitation. **Zone 6:** West has sharp westerly winds, possible atmospheric disturbance; becoming cloudy, cooler, windy. East has an increasing chance of rain. **Zone 7:** West has sharp westerly winds, possible atmospheric disturbance; becoming cloudy, cooler, windy. East has an increasing chance of rain. **Zone 8:** Alaska: Increased wind velocities. Southern coast is generally cloudy, lower temperatures with a chance of precipitation. Central is cool, cloudy. East is windy, rainy. Hawaii: Generally, cooler with a chance of precipitation, some windy or gusty storms.

4th Quarter Moon December 16–23

Zone 1: The zone experiences below-average temperatures with a chance of windy and showery conditions. **Zone 2:** Northern sections see lower temperatures with a chance of showers and windy conditions. Southern areas warmer with a chance of showers. **Zone 3:** The zone mainly experiences lower temperatures with a chance of precipitation. **Zone 4:** West is fair, then becoming windy with possible showers. Central sees rising humidity and chance of showers. Period ends with lower temperatures, chance of showers, and wind. East is cold, fair, and windy with a chance of showers. Warming around the twentieth with possible showers, then colder. **Zone 5:** West is fair then becomes windy with possible showers. Central area sees rising humidity and chance of showers. Period ends with lower temperatures, chance of showers, and wind. East is cold, fair, and windy with a chance of showers. Warming around the twentieth with possible showers, then colder. **Zone 6:** The zone experiences a warm-up, possible windy conditions. Afterward, coastal areas breezy. Inland temperatures below average, possible showers. Eastern lower temperatures with possible showers. **Zone 7:** The zone experiences a warm-up, possible windy conditions. Afterward, northern coastal areas breezy. Inland temperatures below average, possible showers. Eastern area sees lower temperatures with possible showers. **Zone 8:** Alaska: Western zone mostly cold, clear, some wind. Central sections cold with possible showers and wind. Eastern area is cold and windy. Hawaii: Period begins with thunderstorms, then lower temperatures, possible showers.

New Moon December 23–29

Zone 1: Rising temperatures and fair over the Mid-Atlantic region, then precipitation. Elsewhere, southerly winds, warmer, fair with an occasional shower. **Zone 2:** Northern rising temperatures and fair over the Mid-Atlantic region. Then front brings a chance of precipitation. South is windy or gusty, storms early, otherwise warmer, fair. **Zone 3:** Generally, the zone is cloudier with lower temperatures. Southwest zone cold with increasing showers. **Zone 4:** Western regions fair with rising temperatures. Central area windy, warmer with a chance of showers. Eastern sections cold, sometimes windy, with possible showers. **Zone 5:** Western regions fair with rising temperatures. Central area windy, warmer with a chance of showers. Eastern sections cold, sometimes windy, with possible showers. Southeast section has potential for stronger storms around the twenty-ninth. **Zone 6:** Front enters West Coast bringing wind and rain. Contrary air masses clash, keeping weather cloudy and rainy. Strong winds from the south bring mild temperatures with showers likely. **Zone 7:** Front enters West Coast bringing wind and rain. Contrary air masses clash, keeping weather cloudy and rainy. Strong winds from the south result in mild temperatures with showers likely. **Zone 8:** Alaska: West and central are windy and stormy. East is briefly windy with precipitation giving way to calm and mild conditions. Hawaii: Generally calm with rising temperatures.

2nd Quarter Moon December 29–January 6, 2023

Zone 1: Cold, windy, chance of precipitation over Mid-Atlantic area. Warmer and dry over New England. **Zone 2:** Cold, windy, chance of precipitation over Mid-Atlantic area. Southern area of the zone sees thunderstorms. **Zone 3:** Strong front and thunderstorms sweep through zone. **Zone 4:** West is colder with thunderstorms. East sees cold front generate storms. **Zone 5:** West is colder with thunderstorms. Central and eastern cold front generates storms. **Zone 6:** A cold front enters western sections, generating thunderstorms that transit eastward. **Zone 7:** A cold front enters western sections, generating thunderstorms that transit eastward. **Zone 8:** Alaska: A western cold front produces precipitation. Central area is cold, with low pressure generating storms. Eastern area sees a chance of thunderstorms. Hawaii: Lower temperatures, cloudy, chance of rain.

Economic Forecast for 2022

Christeen Skinner

Whilst the slow journey of renewal following the "Great Financial Reset" of 2020 has begun, the positions of the planets—and especially at New or Full Moons in 2022—suggest that challenges are far from over.

The rare conjunction of Jupiter, Saturn, and Pluto in Capricorn in January 2020 coincided with the coronavirus pandemic of that year, and businesses in every corner of the world have been challenged. Those that have survived will need to be robust to withstand the cosmic pressures indicated for 2022.

This is not to say that the year is all "bad": indeed, low indices offer buying opportunities when those with cash to invest find attractive business opportunities.

Preparing For Change

At the start of 2022, geocentric Pluto is at 25° 56' Capricorn. This slow-moving planet doesn't travel far before arriving at retrograde station Capricorn 28° 35' on April 29 (EDT) just hours ahead of the first solar eclipse of the year. Pluto then stations direct on October 8 (EDT) at Capricorn 26° 06' before concluding the year at 27° 38' Capricorn.

As Pluto crosses these last few degrees of Capricorn, echoes of both 2008 and 2020 will likely be heard with some corporations and governments showing clear signs of stress and threatening collapse: a theme that will doubtless continue until Pluto makes Aquarius ingress in 2023.

The fixed star Terebellum, a star in Chiron's tail, is at approximately 26° Capricorn. Terebellum features in the charts of those who show a "mercenary" nature and is linked to both power and success. We might reasonably wonder that as Pluto aligns with this fixed star there would be some evidence of "comeuppance."

Certainly before Pluto completes its transit of Capricorn, and just as was forewarned by its entry into that sign when global banks were on the verge of collapse, the demise of many corporations is probable. Alongside this we may witness a plethora of lawsuits and potential collapse in share prices—with significant effect on indices. These may be particularly evident at both Pluto's retrograde and direct station: respectively April 29 and October 8.

Other highly significant features of 2022 are the conjunctions of Sedna and Ceres at 28 Taurus. (The retrograde conjunction is on January 4 and the direct conjunction on January 23). Sedna, which orbits beyond Pluto, has an orbit of 11,408 years and has been moving through Taurus since the mid-1960s. It formed a conjunction with Ceres in Taurus in 1970 and has been making subsequent Taurus conjunctions with that asteroid approximately every four years.

Ceres is the largest of the asteroids orbiting between Mars and Jupiter and is associated with growth and farming whilst Sedna is linked to the sea. Since the 1970s, interest in aquafarming has grown. Though this industry has been present for thousands of years, rapid developments have been made in the last half century. Half of the world's seafood consumption now comes from aquafarming. This sector could attract attention in 2022.

Investors might also like to note the potential influence of Jupiter as it moves through the zodiac. During Jupiter's 11.86-year orbit of the Sun, it spends an unequal time in each zodiac sign dependent on its distance from the Sun. Entry into a new sign can occur at any time of the year and the impact is usually noticeable within days. This planet, associated with expansion, prompts growth in the business sectors linked to the zodiac signs involved.

When more than one sign is involved—as in 2022—then the boost to the two different sectors increases the possibility of growth to all stock market indices. At the start of 2022, Jupiter is in Pisces. Jupiter moves on into Aries on May 11 (EDT) where it benefits businesses connected to the military, surgical hardware, and cutting equipment of all kinds (Aries).

On October 28, Jupiter returns to Pisces and attention should return to water, alcoholic beverages, pharmaceuticals, media, and oil: all sectors likely to have seen growth as Jupiter began its passage through Pisces in 2021. Jupiter then returns to Aries on December 20.

Astro finance is an attempt by an astrologer to decode planetary positions and patterns and discern correlation and potential influence on global finance. Aside from change of sign, the distribution of the planets at each New and Full Moon is given consideration.

You may know from your own chart that there are well-recognized patterns: a splash, a bundle, the seesaw, a locomotive, a bucket, etc. The year 2022 is special in that, of the twenty-five charts of New and Full Moons to be considered, ten would be described as "bowl" patterns, five are "seesaw" shaped, five form "locomotives," three are "slings," and the remaining two would be considered "bundles." In each case, we find concentrations of activity in just a few areas of the zodiac.

The dominating influence of bowl shapes (40 percent of these lunation charts), where the familiar planets of Mercury, Venus, Mars, Jupiter, Saturn, Uranus, Neptune, and Pluto together with the Sun and Moon, are all contained within 180° and suggests "all or nothing." Of course, we have known for many years that the distribution of wealth, like the planets, has been unequal. In the few months of 2022 when the seesaw is in operation, there may be signs that the slow process of correction is underway.

The seesaw shape is prominent from the New Moon on August 27 through the New Moon on October 25. Through these eight weeks, at the end of the third and through the first half of the fourth quarter of 2022, there is greatest potential for financial correction. A key date will likely be the Full Moon on September 10, when Saturn and Uranus are within two degrees of right angle to one another.

Research reveals that when these two planets are within orb of either conjunct, opposed, or at right angle to one another, there is negative mood in the marketplace and subsequent loss in index value. (Examples include 1930–1931 and 2008–2010.)

As viewed from Earth, the right angle between Saturn and Uranus occurs several times from 2021, owing to one or other planet being retrograde. They make their last square aspect in 2022 before the two planets conjoin in 2032. Supporting the idea that this particular right angle will coincide with high market drama is that, unlike in 2021, Uranus will be conjunct to the lunar north node—as it was in 1931, which was a year of acute financial difficulty.

The year 2022, then, is likely to be a difficult time at all levels: political, social, and economic. Strengthening the possibility of this affecting prices on the New York Stock Exchange are other factors: In the chart for the New York Stock Exchange, Mars is positioned at 18° 44' Virgo. The passage of slow-moving planets over this degree, and indeed New and Full Moons close to this degree, have, in the past, coincided with identifiable turning points. On September 10, 2022, there is a Full Moon at 17° of the Virgo-Pisces axis.

As if all this were not enough, the final clue to the potential for acute market drama in September is heralded by Mercury's station at 8° Libra that same day. Note that not all degrees of the zodiac are equal with some: the equinoxes and solstice points at 0° Aries, Cancer, Libra, and Capricorn having extra power. Analysis reveals that major events in the markets are often coincided with planets transiting 8 or 19 degrees of the cardinal signs. (Reference my book *Exploring the Financial Universe*.)

Retrogrades

Mercury has three retrograde periods in any year. In other words, as viewed from Earth, it appears to stand still in the sky, then appears to move backward over degrees recently covered, before once again standing still and then appearing to move forward. Though the retrograde period lasts only a matter of days, allowing for the planet to make its "loop" and then return to the retrograde station, the entire retrograde and its shadow lasts some weeks. Much attention is given to these periods, with many people of the opinion that these are not good times for communication (a Mercury keyword). It is as important to focus on those weeks when Mercury's speed is fast, as during these periods commercial activity usually increases and indices tend to rise.

Of course, no single planet's movement should be considered in isolation: Mercury may be moving forward at speed whilst Venus or Mars is retrograde. The year 2022 begins with Venus retrograde in Capricorn but, once it reaches its station on January 29, that planet continues its journey through the zodiac without stationing retrograde again that year. Mars turns retrograde on October 30 and is retrograde for the remainder of the year.

To launch a new business, it is wise to avoid those periods when Mercury, Venus, or Mars are retrograde. The most delicate and testing time for any new business are the first two years (a complete Mars cycle). Should the business survive, then further challenges are probable at seven years (a quarter of the Saturn cycle) and at fourteen years (the half cycle). A commonly used forecasting technique works on the principle of allowing "one day per year." It is advisable then to launch at least fourteen days before a planet turns retrograde so as to avoid potentially adverse conditions.

There are exceptions to these rules. These would be considered by your astrologer if you are launching or inaugurating in 2022. The astrologer would take into account your chart, that of your company, and the nature of the product or services to be provided.

The recognised outer planets turn retrograde annually so that it is most unusual to have all the "regular" planets all in forward motion. (Please note that we will soon be including minor planets orbiting beyond Pluto in our analysis. Research into the possible influence of these dwarf planets is underway.) In 2022, however, and after Mercury turns direct on February 4 for nine weeks until early May, all the regular planets are in forward motion. Those wishing to launch new business enterprises should consider the midpoint of this period as offering excellent cosmic headwind. Their fledgling businesses would have the advantage that—by both direct and converse progression—they would not experience a "retrograde effect." From May onward, there is always one or more planet in retrograde motion.

This does not mean that there is no "good" date to launch an enterprise after May. It is, after all, rare to find an enterprise that wasn't established with at least one planet retrograde. What should be avoided, if at all possible, is having either Venus or Mars retrograde. Venus retrograde (as in the first few weeks of 2022) can result in difficulties with essential partners and suppliers. Competition is not a bad thing: note how often restaurants open side by side. They effectively "support" one another in creating a lively area. Camaraderie has benefits. Not so with Venus's retrograde where competitors pull against one another to negative effect. Given Venus's relationship with cash flow, a retrograde Venus usually means that there will be more flowing out than in.

A retrograde Mars is indicative of easily drained energy and resources. In 2022, Mars retrogrades during the fourth quarter and in Gemini. Businesses launched against this background will likely find that they are subject to negative discussion on social media platforms and experience constant struggle to get their message across. Mars in Gemini brings the potential for "fighting talk" and wars of words and subsequent legal action. Whilst this might be boom time for law firms, it is not so good for those using their services. Fighting "wars of words" will likely prove expensive and exhausting.

Eclipses

There are two solar and two accompanying lunar eclipses in 2022. The solar eclipse on April 30 is in Taurus and is followed at the accompanying Full Moon on May 16 by a lunar eclipse in Scorpio. The latter is hugely significant in that it occurs just hours before the "birthday" of the New York Stock Exchange. The second solar eclipse, on October 25, is followed by a lunar eclipse in Taurus. With the Taurus-Scorpio axis so emphasised, it is probable that financial matters will be front-page news during both two-week periods—and perhaps not in a "good" way (though this is likely to bring buying opportunities).

Solar eclipses may be viewed as a rope of knots (events) that stretch across many years. Each is part of a cycle. Every nineteen years, there will be an eclipse at approximately the same zodiac degree but each time have visibility in a different part of the world. To comprehend the likely impact, we must assess the position of the planets at the inaugurating eclipse to better understand the nature of the eclipse. We also note the areas of the world in which the eclipse will be visible. Whilst the whole world experiences an altered geomagnetic field as the Moon's face covers the Sun, study has shown that those areas in which the eclipse is visible will likely see greatest social, economic, and political activity.

The April eclipse will only just be visible on the west coast of South America; greatest visibility is across the Southern Ocean and Antarctica. It is entirely possible that the wealth—and health—of this ocean will be of pressing concern to many nations. This eclipse is the sixty-sixth of a series of seventy-one eclipses that does not conclude for another century.

The first of these eclipses took place in 850 CE. At that event, both Mercury and Mars were out of bounds (their declinations beyond the outer limits reached by the Sun as measured from the celestial equator). It is generally accepted that the nature of the starting eclipse echoes throughout the series. Taurus is associated with materials and with money. The Mercury and Mars positions amplify the commercial nature of this series, indicating the potential for reaching new limits (out of bounds).

In the April 30, 2022 eclipse of this series, Uranus is only 4° away from this "sophisticated" New Moon. The impact of this particular lunation should be strong in the financial world with new and revolutionary concepts and ways of financial working developing as the year progresses. We should expect digital currencies in particular to gain ground.

In geographical contrast, the October solar eclipse is visible across much of Europe, Algeria, Libya, Chad, Sudan, and Ethiopia. This Scorpio eclipse is the fifty-fifth of a series of seventy-three in Saros Cycle 124.

The first of these eclipses took place on March 6, 1049 when Pluto reached declination of over 26° and was in opposition to Mars. Mars and Pluto are the natural rulers of Scorpio, underlining the potential for this series of eclipses to be linked to power struggles. From the economic perspective we should expect this October eclipse to coincide with increasingly spectacular boardroom power struggles, and commercial or even trade war.

In the initial chart for Saros Cycle 124, Uranus and Neptune, too, had reached the opposition of their cycle. Uranus and Neptune had yet to be discovered and astrologers or sky-watchers of 1049 would not have recognised this cycle and the potential links to exploration of new worlds. This is not the case in 2022 with the reverberations of this cycle—which we now know coincides with developments in internet, social media, and linked marketing. We might reasonably anticipate that this October eclipse will coincide with the formation of new and energetic companies—perhaps tentatively planning the viability of exploring worlds beyond our solar system.

Accompanying Lunar Eclipses

There are two lunar eclipses in 2022, both occurring at the Full Moon following a solar eclipse.

The May 16 lunar eclipse accentuates the Taurus/Scorpio axis and takes place just before the anniversary or birthday of the New York Stock Exchange—itself close to the birthdate of the Tokyo Stock Exchange and precisely six months before the birthday of the Johannesburg Stock Exchange. A lunar eclipse often marks an ending, a turning point or moment of crisis. The fact that these three major exchanges will all be affected by this eclipse suggests that this will be an important period for related indices: most likely coinciding with loss of value.

The November 8 lunar eclipse similarly accents the Taurus/Scorpio axis. The chart for this event has the Sun with Mercury in Scorpio, whilst the Moon and Uranus are in opposition and all at right angle to Saturn. This suggests a "slamming on of the brakes"—most likely affecting cooperative banking systems and perhaps also mutual fund management. Nor should we discount the possibility of struggles within the general banking industry and sudden losses in their stock value. It is these that will likely be the key factors in the decline of major indices, which may begin their negative slide as Mars retrogrades on October 30.

First Quarter

There are similarities between the first quarter of 2022 and that of 2020. Recall that Pluto entered Capricorn back in 2008 when the foundations of banking and many corporations were shaken to the core in what is now known as the Global Financial Crisis. Financial astrologers had made this forecast and also had major concerns about 2020 when both Jupiter and Saturn would join Pluto in that sign. As we now know, the COVID-19 pandemic gave rise to what may now be seen as a Global Financial Reset.

Until Pluto moves on into Aquarius in 2023, echoes of those earlier times should be heard. This may be particularly apparent in January 2022 when several striking and relatively rare cosmic alignments occur, including the passage of the minor planet Chiron over 8° Aries. Historically this has been a sensitive financial degree and has a justified reputation for correction. At the very least, traders may be tensed in preparation for downturn.

As you may know, there are many perspectives to take into account. One of these concerns is what are known as parallel aspects: measurements of declination from the celestial equator.

January 2022 begins with Mars out of bounds and at maximum declination, bringing high levels of energy and volatility as it moves through Sagittarius in parallel aspect to Pluto (in Capricorn). Sagittarius is associated with long-distance travel, further education, legal matters, and religion. The possible manifestations of this aspect are myriad and include acts of religious terrorism. Nor should we discount the implementation of tougher international air travel regulation that in turn affects the share prices of businesses working in that sector. Companies that have associations with both legal matters and commerce linked to religions (pilgrim travel for example) could also be adversely affected.

Again echoing 2020, in mid-January, Mercury, Venus, and Saturn are all in parallel aspect. Saturn has a justified reputation for bringing delay and even obstruction. Mercury and Venus need to work together for there to be equitable commercial exchange. It is entirely possible that rules and restrictions laid down by hardline governments will make it exceedingly difficult for some travel companies to operate. At the Full Moon on January 17, Mercury is in latitude parallel with Mars (still out of bounds and with the Moon in Sagittarius). This underscores the probability of the travel sector fighting for permission to operate.

In January 2022, Venus is retrograde. That planet reaches maximum latitude on January 26. Given the parallel aspects listed above, it is entirely possible that a major commercial deal, whose promise initially causes indices to rise, will come unstuck. That this event coincides with Mars's return to Capricorn is further evidence of the high probability of stocks (especially the banking sector) reaching their high for the year and for economic reporters to suggest that a repeat of the first quarter of 2020 when prices fell in March is likely.

Yet there is also a Jupiter/Uranus sextile that becomes exact in February. This is a most promising aspect, likely to be beneficial to the growing cryptocurrency sector and for those companies focused on space-age technology. That said, it is imperative that these corporations have solid funding. February is likely to prove a challenging time for any business whose cash flow is unable to cope with the restricted capital hinted at in the close conjunction of the Sun and Saturn at the New Moon on February 1.

The parallel between Mars, then in Capricorn, and Pluto becomes exact again on February 24. Fissures in banking sector stocks should be apparent. Within hours of this event, Jupiter reaches its first semi-square aspect with Pluto: a cycle that began in 2020. Businesses that were launched at the 2020 conjunction could find this a difficult time. Unless they have sufficient capital, they may find they are severely strapped for cash, with some businesses threatened with bankruptcy.

On several occasions since the millennium, the early part of March has seen dramatic falls in stock market indices: notably both the Dow Jones index and the S&P. The year 2022 will likely join that list. Some may find this forecast surprising, as Jupiter, then moving through Pisces, is conjunct with the New Moon on March 2. Jupiter has a reputation for bringing good fortune. Yet in that same chart, Mars conjoins with Pluto in Earth sign Capricorn, as Mercury conjoins Saturn in Aquarius. It is entirely possible that indices will be "brought down to earth."

Strengthening the argument that this could see echoes of past lows, a few days later, on March 6, Mars moves into Aquarius where it joins both Jupiter and Saturn. Though not in exact aspect, all three will be at right angle with Uranus slowly moving through Taurus. It is certainly true that both the Mars-Jupiter and Mars-Saturn cycles are often at key phases at times of war, yet these same aspects have also coincided with significant market volatility. Perhaps the threat of trade war will be a major factor in loss of share value.

The chart for the Full Moon on March 18 is a sling formation with the Sun and Moon both at right angles to the Galactic Center. This is further evidence of volatility and emotional trading. It is normal for there to be a shift in sentiment at the equinox. Mars reaches the exact square to Uranus on March 22 within hours of the equinox, suggesting a possible high after earlier lows.

Second Quarter

The dominant feature of April 2022 is the conjunction of Jupiter and Neptune in Pisces. The aspect is exact at the Full Moon on April 16 and traditionally should benefit industries connected with oceanic exploration, marine equipment, media, oil, and pharmaceutical companies. In the twenty-first century, we now include space travel: voyages beyond the known world. Clearly much depends on the charts of the specific companies involved, but businesses working in these sectors should experience promising development. April 2022 is a time to look for well-priced shares in these sectors.

Less positively, on April 16 Pluto in Capricorn is within orb of right angle to both the Sun in Aries and Moon in Libra. Pluto is the planet associated with corruption, and it is likely that a proposed amalgamation will come under considerable scrutiny. Should there be a proposed merger, this would likely not succeed.

The solar eclipse on April 30 is the first of a series of New and Full Moons whose charts are in bowl shape. Concentration of energy in one hemisphere of the zodiac immediately infers focus but imbalance. This New Moon is conjunct Uranus (planet of the unexpected) and could coincide with shocking political directives. Whilst these may not have immediate effect on share prices, delayed reaction coinciding with the Full Moon on May 16 is likely.

This lunation takes place just a day before the anniversary of the inauguration of the New York Stock Exchange. In the chart for this Full Moon—also a lunar eclipse—it is both Vesta and Saturn's turn to be at right angles to both Sun and Moon, signalling the likelihood of a downturn affecting not just equities but also currencies. The bowl shape of this chart is led by the Moon, which will then be in Scorpio, the sign of its fall. This underscores the probability of traders being at low ebb and pulling prices down to match their mood.

The bowl shape of the Gemini New Moon on May 30 is led by Pluto in Capricorn: potentially drawing attention to the banking industry and the control it might have on commercial (particularly Gemini type) trading. Businesses and companies likely to be seriously affected would include the car industry, local travel, local newspapers, and telecommunications.

It is exceedingly rare for a series of Full Moons each to configure with one of the outer planets. The year 2022, then, is a marked difference. In April, Pluto was dominant, in May it was both Vesta's and Saturn's turn. At the Full Moon on June 14, it is Neptune that takes up position at the Sun-Moon midpoint. Once again, this is a bowl-shaped chart led by the Moon: implying strong emotional reaction. With Neptune involved, many could feel all at sea and, yes, indices could once again fall. At this Full Moon, Mars conjoins with Chiron in Aries: an aspect indicating pending correction.

Neptune is stationed at the following New Moon on June 28. In this chart, Jupiter is at right angle to the New Moon whilst Mars and Pluto are also in square aspect. The bowl shape in this chart is once again led by Pluto. This extraordinary planetary picture suggests great strain in the banking sector especially. Smaller companies could find it difficult to obtain funding: a theme that continues through the next quarter.

Third Quarter

Pluto conjoins the Full Moon on July 13. For the last decade, lunation alignments that have brought this "planet of power" into focus have coincided with news concerning exposure of corruption. Of course, this need not affect the world of finances—but it often does.

For some years, Uranus has been travelling through Taurus. Its last transit of this area of the zodiac was in the 1930s during the Great Depression. In July 2022, Uranus is exactly aligned with the lunar north node, marking a moment of destiny. High drama is to be expected. The chart for the July Full Moon is once again bowl-shaped, with the Moon as leader of the planet grouping. This suggests overt emotional reaction. At the very least, volume of trade should be up with prices volatile and closing to the downside.

A negative trend is confirmed at the New Moon on July 28 when Mercury is within orb of opposition to Saturn. Both are at right angle to Mars, in turn conjoining both the north node and Uranus. The chart for this lunation is locomotive in shape with Pluto leading. In economic terms, Pluto as god of the underworld could lead markets through a tunnel that lasts for some months, i.e., it is more likely that prices will be going down than going up.

A negative trend is also apparent at the Full Moon on August 11. Once again this is a locomotive pattern with Pluto leading. The "tunnel" at this point could be dark as Saturn (depression) is conjunct the Moon while squaring Uranus and the lunar north node. In the last century, each hard aspect between Saturn and Uranus has coincided with market falls. This could again be true in August 2022.

The theme continues at the New Moon on August 27. This chart is seesaw in shape, and as we know, maintaining balance on a seesaw is not easy. This New Moon is at right angle to Mars moving through Gemini, as Venus in Leo opposes Saturn in Aquarius and squares Uranus in Taurus. This T-square in fixed signs implies rigid controls in the form of rules and regulations that disable normal trade. Black markets should thrive.

Pivotal in 2022 is the Full Moon (17 Pisces) on September 10. Not only are Saturn and Uranus still in square formation, but the Sun opposes both the Moon and Neptune as Mercury stations retrograde at 8° Libra: a cardinal sign. Each of these factors alone sets financial alarm bells ringing.

Yes, it is possible that one force will cancel another. That, though, seems most unlikely. The actual degrees involved draw attention to the position of Mars at 18 Virgo in the chart for the New York Stock Exchange. In the past, this has proved a super-sensitive degree. Neptune's opposition to this brings the potential for great loss.

It is probable that this Full Moon will prove a turning point. Technical analysis closer to the time should indicate just how extreme price movement might be. From the astro-finance perspective, there seems high probability that there will be a downward slide between this Full Moon and the New Moon on September 25 (EDT).

This final lunation of the third quarter of 2022 offers yet another seesaw shape: dominated by Saturn still at right angle to Uranus. Until this aspect is cleared, growth seems most unlikely. What is interesting about this New Moon in Libra is that the Sun and Moon are within 3° of opposition to Jupiter. This suggests exaggeration (Jupiter) but also the potential for major mergers. It is the promise of these that could avert markets falling further.

Fourth Quarter

The first New Moon of this quarter is interesting in that the Sun is conjunct Venus in Libra opposing the Moon conjunct Chiron in Aries: a seesaw pattern. In that same chart, Mars is applying to its square with Neptune. It is tempting given Chiron's placement to assume correction. Technical analysis closer to the time would confirm this. What seems likely is that there will be concern about the value of pharmaceutical, oil, and media stocks whose value may have plummeted. Yet these could rise when Jupiter returns to Pisces at the end of October.

This quarter of the year includes both a solar and lunar eclipse. The solar eclipse on October 25 occurs between Saturn's direct station on October 23 and Jupiter's return to Pisces on October 28 suggesting a rocky, possibly turbulent, few days. As planets move from one sign to another, there is a ripple effect that often

affects markets. It would be advisable for traders and investors alike to be extra focused and to ensure that they have appropriate financial safety nets in place. Adding to the cosmic complexity, Mars turns retrograde within orb of opposition to the Galactic Center. At the very least, this signals considerable volatility.

Given Mars's position, there is always the possibility of radio interference in trading. This could, of course, take many forms from computer virus to legal challenges. There may be unwillingness on the part of investors to go back into the market. Yet it could be argued that after a bruising nine months of the year, prices are now at an attractive buying level.

Investors could use this last quarter of the year to think ahead and look at the sectors linked to Jupiter's upcoming transit of Taurus in 2023. Taurus is associated with banking stocks and with confectionary. It may be that stocks in these sectors are attractively priced in late October or early November.

By the lunar eclipse on November 8, Mars is out of bounds. This locomotive-shaped chart is led by Mercury, the planet of commerce, as the Sun, Mercury, and Venus oppose both the Moon and Uranus with Saturn midway between the two groups. This should prove a defining moment and very likely a change in stock market trend.

Indeed, at the Sagittarius New Moon on November 23, both Mercury and Mars are out of bounds whilst the locomotive shape is led by the optimistic Sun in Sagittarius. At last there could be light at the end of 2022's dark financial tunnel. With the presence of Jupiter in Aries boosting related stocks (cutting tools of all kinds, military hardware, and sports equipment) by the final Full Moon of the year on December 7, traders and investors alike should feel encouraged whilst issuing sighs of relief that a dark period is at an end.

In summary: Whilst the effect of recession and even depression could be felt across the world, and investors might despair that their savings are dwindling, by the close of that year a turning point should be reached. Those cash rich and who still have investment or trading courage could find that the last six weeks of 2022 bring plentiful opportunity to buy in to the market at optimum prices.

New and Full Moon Forecasts for 2022

Sally Cragin

If you're reading this at night—right now—go out and see if you can see the Moon. I'll wait. It shouldn't be hard to find…

Are you back? Good. Here's a question. When you take a moment to look at the Moon, do you find you are filled with wonder and reflection? If so, you are in tune with your ancestors no matter what your cultural heritage may be.

Once you get familiar with the mechanics of these movements (more predictable than any watch!), planning activities, scheduling events, and doing tasks such as gardening and cleaning become easier.

The New Moon to First Quarter

From blackness comes a thin silver sliver. This enlarges from right to left as the earth's shadow diminishes.

Key concepts: increase, enlarge, and expand. This is the time of a "fresh start."

The First Quarter to Full Moon

The lopsided smile enlarges to become the glorious Full Moon. Some folks find this emotionally taxing, others hit their stride.

Key concepts: Increase, enlarge, invest, expand, bring to a climax, get others involved.

The Full Moon to the Last Quarter

Slowly, the shadow of the earth can be seen on the right side of the Moon, gradually diminishing our view. Projects begun at the New Moon may undergo another development.

Key concepts: Diminishing, retreating, simplifying, crystallizing.

The Last Quarter to the New Moon

Where's the Moon? For now, it's vanished, as did the smile of the Cheshire Cat in *Alice in Wonderland*. This can be a time of low energy, but it is excellent for cleaning and being frank with a loved one.

Key concepts: Relaxing, streamlining, concluding.

The Dark of the Moon

This is the day before the New Moon. Decisions made on this day, including declarations or conclusions, may be reversed on or after the New Moon. This day (or preceding days) might also bring new information to light.

The Bigger Planets and the Moon

This year, Saturn continues its journey through Aquarius, so when the Moon is in Aquarius (full, new, waxing, waning), you may feel that "someone" or "something" is limiting your capacity to dream or be fully creative. Or that discouragement comes more easily. Try to shrug this off. Those of you born 1931–1933, 1962–1964, and 1991–1993 are having a Saturn return, which brings numerous opportunities to simplify and improve your lives. (Those New Moons will help you do this.)

Jupiter moves from Pisces (January–May 10) to Aries (May 10–July 28). But Jupiter will retrograde until November 23. During that time, Jupiter moves back into Pisces (October 29–December 20). Aries and Pisces birthdays: look for opportunities for the universe to be generous to you! A longer period of good luck and opportunity will come to those born February 1998–February 2000, March 1986–March 1988, March 1974–March 1976, April 1962–April 1964, December 1950–April 1952, January 1939–May 1940, January 1927–May 1928. For you folks, the Full Moon could bring interesting new people who want to be your cheerleader.

Sunday, January 2, New Moon in Capricorn

Make those New Year resolutions today! Behavior undertaken on the New Moon (versus the "dark of the Moon") is more likely to stick. Money matters matter, and folks who enjoy complaining may seek you out, especially those of you with faces filled with trust. Spend time with folks who are much more mature than their years may suggest, because frankness counts. Capricorn: heed those urges to workaholism. (When's the last time someone told you that!) Start projects during this New Moon that unfold over the next thirty days. Libra, Cancer, Gemini, Leo, and Aries: are you nurturing a grudge? Is it getting you somewhere or getting in the way? Scorpio, Sagittarius, Aquarius, Pisces, Taurus, and Virgo: build on what you've started—you have more pieces in place than you think.

Monday, January 17, Full Moon in Cancer

The Moon is ruled by Cancer, so emotions for all (sentimentality and nostalgia) could be intoxicating. With Mercury retrograde, miscommunication comes easily. Hold your tongue—even if correcting others' misapprehensions seems like the "right move." The Wolf Moon can also bring out a fierce loyalty in us all, and if you need to "get away from it all," schedule a massage or bake some bread. Cancer rules baking, and getting out frustrations while pounding bread dough is soothing (and makes for a better loaf!). Cancer: your insights are deep, but you have got to make time for yourself during the Full Moon. Others are attracted to your charisma, which could be draining. Capricorn, Aquarius, Aries, Libra, and Sagittarius: mind your tone, as impatience or defensiveness could be perceived by others as inappropriate. Pisces, Scorpio, Gemini, Taurus, Leo, and Virgo: luxury beckons—don't spare yourself something that makes your life more comfortable.

Tuesday, February 1, New Moon in Aquarius

Remember, Saturn the planet of limitations and responsibilities is in Aquarius. This could be a time of innovation, but for some it may feel as if the walls are closing in. Planning for the far future could be a solace—do you have your garden seeds picked out? Or your summer bathing suit? Aquarius: the next thirty days give you an opportunity to take enormous chances that benefit your career. However, others may discourage you, so do ask: Who do I trust to confide in? Sagittarius, Capricorn, Pisces, Aries, Gemini, and Libra: express yourself and share your passion with others. Work on friendships with folks from a different cultural background—you'll have a lot to share with one another. Taurus, Leo, Scorpio, Virgo, and Cancer: the space cadets may want to travel on your ISS (individual space station). Be cautious about making room for them.

Wednesday, February 16, Full Moon in Leo

The Snow Moon brings merriment, laughter, and games-playing (which can be a good thing). Leo encourages socializing, as well as public relations. Think about promoting yourself, your cause,

or someone who needs your light to shine on them. An excellent time for wardrobe improvement or trying a bold new coiffure—Leo Moons can increase vanity, but if you look fabulous, who cares! Leo: if you've been grinding your gears for the past three months, this Full Moon might be the boost you need to simplify your life. Gemini, Cancer, Virgo, Libra, Sagittarius, and Aries: your communication skills are superb and don't be afraid of overstating a situation—or even exaggerating—if you need to make a point. Taurus, Aquarius, Scorpio, Pisces, and Capricorn: Do not share everything you know—more information is coming, and it could be garbled right now.

Wednesday, March 2, New Moon in Pisces

Astrologically, March comes in like a lion (a stubborn one) and goes out like a lamb (who likes to wander among the clover). This New Moon helps those who favor unconventional healing or who work among society's forgotten (poor children, the elderly, the disabled). Making or appreciating art and music is also emphasized, and if you haven't rocked out to your favorite songs, put on your dancing shoes. Pisces: you may be feeling vulnerable, but it's more likely that you've got spring fever and are looking for playmates. Go wild! Virgo, Sagittarius, Gemini, Libra, and Leo: you may feel like you're moving in slow-motion. Or—maddeningly—that others are. Easy does it is the better way. Cancer, Scorpio, Aries, Aquarius, Taurus, and Capricorn: Small steps are better than big leaps, and working on your own may be more satisfying.

Friday, March 18, Full Moon in Virgo

The Worm Moon helps us all be more organized, although with Venus, Mars, and Saturn cruising through Aquarius together, we may have ideas that are just beyond our reach. Virgo Moons are excellent for health diagnoses, spring cleaning, and holding yourself to a high standard when it comes to physical exercise (especially after a long winter). Virgo: you're a genius at untangling garbled information, and others may need you to do their work. Ask yourself how will they get better if you do the work? Push yourself and make big plans for the next month. Pisces, Aquarius, Aries, Gemini, Scorpio, and Sagittarius: irritability could bedevil you and others' inability to understand simple concepts could make your head spin. Keep it simple. Capricorn, Taurus, Cancer, Leo, and Libra: you may have useful breakthroughs regarding being efficient on small tasks.

Friday, April 1, New Moon in Aries

Edna St. Vincent Millay said it best: "April / Comes like an idiot, babbling and strewing flowers" (Millay). The New Moon on April Fool's Day could throw a monkey wrench into your organizational momentum. The key is keeping your sense of humor—while moving forward. Impulsive purchases could be a stopgap fix for feelings of emotional need; wait until next week to buy something with lasting value. Aries: you are beginning a thirty-day cycle of empowerment. If you've been unhappy with your current position, an alternative path will be more visible. Cancer, Libra,

Capricorn, Scorpio, and Virgo: impatience could bedevil you, and fussing about trifles could derail. Leo, Sagittarius, Taurus, Gemini, Pisces, and Aquarius: develop anything "new" in your life (friendships, alliances, good habits). You'll have more oomph.

Saturday, April 16, Full Moon in Libra

After the Worm Moon comes the very pretty Pink Moon. Some flowers will be up and blooming—as will relationships, since Libra rules partners and alliances. Understanding those closest to you should come easily. Emotional insights come easily but so can ambivalence. Remember: Libra is the sign of the scales, and if a side is tipped too far in one direction, the other wobbles. This is a fine time for negotiation and prioritizing. Libra: you may feel like you're "talked out," but others may need your counsel—or just your careful listening. Capricorn, Aries, Cancer, Pisces, and Taurus could strike others as "disengaged," whereas what's really going on is extreme fatigue. Leo, Virgo, Scorpio, Sagittarius, Aquarius, and Gemini: a flirtation could erupt into passion, testing your ability to be true to yourself.

Saturday, April 30, New Moon in Taurus

A phenomenal weekend for gardening or making your garden more elegant. (Gnomes? Solar-powered fountain? Bring 'em on!) However, this solar eclipse could be accompanied by some financial hiccups. Speculators are playing with fire. Taurus is about consistency, but the New Moon gives us all license to alter the rules, particularly if stagnation has been a theme. Taurus: look for enrichment on a spiritual plane, which means simplifying some area or relationship that may be more complex than you have time for. Leo, Scorpio, Aquarius, Libra, and Sagittarius: being conservative now with your spending will help you have a more enjoyable summer. Gemini, Cancer, Aries, Pisces, Capricorn, and Virgo: folks you can rely on are nearby—they're just quieter than the ones making noise.

Monday, May 16, Full Moon in Scorpio

This beautiful Flower Moon prompts a renewed appreciation of beauty. With the Moon in Scorpio there're no "punches pulled." Scorpio Moons bring out our ability to be brutally truthful—but Mercury retrograde could garble even the most concise communication. Scorpio: accept attention coming your way, particularly from those who want to learn from you. As much as you prefer the sidelines, the spotlight is finding you. Taurus, Leo, Aquarius, Aries, and Gemini: look closely at your financial situation. If you're overextended, this should become clear. Virgo, Libra, Sagittarius, Capricorn, Pisces, and Cancer: others may seem stressed and then look at you for solace—and are then unwilling to take your (hard-won) advice. Don't take this personally—Full Moon madness is contagious!

Monday, May 30, New Moon in Gemini

The second New Moon in a month is the Black Moon, which sounds more ominous than it is. New Moons provide us opportunities to get a fresh start, discard what's not working, and take tentative steps forward. Mars has moved into Aries, getting into alignment with Jupiter, and new beginnings are the story for all as Jupiter begins a new twelve-year cycle. Gemini: your intellectual curiosity will take you to some interesting places—and romance is looking for you (even if you're hiding). Prepare for infatuation, which may last as long as thirty days! Aries, Taurus, Cancer, Leo, Libra, or Aquarius: lean on your partner. Virgo, Sagittarius, Pisces, Capricorn, and Scorpio: the universe is looking for opportunities to confuse you—don't let it! Stick to "the plan."

Tuesday, June 14, Full Moon in Sagittarius

The luscious Strawberry Moon reminds us to enjoy the simple pleasures of life. Strawberries are in season now, as is asparagus, and since Sagittarius rules longer trips, make a date to walk or bike or carpool to your local farm stand to stock up on healthy food. Sagittarius rules higher education, so even if you're not graduating this season, ask yourself: What knowledge will benefit my life right now? Sagittarius: Full Moons can be exciting, useful, and unpredictable periods that remind you how creative you are. Whatever direction you're going in—double the pace. Pisces, Gemini, Virgo, Cancer, and Taurus: getting the wrong idea or "leaping before looking" could be tempting—and risky. Libra, Scorpio, Capricorn, Aquarius, Aries, and Leo: feeling "righteous" could bring enormous pleasure. Is there a way you can find a better balance in your life?

Tuesday, June 28, New Moon in Cancer

An excellent Moon for getting a massage, baking, making or purchasing ceramics, and being cozy at home. Cancer is the cardinal water sign, and this Moon could bring out everyone's desire to slip into a warm bath—or lake, brook, stream, or ocean! Home interests are emphasized—look at your domain and see it through another's eyes. Is it a welcoming place where there's a comfortable chair for all? Cancer: you may be feeling raw, but keep your feelings under wraps, because others are likely to accuse you of overreacting (though next week they'll admit you were right) What project can you begin that achieves fruition in thirty days (or six months)? Scorpio, Pisces, Taurus, Gemini, Leo, and Virgo: your abilities to nurture others are strong and bring pleasure. Libra, Capricorn, Aries, Aquarius, and Sagittarius: others may feel you're not taking them seriously or listening. Avoid conflict by adopting some anodyne acknowledgments such as "You may have a point there" and "That's something to think about."

Wednesday, July 13, Full Moon in Capricorn

The Buck Moon in finance-minded Capricorn suggests your philosophy should be "the buck stops here." Frugality will serve you well. So will bringing to a climax any project that was begun in the last month or that has had numerous steps (and setbacks).

Mars in Taurus and the Moon harmonize, which encourages practical thinking. Capricorn: your desire to climb that mountain on your own could backfire. There's a flood of folks wanting to help (which could prompt a giggle). Aries, Cancer, Libra, Leo, and Gemini: mind your p's and q's—others may think you're speaking roughly when you're being frank. Taurus, Virgo, Scorpio, Sagittarius, Aquarius, and Pisces: invest in yourselves. This can include making time to get guidance or encouragement on a business endeavor.

Thursday, July 28, New Moon in Leo
The Lion's Moon could find us all purring versus growling. If you've not taken any time out this summer, this weekend could be the time to visit a place that delighted you when you were a child. Leo can bring out the self-centered child in us all, so try and keep your sense of humor when others express a more-exalted-than-usual sense of themselves. Leo: your feelings of affection for others could defuse a tough social situation. Think about starting a project that could be completed in a month. Scorpio, Aquarius, Taurus, Capricorn, and Pisces: is someone rubbing your fur the wrong way? Overly sensitive feelings could surprise you in their forcefulness. Take five and move on. Sagittarius, Aries, Virgo, Libra, Cancer, and Gemini: your love of life is strong and brings joy. But you may have more to say to others than they want to hear.

Thursday, August 11, Full Moon in Aquarius
The Sturgeon Moon is in tune with Saturn in Aquarius, bringing us all teachers we weren't expecting to have in our particular classrooms. Your desire for freedom versus "being taught" is huge. So is your ability to come up with ideas to save the world (yes, we can still use as many of those as possible). This is a time for some to exaggerate but for others to see the future, say the truth, and astonish us. Aquarius: your curiosity is at a peak—but stay

skeptical. Others may try to convince you of an absurdity—if you're on point, you'll be giggling instead of believing. Aries, Taurus, Leo, Scorpio, Virgo, and Cancer: you could be really impatient if others change plans. Or others could feel that way about you changing plans. Gemini, Libra, Sagittarius, Capricorn, and Pisces: make opportunities to be creative in an arena you don't usually venture into (bakers, try your broiler, and quilters, try ceramics).

Saturday, August 27, New Moon in Virgo

Perfectionistic impulses take center stage! Virgo helps us be precise—which is excellent in baking and engineering—but could prove vexing in personal relationships. Fortunately, logical impulses can prevail, particularly for folks who are "slow and steady." This New Moon encourages us all to look at our personal health and the state of our career. Are you getting as much satisfaction from your work as you think you should? This Moon shines a light on those areas. Virgo: try something new, go someplace new, talk to someone new. Your soul craves renewal. Sagittarius, Pisces, Gemini, Aquarius, and Aries: others may think you're more decided on a topic than you are. Watch how you express yourself. Capricorn, Taurus, Cancer, Leo, Libra, and Scorpio: look at how you structure your leisure days. Are you putting enough "breathing space" into your activities?

Saturday, September 10, Full Moon in Pisces

The Corn Moon should find us all well-nourished from summer crops and turning our attention to spiritual matters. Pisces Moons encourage the enjoyment and production of the visual and aural arts, and the Full Moon makes us soul-hungry. Who in your life has been struggling and needs a hand? Where have you been deficient in nourishment? Pisces: look back to early March. What themes or personalities emerged then that are resolving now? Gemini, Virgo, Sagittarius, Leo, and Libra: lack of discipline is the theme for you—if your expectations are to be efficient, you may need to isolate yourself. Cancer, Scorpio, Capricorn, Aquarius, Aries, and Taurus: pursue romance at all costs! As practical as you are, your sensual side needs attention.

Sunday, September 25, New Moon in Libra

Not a time for solitude; partnerships are the focus. Are you working on a new (work or love) relationship? Give this your full attention—the New Moon encourages deepening intimacy. Marketing is also key. Those involved in sales have an excellent opportunity to look for and develop a new audience or a more efficient sales pitch. Libra: look back to April 16 and see if new projects that emerged at that time have continued to develop. If so, you're in tune with the Moon. Capricorn, Aries, Cancer, Pisces, and Taurus: you could be extravagant in the efforts to impress another. Gemini, Aquarius, Leo, Virgo, Scorpio, and Sagittarius: being indecisive may mean that you should be selecting both options, not just one.

Sunday, October 9, Full Moon in Aries

It's time for the Harvest Moon to shine a light. How did your garden grow? The twelve-sign lunar cycle begins again with this first sign of the zodiac, which emphasizes me, myself, and I. Others might see selfishness, but the wise reader will put their own needs first—once they've been identified. Aries: you could feel scattered, but only because so many want your attention. Don't let their needs get in the way of your own. Sagittarius, Aquarius, Pisces, Taurus, Gemini, and Leo: be an activist—be loud and proud about what you care about! Cancer, Libra, Capricorn, Virgo, and Scorpio: an impulsiveness could bedevil your conversation today—think twice before you speak.

Tuesday, October 25, New Moon in Scorpio

Scorpio Moons are the Moons of sensuality, indulgence, and financial shenanigans. They can also help stir up drama. People who are generally straightforward may seem to have a "side-eye" shiftiness, but this temporary development just means you need to put more skill into reading communication, particularly with your partner. Folks may seem less firm or decided than they are, and hearing a section of the story will be a common experience. Scorpio: between now and next May, you have the opportunity to take a chance in your career that may (to others) seem like you're being a risk-taker. Which is why you should move forward. Virgo, Libra, Sagittarius, Capricorn, Pisces, and Cancer: don't believe everything you hear; this New Moon is urging you to dig deeper—diplomatically, that is. Aquarius, Taurus, Leo, Gemini, and Aries: it will be difficult to stay firm, especially if you feel backed into a corner. The question is, does that corner have a hidden exit?

Tuesday, November 8, Full Moon in Taurus

Widely known as the Hunter's Moon, this lunation will find few of us with a blunderbuss in the woods stalking our cutlets in the raw. However, Taurus is all about "having," so shopaholism could distract you. Taurus: look back to the week of April 30. What projects or personalities have become more significant? If these are in your estimation successful, keep moving forward. But if not, this week is excellent to cut the cord. Libra, Scorpio, Sagittarius, Leo, and Aquarius: "it's okay to be stubborn" could be a theme. If you folks are resisting change, you're in tune with the Moon. Virgo, Capricorn, Pisces, Aries, Gemini, and Cancer: your love for beauty and for sharing lovely experiences could bring you closer to a loved one.

Wednesday, November 23, New Moon in Sagittarius

Adventure and the sign of the archer go together beautifully, and this lunation is excellent for travel during this holiday weekend. Reassessing an educational plan or direction is also smart—and your true feelings about what you've been studying should emerge. Sagittarius Moons also favor humor, so stick to those who tread lightly through life (which may mean rearranging the

seating on Turkey Day). Sagittarius: look back at your calendar to the summer solstice. What have you stopped, discarded, moved on from? And what do you wish you had left behind? Pisces, Gemini, Virgo, Taurus, and Cancer: it will be too easy to put out a foot wrong or bump into things—literally or figuratively—right now. Tread carefully. Aries, Leo, Libra, Scorpio, Capricorn, and Aquarius: you may be called in as a third party to help people figure out what's really going on. Not your most comfortable spot—but your instincts are spot-on.

Wednesday, December 7, Full Moon in Gemini

Chatty Gemini energy is at its peak during this Beaver Moon. This is enjoyable, but don't overlook the solemnity of Pearl Harbor Day—and the honor we need to pay our servicemen and service-women. This Moon favors partnership but alliances that are not meant to last for long. Gemini: reflect on the long-term projects you embarked on around the end of May or start of June. They should be getting more complex, and if you need assistance, now is the time to ask. Virgo, Sagittarius, Pisces, Scorpio, and Capricorn: if you feel rushed or are moving more quickly than you like, you're in tune with the Moon. But you should still say "Can we slow down please?" Libra, Aquarius, Aries, Taurus, Cancer, and Leo: others may be looking at you and wanting more intimacy than you have to share right now. Do not feel guilty about this!

Friday, December 23, New Moon in Capricorn

Our final New Moon of the year is in practical, businesslike, "plan ahead" Capricorn, so if you're tempted to put a build-it-yourself toy under the tree, the Moon is smiling at you. Capricorn Moons are excellent for adjusting finances and really "seeing" what's wrong with a structure or preexisting formula. Capricorn: did some event occur during the second week of July that sent you in another direction? This New Moon can help you adjust your trajectory. Aries, Cancer, Libra, Leo, and Gemini: slow your pace. There is another time for all your plans, and remember there are twelve days of Christmas, not just one. Taurus, Virgo, Scorpio, Sagittarius, Aquarius, and Pisces: you may need to work hard to make others feel more comfortable—but this may not be apparent to you right away. Look for the wallflowers and give them a little love.

Reference

Millay, Edna St. Vincent. "Spring." Poetry Foundation. Accessed October 1, 2020. https://www.poetryfoundation.org/poems/44728/spring-56d223f01f86e.

2022
Moon Sign Book
Articles

How Your Moon Helps You Cope With Challenging Times

Alice DeVille

At various life intervals, you sit up and take notice. A full load of lemons lands in your lap, and you're not sure you can make drinkable lemonade. Shock, awe, and confusion. That's what's left. Ignoring it will only prolong the discomfort or escalate the problem. Challenges may appear in the form of accidents, bankruptcy, broken engagements or divorce, conflicts in business and personal relationships, death of loved ones or close friends, financial difficulties, diverse fraud scenarios, gossip that ruins credibility, homelessness due to lack of assets or damage from natural disasters, illness, loss of employment, mental pressure, psychological outlook, and the ravages of war and military conflicts.

For example, COVID-19 has been a serious problem for the last few years and is still affecting those in 2022 who may only now be returning to work or healing financial shortages. Another societal long-term challenge has been dealing with the September 11 attacks, a day that changed so many lives when terrorists struck the World Trade Center in New York, killing several thousand people in New York City, Arlington, Virginia, and Shanksville, Pennsylvania. Going forward, the horrific attack on the US Capitol on January 6, 2021, that was instigated by the sitting president and carried out by home-grown terrorists, seditionists, and white supremacist groups intending to overturn the outcome of the election was and will continue to be another challenge.

More singular examples include when an individual loses a parent, an experience that leaves a lasting void in their hearts, when a child is struck with a serious illness and does not survive after treatment, a bride is unexpectedly left at the altar on her wedding day, or the bride-to-be tells the groom a few days before the wedding that she cannot marry him. Financial issues such as identity theft may cause the victim to endure several painful years of sorting out details and charges and tracking down fake accounts. More of this theft occurs when people become desperate due to lack of funds, unemployment, or health issues.

The Moon and Your Coping Mechanisms

Did you know your natal Moon offers clues about how to cope with unexpected stressful conditions and execute a plan to address their onset? The Moon elicits an instinctive response aligned with the sign of your natal moon and guides the approach you are likely to use in assessing emerging situations. It supports the rapport you have with others whose help is necessary to get the job done. Your Moon personalizes other planets it comes into contact with when searching for relief.

Expressing Personal Lunar Solutions

Prepare yourself for learning more about the tools you have at your disposal. Locate the sign of your natal Moon and the house where it appears in your astrology chart. The passages below help you identify a winning approach to your coping aptitude.

Aries Moon: One of the most action-oriented signs, you pride yourself on quick reaction time whenever upsetting conditions jolt life's serenity. Decisiveness is a winning asset you wear proudly and use when necessity calls. You thrive on risk-taking by demonstrating your strong instinct to respond to the emotional fallout that occurs. In a military setting, you race to the scene to implement a strategic plan for restoring order to drastic, dangerous conditions that could instigate war. Most of you enjoy navigating, so it is important to develop excellent driving skills as well as the knowledge of life-saving and rescue practices. Certification in first aid techniques that include CPR is a must. If you haven't added these qualifications, they are available in most communities through groups such as the Red Cross with options to attend classes online or in person.

Taurus Moon: As the owner of this powerful Moon sign, you crave security in both your material and emotional world. A threat to either leads to quick defensive behavior to protect your turf and your loved ones from unwanted hardships, including financial shortfalls, home invasion, theft, illness, or injury. Ordinarily a person who follows a conventional path, you're a model of determination who does a 180 when you see how problems at your hearth and home upset much-desired equilibrium. Your gifts are common sense, tact, and speaking up to challenge perpetrators of erratic actions. You're not afraid to confront a troublemaker to demand they stand down. Another asset is your expertise in balancing the budget and keeping an eye on expenses affiliated with unanticipated purchases targeted for remedial action.

Gemini Moon: Whether it's a quick quip or a detailed written response to a trying set of circumstances, you know how to drive home a point and negotiate the best outcome for your dilemma. Nervous energy works to your advantage when the situation calls for multitasking. Communication blends with your rapid emotional thought processes when you respond to the issue and argue with the rational side of your brain. Your analytical mind is a huge asset in settling conflicts in sync with your outstanding verbal skills and instincts for getting to the heart of the matter.

Cancer Moon: Very few can best your emotional and intuitive style, which helps you decide whom to trust and include in your intimate circle as well as how to tackle emerging problems. Memories from past experiences with family dynamics guide your approach to soothing harsh conditions, providing stability to those in need of a hug or safety from threatening confrontations. Cancer Moons have the nurturing vibe to find ways to feed the hungry, find shelter for the homeless, or start a fundraiser to assist victims of pandemics or other natural disasters, including those who survive fires and floods.

Leo Moon: No better situation exists than for you to put your leadership skills to the test when unplanned circumstances invade your life. Your package comes equipped with happy enthusiasm, creative license to explore options, and spontaneity to ignite the spark of action in those you recruit for the counterattack on disaster. Confidence ranks high in your world even if you have inner doubts. You draw on your cache of exuberance to respond to emergencies and coach others to find their passion and bring out their inner power as they express strength and empathy for trying conditions.

Virgo Moon: "Outstanding" is the best word to describe your organizational acumen. Once you see the big picture, you're off and running to develop a plan that covers all important facets of the problem, including files and a shared portal to enhance accessibility

to key information. Your instincts for providing order may lead you to create policies and procedures that guide users in relevant manuals. Service-oriented work attracts you and makes use of your fundamental approach to caregiving in diverse fields such as catering, education, elder care, equipment management, fitness, medicine, nutrition, and pets. You're a natural supporter of blood, charitable, clothing, and food drives, where you often have a key role.

Libra Moon: If ever there were a Moon sign that signified a model peacemaker, it is the gracious person who is born under a Libra Moon. Your qualities give you natural empathy and the ability to understand the problems of those who come to you for advice and counsel. You excel as a mediator since you are always looking for ways to reach a compromise and promote a winning environment. With your diplomatic style of delivering a message, you elicit harmony under turbulent conditions. Adherence to laws is important to you as you skillfully navigate vague references in search of verifiable facts that help you address emerging challenges. You take a fair and balanced approach in giving involved parties a chance to present their side of an argument and refuse to be rushed into making a decision without adequate situational analysis. Equal access to shared information drives your action-oriented Moon toward settling a crisis peacefully.

Scorpio Moon: Sometimes people think you are looking for a fight when you recognize a challenge has exploded in your life. If they only knew how intuitive you are and how quickly you understand the situation. Maybe you don't disclose everything that is on your mind, but your deep psyche doesn't miss a trick. Yes, you can be confrontational when you see behavior problems, laziness, or apathy while others are suffering, the house is burning, and the need for action is fully apparent. You cope with dilemmas by asking questions first and then reaching into your bag of solutions to grab the one that fits current reality. You research new situations, investigate mysteries, solve crimes, get the truth out of fabricators, and elicit an emotional response from a poker-faced stoic who is sticking with a story that is self-destructing. Put your exceptional emotional resources to the test and end the drama.

Sagittarius Moon: Enthusiasm is your middle name and aids you in responding to challenging circumstances with a positive, optimistic light. You exude natural diplomacy when you mediate stressful conditions that require you to stretch your intellect in a quest for options that lead to winning solutions. Throw a little adventure into the mix that includes travel and you stabilize your Sagittarian restlessness while suppressing any worry gene that has you on edge. Those of you with natural writing ability will publish articles, write books, and explore appropriate public relations opportunities. Your gift is not that you know everything about a given subject but that you know how to coordinate and present details effectively.

Capricorn Moon: A government career was tailor-made for you with your flair for ambition, strategic goals, and desire to lead. Service-oriented assignments suit you best. Timing is everything in how you might fill vacant positions that call for experts who have a handle on critical agency needs. You wrote the book on responsibility and are only too happy to take charge of a project to make sure plans are carried out efficiently and effectively. You'll put common sense to work for you in analyzing emerging conditions and take well-calculated risks when you're satisfied with the scope of the mission. Overseeing a pandemic is right up your alley as you develop critical steps along the way that call for long-range planning and target meaningful objectives. Although some may find you aloof, you have a sharp sense of humor that breaks the ice under stressful circumstances that pop up intermittently in your life.

Aquarius Moon: Leave it to the gregarious Aquarius Moon to have the inside track on how to guide humanity through a crisis. First, let your contacts know that your frosty exterior hides a kinder heart that hears the call of distress when sudden events upset the status quo. People need people and you are just the one to drive home this message when you quickly take the lead, hold urgent meetings, set up special task forces to inform key players, schedule rallies, and initiate the aid of organizations like the Red Cross and Centers for Disease Control and Prevention (CDC) when masses of people face health and safety crises. Your knowledge of systems technology also makes you a sought-after talent in positions that call for expertise in cybersecurity. In a flash, bright ideas and solutions come to you. Your inventive mind lays out the plan, allowing those involved to welcome a true change agent to the team.

Pisces Moon: Your Moon, with its desire to heal the pain and fallout from unplanned challenges and setbacks, steps into

the arena to help those in need with a new formula for navigating the workplace. In recent years, the entire work dynamic has undergone a major shift. The gift you own is your uncanny ability to sense the emotional fallout from sudden change that makes regrouping and quick implementation of new processes a necessity. You take the lead in developing the formula for successful telecommuting via interpreting the emotional responsiveness from your clients, cooperators, colleagues, patients, and stakeholders. Working behind the scenes, you teach others how to accomplish the workload remotely without letting distractions get in the way. Your highly emotional Pisces Moon leads the charge in rehabilitating practices that are out of touch with realistic public needs and changes the landscape of the work world in the years ahead.

Moon Stones

Elizabeth Barrette

The Moon is one of the strongest astrological influences and touches on everything from gardening to psychology. Its waxing and waning cycle encourages things to grow or shrink, become more or less active. It sets up opportunities, harvests, and resting times.

Stones are part of the planet earth, but not all of them also correspond to earth as a heavenly body. Some stones relate to the Moon instead, often also matching to water, air, or both. You can empower an astrological reading, a feng shui layout, a garden schedule, etc., by "stacking" together multiple items with the same correspondence. You could also assemble a set of items that represent the heavenly bodies, the elements, or another group of concepts.

Stones Associated with the Moon

Moon stones tend to be pale and glossy, but some of them are dark. Colors include clear, white, yellow, blue, gray, and black. Many have special effects dealing with light. They may have chatoyancy, a striated reflective quality seen in cat's eye. Fluorescent stones glow under ultraviolet light, like fluorite. Iridescence makes rainbow effects as light passes through layers, for example in pearl or mother-of-pearl. Labradorescence shows a flash of blue and gold light, as seen in labradorite. Opalescence combines shiny, milky, and hazy qualities in a translucent matrix like moonstone. Schiller is a play of color inside a stone, such as white opal. Some people count glass, especially if it is imbued with opalescence or molded into a lunar shape. Gems that come from the sea, such as coral, are considered Moon stones. So are ones that resemble water, like aquamarine. Those beloved of Moon deities also count as Moon stones for many mystical purposes.

Cat's eye: While various stones are called cat's eye, such as cat's eye moonstone, the original version is a form of chrysoberyl. It comes in many colors, but the most popular for lunar use are blue, yellow, or gray. When cut in cabochon, this chatoyant stone shows a bright line down the middle.

Coral: This is the polished skeleton of colonial sea creatures, and as such, should be taken only from sustainable sources. Coral strengthens the connection between the oceans and the Moon, particularly white coral. Through the sea, it also links to blood, especially red coral. This stone makes splendid cameos, and any one of a woman's face can stand for a Moon goddess.

Fluorite: This banded stone comes in many colors, often shades of green, blue, and purple. It fluoresces under ultraviolet light. It is soft enough to carve easily, so it comes in diverse shapes.

Glass: This is a crystalline material made from silica sand melted with other materials. Most glass used in jewelry is manufactured, enjoyed for its shape and brilliant colors. However, natural glass appears as obsidian and a few other things. Black, gray, and red are most often used.

Labradorite: Its distinctive gray with flashes of vivid blue and gold gave rise to the term "labradorescence." This evokes the changing nature of the Moon, ideal for transformative work. When held, it raises consciousness during meditation, making a sphere a nice choice. Labradorite jewelry enhances intuition and psychic powers.

Obsidian: This black volcanic glass symbolizes fire and darkness. An obsidian sphere stands for the dark Moon. The stone takes a high polish, so it can also be used to make a round mirror.

Opal: Although more associated with fire than water, opal is a diverse stone. Some opals have few or no sparks, just a milky white face; and there are translucent bluish ones that have broad opalescence rather than pinpoint schiller. Opal relates to all elements and planets, but individual opals tend to correspond based on their features. So bluish or white opals relate to the Moon. They are good for drawing money, luck, or power in the waxing phase. Very rare, but very powerful, is opalized seashell, it combines the power of the sea with the moon and the opal itself and the hidden history of mother-of-pearl. Use it for potent transformation.

Pearl and mother-of-pearl: These are two forms of the same thing: nacre. A pearl consists of layers of nacre wrapped around a grain of sand or other irritant. The white sphere of a saltwater pearl is a perfect representation of the full moon. Freshwater ones sometimes form crescents. Mother-of-pearl covers the inside of a shell with nacre. It excels at making home a safe and comfortable place.

Quartz: This stone comes in many forms and colors. Clear, white, gray, and pale pink are most often used for the Moon. Clear and white quartz are among the most popular for spheres or half spheres. Rose quartz can stand for the Strawberry Moon. Smoky quartz is a good choice for the dark phase and has grounding qualities. Girasol quartz looks much like moonstone due to its milky opalescence. It promotes calm and self-healing. Another popular carving stone, quartz is among the easiest to find as little animals. Look for lunar ones such as cats, dogs, rabbits, or horses.

Selenite: Typically white or pale blue, this stone boasts spectacular chatoyancy. Due to its affordable price, it is often carved into big spheres (which stand for the Moon) or obelisks. I have a gorgeous piece done as a unicorn horn. Long natural crystals make fine wands if you don't mind the rough, fibrous texture; or you can get a round polished one. Selenite wands excel at directing energy. The stone in general works for cleansing and purification, and it's popular in energy work.

Lunar Jewelry

Among the easiest ways to combine the Moon with stone work is through lunar jewelry. The Moon is enormously popular as an image in jewelry. It most often appears either in the full or crescent phase. Others such as gibbous rarely appear but can be commissioned. Sometimes a face is carved into the stone. In Western tradition, this is typically the man in the moon. In Pagan lore, it can be any of the lunar goddesses. In Japan, the Moon is a rabbit. Because rabbits and hares have other associations with the Moon in many cultures, this imagery is relatively easy to find. Full-body goddess pendants are also common.

Lunar jewelry is almost always made from silver and stones of the Moon. Other metals are used very rarely, but occasionally you will see multicolored effects of several metals, or another "white" metal such as platinum or white gold. Worthy of consideration is niobium, which is more common on the Moon than on Earth and has mythic associations with water. This hypoallergenic metal can be anodized into any color or a rainbow effect, and many jewelry findings (earring hooks, jump rings, etc.) are readily available. Some stones, especially pearls, are often strung as bracelets or necklaces by themselves.

Stones and other materials can be carved or pressed into round cabochons, crescents, or Moon faces. Ivory used to be a favorite for carving but is no longer sustainable; a plant-based replacement, the tagua nut, works beautifully in jewelry. One of my favorite necklaces has a tagua crescent face on a silver background of stars and tiny gems. Glass is another favorite because it is so easy to mold and color, and it's cheaper than most stones.

Lunar jewelry is used for a variety of purposes. It can show devotion to a lunar deity. It can signal your interest in astrology to other people. It carries a little piece of Moon energy with you. It may embody a positive affirmation, a mantra, or a psychological goal. It can even stand for the Moon card in tarot. Use it for whatever lunar things you wish.

Uses of Moon and Stone

Charging stones can make them more useful for astrology, feng shui, or tarot. The Moon contributes energy and versatility. The stone contributes containment and stability. Together, they accomplish more than either could alone.

Stones may be charged by leaving them in moonlight. A single night is enough for many types of use. However, leaving the stone out for all the nights of a phase will attune to that phase in particular, allowing the stone to be used in place of the Moon when that phase is unavailable. Leaving the stone out for a full lunar month attunes it to the cyclic nature of the Moon. You can then call on any phase, or on the power of change itself. It is important to cover the stone during the day to minimize exposure to sunlight. This is especially useful in feng shui if you are using a stone to increase something auspicious or decrease something inauspicious, or in astrology to capture an uncommon occurrence such as an eclipse.

The shape of a stone also influences its symbolism. A round stone will best represent the full (if white) or dark (if black) phase. A round stone with a face customarily means full. A crescent may be reversible if it has neither a face nor a directional setting, but most crescents show either the waxing or the waning phase. Spheres can represent the full phase or the Moon in general.

Moon stones make an important part of the heavenly bodies sets sometimes used in astrology. A sphere of some relatively durable stone, such as milky quartz, makes an excellent focus in a Moon garden. You can also use a crystal. Large, dark stones such as basalt absorb heat. These provide basking places for wildlife and can keep a birdbath in liquid form longer as the weather cools. Make a whole garden from Moon stones and it will hold enough heat that you may succeed in growing plants from a warmer climate. If you have a fountain, it may be filled with pebbles of different types.

Moon Stones in Feng Shui

Many lunar stones work well in feng shui. Good choices include black obsidian for the dark Moon, clear quartz for the full Moon, and Moonstone in general. Their placement in your feng shui layout influences what effect they have.

Black obsidian combines the feng shui elements of fire, earth, and water. Its dark color allows it to trap negative energy, making it an ideal cure for anything that directs a bad flow of qi into your home, such as a straight road pointed at your door. This stone also strengthens the north bagua area, which supports your career and life path.

Clear quartz has various applications. First, a cluster of quartz crystals represents a happy family and thus lends itself to a harmonious home when placed in a common area. A single quartz crystal clears any bagua area where it is placed. You can move it from one to another depending on where you feel a need for extra help.

Moonstone activates the feminine yin energy. Placing it near the bed encourages receptivity and intuition. In the health area at the center of the home, it brings balance and reduces stress. At the office, it promotes creativity in the career.

Conclusion

Working with the Moon can enhance your understanding of cycles in general and astrology in particular. You discover how to work with the natural flow of energy, not against it. However, the cycles may not always match up with what you need in the moment. For those times, a knowledge of stone lore makes it possible to tweak the energy so it does what you need—a bit like rerouting water from a river to irrigate a field when the weather doesn't provide the right rainfall. Stones also help you focus on different aspects of the Moon. Keeping a good selection of lunar stones will widen what you can accomplish.

Self-Care and the Moon

Amy Herring

I sit down on the comfortable couch and reach for my favorite pillow, the one with the star pattern all over it. My therapist closes the door and sits down across from me, smiling brightly. We exchange pleasantries as we get settled. I lean back and cross my legs, bracing myself slightly in anticipation of her next question: "How have you been doing on your self-care this week?"

I roll my eyes and sigh, although I've gotten better at doing that solely on the inside now as our sessions continue. "Self-care" is one of those phrases that immediately evokes images of pedicures or bubble baths in me—something people do in commercials for body wash or chocolate. It sounds too self-indulgent, especially on a daily or weekly basis. But I remind myself that self-care is not self-indulgence or pampering (not that there's anything wrong with those things!). Self-care means doing things that sustain our mental, emotional, spiritual, or physical health. It involves giving yourself what you need, just as your parent or primary nurturer did for you when you were too young to do so yourself. Just because we are grown doesn't mean we no longer need to be cared for, but that we are more capable of caring for ourselves than we were at the beginning of life.

However, we aren't always as kind and attentive to ourselves as our caregivers hopefully were. Much of what we are taught when we were young is intended to instruct us on how to care for ourselves when we are grown, but sometimes we skimp on even the basics. It's sometimes easier to go about our days reacting and responding to the requests and needs of others, whether they are coworkers, friends, significant others, children, parents, or all of the above. We can find ourselves last on the list by default, until we've met all of our other obligations and can use the time that is magically left over to tend to all our own needs. (This happens all the time, right? It's normal to forget to eat while you're feeding everyone else, right? Oh, dear). Emotional breakdowns or burnouts can happen if we do this for too long, and the inner child, the one we're afraid is just a petulant, whining toddler becomes just that, throwing the tantrum needed to get our attention.

Moon and Mothering

When it comes to self-care, the natal moon has the lion's share of the market. The moon represents our inner child, the part of us that is still vulnerable and still in need of protection and care. More importantly, the moon's position in one's natal chart will show the kind of nurture (beyond the human basics) that will feel the most comforting, what we most hunger for, and how we respond when we're running low on that comfort. The moon is both mother and child, our instinct to nurture as well as our need to be nurtured.

Astrologers have traditionally looked to the moon in a person's natal chart to understand their mother. In psychological and archetypal traditions, the moon does not necessarily represent the personality or condition of our literal mother but is an archetype for the nurturing instinct, including both the need to give and receive nurturing. The archetype of mother embodies not the individual personality of any one mother, but the universal concept of mother: one who gives birth, nurtures, protects. We all have the mother archetype within us, no matter our sex, gender, age, or whether we give birth to literal or metaphorical children. Any time we create, nurture, or give comfort, we are drawing on the mother archetype within.

Among the wealth of lunar wisdom we can glean from the moon, we can look to the symbolism of our moon's placement in our natal chart to know how to mother ourselves. "Mom" not only knows what's best for us and encourages us to do what is right for ourselves, but she also knows how to pamper when you need a little comfort to get yourself right again.

Your Moon Sign

We all need shelter and safety, healthy food, enough rest, downtime, and playtime, but beyond the human needs that we all share, your moon sign can shine a light on how you can give yourself the specific types of comfort and care you need.

Aries

You naturally tend to acquire a buildup of emotional energy, and finding enjoyable ways to utilize and release that energy is a path to self-care for you. Getting your body moving is a direct way to do so, whether in targeted pursuits like organized sports or exercise, casual fun like a day at the beach, or everyday activities like cleaning or yardwork. Not only is physical activity an important way to take care of one's health for anyone, but for you it is also a way of clearing the emotional decks—like the air after a storm. This can be especially true when stress or frustration is particularly winding you up.

Making time to express yourself in this way also means it is less likely to find a suboptimal route of release, like a misdirected outburst of anger or impulsiveness. Directing that tense energy elsewhere may be all that is needed if it's just about blowing off steam to release tension and lift your spirits. However, also important to self-care is the expression of purposeful anger too. Sometimes you have to fight for what you need and what you deserve, which is a profound act of self-care.

Taurus

Take care of yourself by giving yourself permission to go at your own pace. This may sometimes mean deadlines get pushed back or that you don't get to everything you'd planned on doing, but being forced to rush is a direct path to Grumpytown. The more you feel pushed to rush, the more you will instinctively counter it through resistance, even if it's you trying to push yourself.

Take care of your heart in a very tactile way—through the sensory experience of life. Pleasurable physical experiences can certainly bring us comfort and elevate our mood (eating our favorite food, for example), but beyond that, a Taurus moon needs to feel security through stability and groundedness, which comes most readily through the body.

Gemini

You have a big appetite for information, whether it's news headlines, word games, or interesting conversation. You may not be inclined to turn any information away because curiosity is a strong instinct, but practice self-care by recognizing the point at which information ingestion becomes overwhelming noise. Brain candy without substance can leave you feeling distracted and empty rather than full and satisfied. This can be especially true if

the topics stir you emotionally because you may not realize their impact on you, just like someone may eat too quickly and keep going before they realize they are already full. You can process more information than most, but when overload does hit you, you can spin yourself up with nervous energy or endless what-ifs until you feel like you don't know anything. Talking to a friend or writing it out can be ways to clear and reset when this happens.

Comfort comes from feeding your brain your favorite casual and entertaining fare. You may also enjoy hobbies that involve working with your hands, building or crafting something like one would put together a puzzle. This is also a great way to reset after information overload: to keep your hands busy and your attention focused while your brain works things out in the background.

Cancer

Hygge is a Danish word that most easily translates to a feeling of coziness—physical and emotional, and it's a word that speaks to the heart of a Cancer moon. Cozying up with favorite people, animals, or things that you love in a safe and protected environment is a comfort to embrace often.

Self-care for you can sometimes seem paradoxical, for it is nurturing to you when you nurture others. When you are able to give of yourself and provide a measure of comfort and nourishment to those you love, be it plant, animal, or human, you get strong returns as well. Being able to give that love and care is something that feeds your heart, but the trick lies in giving from a full heart, not from a depleted one. If you feel neglected, uncared for, or just drained, especially by others but even yourself, giving to others is simply more draining and can cause resentment and emotional shutdown. In those instances, acts of self-care may involve allowing yourself to be cared for by others. This requires the courage to reveal your own needs in a way that makes you feel vulnerable or exposed but is exactly what is needed to cue those you love that you need their love and care too.

Leo

Leo has become the poster child for social extroversion, and while hanging out and having fun with others is a good way to stimulate the inherent playfulness in you, there's another side to you—a side that doesn't necessarily want to play with anyone sometimes. Whether you are an introvert or extrovert is not the point—being social involves a lot of compromise and niceties and show. Sometimes self-care for you is simply closing the door on the world's demands and going off-stage to your own castle, where you can do and be as you please without having to put on your Sunday best. This is also where you can do your best creative work because no one is putting you on the spot. When you need comfort, indulge your inner cat: have things how you like them, let your playful side out when you feel like it, and lounge around like the royalty you are!

Virgo

Worry and anxiety tend to crop up for you when you fear something bad is on its way that you can't (but must!) mitigate or control. Self-care may involve summoning the will and determination to let go of what you can't control and to stop yourself from ruminating on it. A comforting exercise can be putting something small and simple in order that you can control, which helps narrow your focus to something manageable. A small task checked off or some time with a craft or project that you can see tangible progress on can allow you to let go of the breath you find yourself all too frequently holding.

Ironically for Virgo, working is relaxing, especially simple manual tasks. Crossing something off of a to-do list can provide comfort for Virgo, even if it would be classified as work rather than leisure. Virgo doesn't feel comfortable just lounging or sitting idle. Yet, the mindset you employ while working can make or break it in the comfort and self-care category. If work is done in a manic rush to get as much done in as little time as possible or in an attempt to get ahead in some imaginary race, it will wind a Virgo moon up instead of provide calm.

Libra

Being Venus-ruled, you are sensitive to the beauty and peacefulness of your surroundings (or the lack thereof). Spending time in places you find beautiful goes a long way to emotional restoration and equilibrium and goes even further if that place is in your home or somewhere you can feel at home.

You are naturally equipped to detect and manage the tension between opposites or conflicting viewpoints, but it wears on you and can emotionally exhaust you. You cannot please everyone, and you know that, but instinctively you tend to try to keep the peace and sometimes that leads to increased or prolonged tension, not resolution. Care for yourself by avoiding unnecessary tension when you can but summoning the courage to gently and fairly advocate for yourself when the only way out of conflict is through it.

Scorpio

Being the sign of the phoenix, self-care for you often involves catharsis of some kind. Rather than dealing with difficult emotions with distractions or warm fuzzies, you long to go through the other side of the storm, to purge and transform whatever feels stuck or heavy. That often means going further into the discomfort or upset you are feeling and really digging into it, allowing yourself to fully feel it so you can let it go and swim back up to the top.

Pro self-care tip: Be careful about what actual actions you take when you're down at the bottom of that emotional well. Acting from this extreme emotional place can make it more likely to bring about consequences you regret and give you more, not less, to lament. Stabilize a bit before you decide to take any actions as a result of your underworld journey, lest your volcanic emotional state burn your life up or everyone around you.

Sagittarius

You are famous for being naturally buoyant and optimistic, but even you get the blues. Your kind of comfort is expansive, not contractive. When you need to comfort yourself or lift your spirits, you usually need to go out rather than stay in, whether away to the mountains or out on the town, and seek out the new rather than the familiar.

What is comforting to you is that things change. There is a great deal to life that is repetitive and monotonous and that's not your jam. You need perspective and wide-open spaces, figuratively and literally. When you need an emotional reset, distracting yourself by getting out of town can do the trick. Of course, if you're escaping troubles, they'll be waiting for you when you get back. Use this shift in perspective to return with a fresh outlook rather than only an escape, or you'll only be right back where you started—literally!

Capricorn

You have it in you to be a classic workaholic (in life as well as on the job) because you enjoy setting your sights high and achieving those aims. You are also driven to see things through to their conclusion and hate leaving things incomplete. You can stay the course for a long time to achieve a goal or fulfill a commitment, so much so that you are vulnerable to delaying your emotional (and sometimes physical) needs until the job is done or at least until you're "at a good stopping place" (nine hours later!).

This instinct can have you not only working too hard and too long on your own project but others' as well, handling and organizing things you have no need to be involved with except that you are very good at it. Your stamina is such that you can do this for a long time, unfortunately sometimes long enough for it to become a new norm of constant overload. If this happens, you can only get relief by taking some things off your plate, which may prompt a new emotional dilemma: a sense of failure or shirking of duty, two things you dislike very much. The bottom line is, if you don't want to be the one doing everything all the time, you'll simply have to stop doing everything all the time. Take care of yourself by learning how to regularly allow others to handle things, whether it's through delegation or taking a vacation. Work is always there, but you are not a robot. The list of the "urgent and necessary" is never-ending, but your stamina, while immense, is not.

Damage control and overwork are not only problematic, but they often take you off course, drawing you into crises at the expense of allowing you the time and focus to see the larger picture and plan your direction. Solitude can allow you to replenish your stamina and regain your focus, which helps you feel in control, and all of these things provide comfort and allow you to get yourself right again.

Aquarius

An Aquarius Moon once said to me something like "I would hate to think that someone could know everything about me." When asked why, she explained that she is made up of many selves and if someone were to know them all, they might too easily form expectations of her that she wouldn't want to be obligated to meet. An Aquarius Moon needs freedom to be its truest, albeit changeable, self.

Self-care for you involves self-validation first and foremost, even when you are pressured to conform (sometimes in the best-intentioned and innocent ways). Holding your ground can make you seem inflexible and uncompromising, and while it's true that you may want to avoid unnecessary stubbornness, those you are closest to must understand your need to be true to yourself and that to assert the freedom to do so is a fundamental and profound need, not a childish whim.

Time spent alone, especially when you're feeling down, can be a comfort and allow you to sort yourself out freely without worrying about how you are impacting others or whether they'll understand while you're working through things.

Pisces

Pisces is often warned against too much escapism, but the difference between a necessary retreat, which rejuvenates and restores a peaceful spirit, and escapism that leads to ignoring reality to a destructive degree, is significant. Too much banality drains you of nourishment and saps your spirit. Practice self-care by retreating before it has to become an escape and let go of any guilt or comparison to others about how you should be or what you should be giving to others. This doesn't always mean solitude (although it certainly can) but can also be removing yourself from situations when you are overloaded or being too damaged.

When you need comfort or an emotional lift, you need time and space to play. Playfulness is a natural part of your emotional expression, and when the playfulness has gone out of you, it's time to administer the healing salve of imagination. You may have any number of enjoyable hobbies, but the ones that are closest to your heart will have some kind of ability to enchant you, not just entertain you. The hobbies that inspire you most tend to have some otherworldly or fantastical nature that can take you beyond the reality of this world and into an imagined one.

Plant Your Own Shaker Garden

Michelle Perrin, Astrology Detective

From their founding in the mid-seventeen hundreds, the Shakers practiced organic farm-to-table eating, matriarchal leadership, minimalist design, dedicated gardening, and constant innovation, all while living in decluttered environments that would put Marie Kondo to shame. They were also some of the most respected farmers, seed growers, and herbalists in nineteenth-century America, with a reputation for honesty and quality that extended as far as Europe and Australia.

Origins and Background

While most people believe the Shakers to be a slice of homegrown Americana, the movement actually had its origins in eighteenth-century Manchester, England, as an offshoot of the Quakers. One of the earliest and most ardent followers of Shakerism was Ann

Lee, who was eventually arrested for her zealous beliefs. During her subsequent imprisonment, she received a visit from God that she claimed was the Second Coming of Christ, ushering in a period of one thousand years of earthly paradise as predicted in the Book of Revelation. Unlike the traditional church with its Holy Trinity of God the Father, Jesus Christ the Son, and the Holy Spirit, the Shakers believed in a dual God force, where the divine spirit was embodied in one man and one woman: Jesus Christ and Ann Lee. Therefore, the Shakers believed in the total equality of men and women, which was quite revolutionary for the time. Facing continued persecution, Ann Lee gathered a small group of followers and immigrated to the New World.

Shaker Tenets and Belief System

In his seminal 1893 book *A Concise History of the United Society of Believers Called Shakers*, Shaker Elder Charles Edson Robinson set out the core beliefs and values of the faith. The nine tenets included "Honesty and integrity of purpose in all words and transactions," "Absolute freedom from debt, owing no man anything but love and goodwill," and "Purity in mind and body—a virgin life" (Robinson 1893, 32). Unlike the staid Quakers, Shaker gatherings were characterized by ecstatic, free-spirited dancing, which is how they got their name, as they were called "Shaking Quakers" by the general public.

The Shakers were defined by a profoundly American spirit. They possessed an entrepreneurial outlook and business acumen that are rarely found in spiritual communities. While the Shakers lived apart from "the World," they interacted with it for commerce and trade. They were also early adopters of innovation and technology, as they felt these advances made it easier to focus on God's work. They invented a huge array of ingenious labor-saving devices for the home and farm, including a washing machine, double-wide rolling pin for making pies, and the mechanical apple parer and corer. Today, they are perhaps best remembered for their remarkably beautiful furniture and architecture, whose clean lines inspired the toned-down looks of twentieth-century minimalism, as well as artistic movements such as the Bauhaus.

Food and Nutrition

While the Shakers eschewed things that appealed solely to the senses, their food was not tasteless fare. They believed that a nourishing, well-cooked, delicious meal incorporating the full bounty of nature fed the soul and kept the body at its best capacity for work. While they used relatively few seasonings—mostly sage, marjoram, parsley, mint, thyme, and maple products—they had the skill to take relatively few ingredients and prepare an enjoyable meal for all. They were most famous for their apple products, with their most popular items being applesauce, cider, and rose water apple pie.

Remarkable even at the time, they used no chemical or toxic pesticides in their agriculture. They grew their own vegetables, fruit, and livestock, creating an organic farm-to-table experience that we are only now beginning to rediscover and respect.

Business and Commerce: Seeds and Herbal Medicines

The Shakers' strong work ethic was mixed with an equally formidable marketing savvy. Along with crafts and furniture, the seed business and herbal medicine were two sectors in which the Shakers excelled.

Garden Seeds

The Shakers are believed to be the first people to sell seeds by placing them into small, individual paper envelopes. Before this, seeds were sold in bulk from barrels, bins, or large fabric sacks. The Shakers would place their seed packets in small wooden display boxes that could be placed on a store counter so that shopkeepers could stock a much larger array of seeds in a smaller space.

Herbal Medicine

During early Colonial America, most doctors practiced "heroic medicine," a school that relied on extremely drastic procedures such as bloodletting and purging in order to shock the body back into health. By the early 1800s, milder, herbal-based remedies, such as those advocated by Thomsonian medicine (named after its founder, Samuel Thomson), became popular. Thomson learned the healing properties of plants from Native Americans, a practice the Shakers also adopted.

The Shakers appointed men and women in their settlements to study medicine and treat the community. They also invented several herbal remedies that became extremely popular in the US and throughout the world—the most famous being Corbett's Shakers' Compound Concentrated Syrup of Sarsaparilla, which was developed by one of the Shakers' most prominent doctors Thomas Corbett in conjunction with Dr. Dixi Crosby, a professor of surgery at Dartmouth University.

Planting Your Own Shaker Garden

Shaker membership started to dwindle in the early twentieth century, but their influence lives on. If you are interested in creating

your own Shaker-style heavenly paradise here on earth, the following tips are based off the Shakers' own philosophies and practices to help you in this goal.

When creating your Shaker garden, your mission should be driven by a spiritual nature. You should see your garden as the embodiment of the divine force of nature made visible through the hard work of your very own hands. In order to achieve this, start small. Try to create a manageable-sized garden that offers you the ability to observe, cherish, and nurture each and every living organism. The success of your garden is not dependent merely on technique but also on attitude, philosophy, and spirit. An attention to quality, detail, hard work, and discipline is just as important as fertilizer and sunlight.

Getting Started

When looking for a garden plot, the Shakers suggest finding an even plot of land facing to the south or east in full sunlight. It is also a good idea to guard your garden with a wall to protect it from critters and wind.

The Shakers were an orderly, scientific people who believed that it was extremely important to nourish the soil properly before planting. Modern gardeners will often use compost made up of whatever scraps are left over from the kitchen, but it is a better idea to start out by testing the soil so you can provide it with what it truly needs. You can find rapid pH testing kits in any major home and garden center. Once you know your soil type, you can set about giving it the nutrients required for a bountiful harvest. The Shakers fertilized the soil with a combination of one part mineral (lime, sand, or clay), five parts vegetable matter (weeds, straw, leaves, roots, stalks, etc.) and six parts animal excrement, depending on the needs of the soil. The important thing is to determine your type of soil and condition it with the proper natural, organic, chemical-free substances. This fundamental initial step not only nourishes your plants but helps protect them from pests as well.

Plant an Orderly, Well-Ventilated Garden

The primary characteristic of Shaker gardens was how incredibly neat and tidy they were. Shakers planted in a grid-like fashion with a lot of space between rows so that the soil and plants could breathe. They were one of the early believers in proper ventilation as a cornerstone to good health. They included ventilation windows in all their dwellings and treated their plants with the same respect.

Shakers also believed that a garden reflected the mind of the gardener and an orderly garden reflected an orderly mind. Start with a square or rectangular plot and plant in straight, parallel rows. Tie runners or stalks to erect stakes. They were famed the world over for how tidy and clean their settlements were. Their gardens were immaculately kept, and they would pick up every stray piece of grain or kernel that had fallen to the ground. They even respected the land by wearing clean, neat clothing while working, so when tending to your Shaker garden, leave your raggedy old clothes in the closet.

Weeding

Shaker gardeners spent an unfathomable amount of their lives weeding. They saw it as an almost metaphysical exercise. They were not only perfecting their gardens but pulling out impure thoughts from their minds as well. Weeding was a spiritual act that kept the garden and the gardener's soul in a state of divine purity. So instead of seeing weeds as a nuisance, use your Shaker garden as a place where you can go to meditate and eliminate every stressful thought or anxious feeling from your inner psyche with every weed you pull from the soil.

Innovate and Experiment

The Shakers were pioneers of sustainable agriculture. Long before their compatriots, they tried to control soil erosion, took up composting, and were committed to nonchemical forms of pest control. While they used a small number of hand tools for everyday gardening—which they kept clean and in the best condition—they always embraced new, timesaving technologies that would make their work more efficient and productive. They were also open to trial and error, using the scientific method to observe what worked and what didn't. Don't be afraid of failure; view your garden as a creative art form that is always being slowly tweaked toward heavenly perfection. Shakers also over-planted as insurance against pests, bad weather, or crop failure. You may also want to experiment with letting certain plants ripen another month or two before harvesting, as did the Shakers. It takes little added effort, but your mature vegetables will be larger and contain more starch and protein, which will make them last longer and be more filling.

Choosing What to Plant: Usefulness Over Ornamentation

Like the Shakers, you should focus on three types of gardening: food to eat, medicinal herbs and, to a lesser extant, culinary herbs. The Shaker belief that all things should have a use forbade them to grow merely decorative plants. For example, they grew roses for medicinal preparations and cooking—especially as a flavoring ingredient in apple pie—but were forbidden to admire them solely for their scent or beauty.

As the Shakers mainly lived in New England, Ohio, and Kentucky, the majority of the plants suggested below reflect what was popular in their local gardens. The Shakers believed it was not worth the effort to try and grow plants not suitable for the native climate, so if you live in another part of the world, you should use those that thrive in your area.

You may decide to grow a mix of plants or focus on one type, such as a physic garden—a garden for medicinal herbs. The important thing is to grow what you will use.

Vegetables Grown By the Shakers

Potatoes, corn, pumpkins, squash, beans, peas, onions, cabbage, celery, beets, carrots, turnips, lettuce, spinach, asparagus, cucumbers, melons, and nasturtiums (in order to pickle their berries). They also grew peppers and eggplants, but these were less popular in Shaker cooking. Shakers were one of the first groups to popularize the tomato in colonial America. A member of the nightshade family, many people avoided tomatoes out of fear of being poisoned. Shakers grew them and sold their seeds, as well as offering tips for cooking this (at the time) uncommon food. Their efforts helped remove the stigma associated with this staple of the modern garden.

Apple Orchards

Apples were one of the main crops of early colonial America, and the Shakers were famous for their orchards. More than any other foodstuff, Shaker cooking was known for its apple products, which it sold to "the World." Shaker applesauce was considered the best, and at a time when fresh water often carried disease, Shaker hard cider was enjoyed as a thirst quencher and hydration source.

Shaker Culinary Herbs

While Shakers in the twentieth century started experimenting with a greater variety of culinary herbs, they did not use them often in the 1800s. During this period, they tended to stick to sage, marjoram, summer savory, thyme, and parsley, using them in a variety of meat dishes, stuffings, and soups.

Shaker Medicinal Herbs

Shakers originally gathered medicinal herbs in the wild, but as their operations grew, they started planting dedicated "physic gardens" filled with herbs that could be used as home remedies, as well as be made into compounds, balms, ointments, extracts, teas, and other preparations. Many common garden plants that we use today also have other mild therapeutic uses, from relieving anxiety to aiding digestion. The following list contains plants that were often grown in Shaker physic gardens. Before using any homegrown plant for medicinal use, it is best to consult with a trained, certified herbalist.

Basil, lemon balm, mint, spearmint, dill, fennel, coriander, caraway, angelica, peppers, horseradish, safflower, lettuce, roses (for rose water), witch hazel, blackberries, raspberries, sarsaparilla, and valerian. For topical use: arnica, calendula, and marigold.

Conclusion

The Shakers were not only pioneers of the American frontier but also extremely ahead of their time in terms of philosophy and lifestyle. Even in a pre-industrialized world, the Shakers were famed for their minimalism and dedication to social justice. If there were ever a time to espouse Shaker traditions, it is definitely now!

References

Crosman, Charles F. *The Gardener's Manual; Containing Plain Instructions [...].* Albany, Hoffman and White, 1835.

Edson Robinson, Charles. *A Concise History of the United Society of Believers Called Shakers.* East Canterbury, NH: Robinson, 1893.

Moon Signs and Mood Swings

Charlie Rainbow Wolf

Moon signs. They're mentioned throughout the pages of this book, but what do they actually mean? Like the Sun, the Moon—and the rest of the planets and other heavenly bodies—are in constant motion against the backdrop of the constellations, the signs. Each of these signs holds the potential for different traits and characteristics. The Sun takes a year to move through all of the signs, but the Moon only takes around twenty-nine days. Its impact is fleeting because of its speed, but the Moon is the closest heavenly body to your own physical body, and therefore its influence—though brief—is also powerful.

Astrologers read (or interpret) a natal birth chart by looking at the signs the planets were in on the date when someone was born and then comparing the angles—or aspects—they make to each other. When the aspects of the natal chart are compared to the aspects of the planets on any given day, these are called transits. Knowing the influence of the natal Moon is a start; knowing what the Moon is doing now, and how that will impact your moods, is the next step in living by the Moon.

It's easy to know the Moon's phases; you can look up and see it in the sky. However, you will need an ephemeris or aspectarian to know the signs the Moon is in at any given time. Because the Moon moves very quickly around the earth, it only stays in each sign for around two and a half days. Its aspect to your natal Moon will only last a few hours. Therefore, even though quite important, the transiting Moon's influence will only be a fleeting thing.

The Moon Phases

The New Moon is the start of a new lunar month. You won't be able to see it because it rises and sets with the Sun. This is the best time to begin new projects or embrace new ideas.

The waxing crescent Moon is the second phase in a lunar month. It hangs in the sky in a graceful thin curve, appearing in the western sky as sunset approaches. It adds discipline and focus to the energy of the New Moon and is a good time to look at things from a different angle.

The third Moon phase in a lunar month is the first quarter Moon. This is visible from late afternoon onward and hangs in the sky like a half circle or a capital letter D. This phase adds energy and enthusiasm to anything you are trying to accomplish.

The waxing gibbous Moon is the fourth phase in the lunar month and often looks full because of how brightly it is shining. This Moon rises late in the afternoon and is visible most of the night. It often brings a sense of urgency, but you must try to find patience, for it is during this time that important details could be overlooked.

It's easy to see the Full Moon, for it is round and bright. It is the apex of the Moon's journey through its phases, and it is the middle of the lunar month. It rises in the east as the sun sets and sets in the west as the sun rises. This is the time to blend inventiveness with practicality and look more deeply at long-term goals. It's often a good period for team meetings and socializing, for people are apt to be more open at this time.

The waning gibbous Moon—or disseminating Moon—starts the journey from full back to new. It is the sixth phase in the lunar month, with the Moon rising after sunset and setting after sunrise. Its energy brings a bit of reserve, but it's still a good time to share knowledge and what is being learned.

The penultimate phase in the lunar month is the last quarter Moon. This is the time to tie up loose ends, for the energies are slowing down and becoming more reserved. It is the opposite energy to the first quarter Moon, and the half disc hangs in the sky resembling a backwards letter D.

The last phase in the lunar month is the waning crescent Moon—also called the balsamic Moon. It is a time for resting, reflecting, and rethinking what has been accomplished over the last lunar month and contemplating what you want to achieve for the next one. It's not a particularly social time, for the overall energy is reserved and restrained. Like all Moon phases, this one will last about three days and then we move to the New Moon, where the cycle begins again.

Moon Signs

Understanding the Moon's phases is a good start; next, we'll take a brief look at the Moon through the signs. To understand this fully, it is important to consider both the phase and the sign of the transiting Moon. I'll get to that a bit later at the part about how to put it all together. It's quite easy when you get the hang of it—promise!

Aries Moon

Aries is a cardinal fire sign. As the first sign of the zodiac, it rests on the cusp of the spring equinox. Fire signs are warm, passionate, and grandiose—but like a house fire, that energy has to be contained and adequately controlled or disciplined, or the consequences could be quite unpleasant. Here, the Moon takes on a fiery energy that is independent and impulsive. Stay busy and find a way to dispel frustrations before they arise.

Taurus Moon

Taurus is a fixed earth sign. The second sign of the zodiac, it is practical and pragmatic; it is stubborn and dependable. This is not the right time to rush ahead, for the energy is more reserved than animated. Think of the land, how the glaciers slowly formed the peaks and troughs and how the soil quietly supports and nurtures the life upon it—until it starts to shake, and then with a few tremors it can raze everything to the ground. That, in a nutshell, is the influence of a Taurus Moon.

Gemini Moon

Gemini is a mutable air sign. The third sign of the zodiac, it is communicative and full of ideas but has quite a short attention span. There's a restless energy with a Gemini Moon, and focus tends to flit from one thing to another. This is a good time for short-distance travel and for paying attention to all things dealing with communication.

Cancer Moon

Cancer is a cardinal water sign. As the fourth sign of the zodiac, it is on the cusp of the summer solstice. In astrology, the Moon rules the sign of Cancer, so it's very comfortable here. Pay extra attention to home and family during Cancer Moons.

Leo Moon

Leo is the fifth sign in the zodiac, and is a fixed fire sign. It brings gregarious and passionate energy, but there's a bit of ego here. This is a time when luck and creativity are heightened, but make sure to take everything at face value and not jump to any conclusions.

Virgo Moon

Virgo is a mutable earth sign and the sixth sign in the zodiac. Its energy is one of precision, and there can be a lot of criticism and judgement going on in a Virgo Moon. This is the time to organize things and to pay attention to daily routines and health matters.

Libra Moon

Libra is a cardinal air sign and is on the cusp of the autumn equinox. As the seventh sign of the zodiac, it deals with partnerships of all kinds. Libra's energy is social and it likes company, making this a good time to mingle with others.

Scorpio Moon

Scorpio is a fixed water sign and the eighth sign of the zodiac. Passion and tempers may flare with a Scorpio Moon. It is a good time to pay attention to finances and intimate relationships and anything to do with intuition, mystery, or the arcane.

Sagittarius Moon

Sagittarius is a mutable fire sign. As the ninth sign of the zodiac, it brings a focus to philosophy and the higher mind. This is another excellent time for socializing with like-minded people and humanitarian pursuits, but stay flexible, for plans could change abruptly under a Sagittarius Moon.

Capricorn Moon

Capricorn is a cardinal earth sign, the tenth sign of the zodiac, and is on the cusp of the winter solstice. Its energy is practical and pragmatic and headstrong to the point of stubbornness. This is a good time to focus on motivation, ambition, and professional goals.

Aquarius Moon

Aquarius is a fixed air sign. It is the penultimate sign of the zodiac and its vibration is lofty and philosophical. It brings individuality and sometimes even eccentricity, for the energy here is spontaneous and unpredictable. This is a good time to seek out like-minded people and pull together for a common cause.

Pisces Moon

Pisces is the last sign of the zodiac and is a mutable water sign. It's dreamy and romantic, and this Moon is either your best friend or your nemesis depending on how its energies are faced. This is a period when sensitivity is likely to be heightened, and it is a good time to center on esoteric ideas or spiritual pursuits.

Lunar Transits

Knowing the Moon's signs and phases is a start, but this is a blanket influence overall, and not everyone is going to react the same. The reason for this goes back to astrology again; the Moon is going to tug at the Sun and the different planets in the skies as they are now as well as influencing the map of the heavens when you were born—your natal birth chart. This is what makes you an individual and why different people respond to the same situation in different ways.

Analyzing—or reading—a natal birth chart takes a long time. Applying the transits takes even longer! However, to understand the Moon's influence on you as an individual, the best place to start is with your natal Moon sign. You may even already know it, but if not, this information can be found on any reputable online free birth chart calculator. (I recommend Alabe.com or Astro .com. They are free services; you just plug in your date, time, and place of birth, and they will do all the mathematical calculations for you.)

Natal Moon in Aries

Transit Moon Aries	Most favorable, familiar, energetic
Transit Moon Taurus	Mildly favorable, grounding, possibly frustrating
Transit Moon Gemini	Restless, mercurial
Transit Moon Cancer	Challenging, counterproductive
Transit Moon Leo	Very favorable, creative
Transit Moon Virgo	Most challenging, disharmony
Transit Moon Libra	Neutral, mirrors current emotions
Transit Moon Scorpio	Most challenging, distracting
Transit Moon Sagittarius	Very favorable, spontaneous
Transit Moon Capricorn	Challenging, impatient
Transit Moon Aquarius	Favorable, philosophical
Transit Moon Pisces	Mildly favorable, enigmatic

Natal Moon in Taurus

Transit Moon Aries	Mildly favorable, energetic
Transit Moon Taurus	Most favorable, familiar, practical
Transit Moon Gemini	Mildly favorable, communicative
Transit Moon Cancer	Favorable, comfortable
Transit Moon Leo	Challenging, impatient

Transit Moon Virgo	Very favorable, detail-oriented
Transit Moon Libra	Neutral, harmony or superficiality
Transit Moon Scorpio	Neutral, adds passion to current issues
Transit Moon Sagittarius	Most challenging, unpredictable
Transit Moon Capricorn	Very favorable, patient and pragmatic
Transit Moon Aquarius	Challenging, impulsive
Transit Moon Pisces	Favorable, humble

Natal Moon in Gemini

Transit Moon Aries	Favorable, eager
Transit Moon Taurus	Mildly favorable, either anchoring or restricting
Transit Moon Gemini	Most favorable, comfortable, familiar
Transit Moon Cancer	Mildly favorable for family and home
Transit Moon Leo	Favorable, inventive
Transit Moon Virgo	Neutral, good for ideas, bad for patience
Transit Moon Libra	Very favorable, good for socializing
Transit Moon Scorpio	Most challenging, disharmony
Transit Moon Sagittarius	Neutral, adds spontaneity.
Transit Moon Capricorn	Most challenging, impatient
Transit Moon Aquarius	Very favorable, humanitarian
Transit Moon Pisces	Challenging, conflicting energies

Natal Moon in Cancer

Transit Moon Aries	Challenging, too busy
Transit Moon Taurus	Favorable, soothing
Transit Moon Gemini	Mildly favorable for new ideas
Transit Moon Cancer	Most favorable, comfortable, familiar
Transit Moon Leo	Mildly favorable, creative
Transit Moon Virgo	Favorable, industrious
Transit Moon Libra	Challenging, needy

Transit Moon Scorpio	Very favorable, perceptive
Transit Moon Sagittarius	Most challenging, inhibiting
Transit Moon Capricorn	Neutral, can be soothing or oppressive
Transit Moon Aquarius	Most challenging, hectic
Transit Moon Pisces	Very favorable, intuitive and insightful

Natal Moon in Leo

Transit Moon Aries	Very favorable, energetic
Transit Moon Taurus	Challenging, restricting
Transit Moon Gemini	Favorable for new ideas
Transit Moon Cancer	Mildly favorable for domestic activities
Transit Moon Leo	Most favorable, comfortable, familiar
Transit Moon Virgo	Mildly favorable but possibly impatient
Transit Moon Libra	Favorable for partnerships
Transit Moon Scorpio	Challenging, too demanding
Transit Moon Sagittarius	Very favorable, spontaneous
Transit Moon Capricorn	Most challenging, impatient
Transit Moon Aquarius	Neutral, group activities influenced
Transit Moon Pisces	Most challenging, lack of focus

Natal Moon in Virgo

Transit Moon Aries	Most challenging, disharmonious
Transit Moon Taurus	Very favorable, good for focus
Transit Moon Gemini	Challenging, but good for new ideas
Transit Moon Cancer	Favorable, good for home matters
Transit Moon Leo	Mildly favorable, prone to impatience
Transit Moon Virgo	Most favorable, comfortable, familiar
Transit Moon Libra	Mildly favorable for socializing
Transit Moon Scorpio	Favorable, but perhaps moody

Transit Moon Sagittarius	Challenging, too impulsive
Transit Moon Capricorn	Very favorable, good for detailed work
Transit Moon Aquarius	Most challenging, aloof and distant
Transit Moon Pisces	Neutral, good for introspection and spiritual pursuits

Natal Moon in Libra

Transit Moon Aries	Neutral, good for socializing, but could be impatient
Transit Moon Taurus	Mildly favorable, watch overindulgence
Transit Moon Gemini	Very favorable, good for entertaining
Transit Moon Cancer	Challenging, possible mood swings
Transit Moon Leo	Favorable, good for creativity
Transit Moon Virgo	Mildly favorable, don't overthink things
Transit Moon Libra	Most favorable, comfortable, familiar
Transit Moon Scorpio	Mildly favorable, teamwork could become challenging
Transit Moon Sagittarius	Favorable for all personal interactions
Transit Moon Capricorn	Challenging, guard against boredom
Transit Moon Aquarius	Very favorable, philosophical and social
Transit Moon Pisces	Challenging, prone to delusions and fantasies

Natal Moon in Scorpio

Transit Moon Aries	Most challenging, opposing energies
Transit Moon Taurus	Neutral, grounding, possibly frustrating
Transit Moon Gemini	Most challenging, too superficial
Transit Moon Cancer	Very favorable for domestic activities

Transit Moon Leo	Challenging, lack of harmony
Transit Moon Virgo	Favorable, good for attention to details
Transit Moon Libra	Mildly favorable, not a time for making decisions
Transit Moon Scorpio	Most favorable, comfortable, familiar
Transit Moon Sagittarius	Mildly favorable, good for new ideas
Transit Moon Capricorn	Favorable for investigations and research
Transit Moon Aquarius	Challenging, possible disagreements and conflicts
Transit Moon Pisces	Very favorable, relax and unwind

Natal Moon in Sagittarius

Transit Moon Aries	Very favorable, harmonious energies
Transit Moon Taurus	Most challenging, discord and potential delays
Transit Moon Gemini	Neutral, ideas come easily but could leave just as quickly
Transit Moon Cancer	Most challenging, relationships could be strained
Transit Moon Leo	Very favorable, creative and industrious
Transit Moon Virgo	Challenging, too many details
Transit Moon Libra	Favorable for all socializing
Transit Moon Scorpio	Mildly favorable, good for fact finding
Transit Moon Sagittarius	Most favorable, comfortable, familiar
Transit Moon Capricorn	Mildy favorable, good for minutiae
Transit Moon Aquarius	Favorable for philosophical endeavors
Transit Moon Pisces	Challenging, could create unseen consequences

Natal Moon in Capricorn

Transit Moon Aries	Challenging, watch for impulsiveness
Transit Moon Taurus	Very favorable for reaching realistic goals
Transit Moon Gemini	Most challenging, flighty and inconsistent
Transit Moon Cancer	Neutral, handle relationships with practicality
Transit Moon Leo	Most challenging, headstrong and impatient
Transit Moon Virgo	Very favorable for detailed work
Transit Moon Libra	Challenging, indecision may cause delays
Transit Moon Scorpio	Favorable for fact-finding and accounting
Transit Moon Sagittarius	Mildy favorable if you do not get distracted
Transit Moon Capricorn	Most favorable, comfortable and familiar
Transit Moon Aquarius	Mildy favorable for teamwork
Transit Moon Pisces	Favorable for a bit of rest and relaxation

Natal Moon in Aquarius

Transit Moon Aries	Favorable, good for launching new plans
Transit Moon Taurus	Challenging, could be hard to get ahead
Transit Moon Gemini	Very favorable, wonderful for brainstorming
Transit Moon Cancer	Most challenging, emotional discord likely
Transit Moon Leo	Neutral, can be either stimulating or frustrating
Transit Moon Virgo	Most challenging, potential to be bogged down by minutiae

Transit Moon Libra	Very favorable, socializing and teamwork highlighted
Transit Moon Scorpio	Challenging, tempers may flare
Transit Moon Sagittarius	Favorable, spontaneity could be rewarded
Transit Moon Capricorn	Mildly favorable if you remain patient
Transit Moon Aquarius	Most favorable, comfortable, familiar
Transit Moon Pisces	Mildly favorable, great for daydreaming

Natal Moon in Pisces

Transit Moon Aries	Mildy favorable, ideas take on new energy
Transit Moon Taurus	Favorable for putting a foundation under your dreams
Transit Moon Gemini	Challenging, confusion may arise
Transit Moon Cancer	Very favorable for love and romance
Transit Moon Leo	Most challenging, don't get overwhelmed
Transit Moon Virgo	Neutral, could be an anchor or a tether
Transit Moon Libra	Most challenging, watch for deception or dishonesty
Transit Moon Scorpio	Very favorable, insightful
Transit Moon Sagittarius	Challenging, uncomfortable
Transit Moon Capricorn	Favorable for adding practicality to your plans
Transit Moon Aquarius	Mildy favorable, good for networking
Transit Moon Pisces	Most favorable, comfortable, familiar

Conclusion

The above table is just a brief look at how the energies of the transiting Moon might be applied to daily life according to your natal Moon. To further enhance this, add the Moon phase to it; a general rule of thumb is if the Moon is waxing it is a time for growth, and if the Moon is waning it is a time for repose. For example, if the natal Moon is in Pisces, the transiting Moon is in Virgo, and the current Moon phase is first quarter, this is a perfect time to look at practical ways you can start to make your dreams and ideas become reality. If the natal Moon is in Leo, and the transiting Moon is in Cancer, and it is the waning crescent phase, then it is time to slow down, relax at home, and not take on any new plans or projects just yet.

When it's all put together, studying the lunar cycle has the potential to provide not just a glimpse at things to come but also a tool for calculating the most appropriate time for activities and projects. Keep a Moon journal and record your activities and feelings during each lunar phase and transit. This creates a blueprint of your own personal responses to the lunar cycles and a key to further self-understanding.

Modern-Day Foraging: Wild Edibles, Glorified Weeds, or Passing Fad?

Mireille Blacke, MA, LADC, RD, CD-N

After my job in healthcare was eliminated for reasons related to the coronavirus (COVID-19), I felt aimless, without direction or purpose. Losing a job was new to me, and COVID-19 made the world a very uncertain place. As my mood sank, I looked for distractions at home to improve my mindset. It wasn't long before I quite literally tripped over one.

Forcing myself outside to garden, a wayward bug attempted to fly up my nose. Being startled and in no mood for this, I flailed at the determined insect, tripped over the coiled garden hose, then very ungracefully face-planted into the fluffy, unmowed lawn.

Dazed, I sat up, assessing both the remaining bits of bug in my nose and the little dignity I had left. I swore a bit too.

Full disclosure: my backyard is loaded with blueberry, raspberry, and blackberry bushes along with a strawberry trellis and a sour cherry tree. The previous owners get full credit for installing those. Usually birds, rabbits, squirrels, and one plump woodchuck ("Woodchunk") enjoy the fruit-fest before I do. Sitting there that day, I saw blatant evidence of scavenging in little gnawed berries and naked stalks. Why didn't these fruit thieves feast on the endless sea of white clover where I tumbled? Upon closer inspection, I saw that they, or something, did.

Inspecting my pilfered berries and clover, an article about modern-day foraging sparked my memory; maybe investigating this would boost my foul mood, give my therapist a break, and possibly even outwit Woodchunk.

The Foraging Renaissance

Mainstream interest in foraging for food experienced a revival in recent years. Rising unemployment rates and food shortages stemming from the pandemic's first wave in 2020, generated even more attention on foraging for wild edibles. Exchanging new-found time and effort (aka sweat) for readily available, fresh food when dollars were limited seemed like a fair trade. Add physical activity and a likely mood boost to the equation: even better! With the world in crisis, this was worth investigating.

Words of Warning: Legality and Safety

There are contemporary barriers to wild edible foraging that our ancestors didn't have to face, such as federal, state, and local legal restrictions, in addition to potential modern-day food safety concerns.

Local, State, and Federal Laws

Prior to foraging, research local laws in your area to verify that it's legal where you live. Expect different regulations, requirements (e.g., permits), and restrictions regarding foraging on public land and parks compared to private property, properties of city or state parks departments, and federally protected properties. Be environmentally responsible and make sure none of the plant species you plan to collect are protected from foraging by law.

Safety: Poisonous Plants

Like me, you may stumble across plants that resemble the non-toxic wild edibles pictured in reference guides, but they're actually poisonous and should be avoided altogether. It's often quite difficult to identify a high-risk choice (e.g., moonseed) from the safe wild edible resembling it (e.g., grapes). But confusing the botanical identifications in this case could be fatal. Simply, it benefits the forager to learn to identify toxic and deadly plants. As an amateur, I would consider it too risky to forage for mushrooms without an expert present. It's also important to ID any nasty wild plants that may surround your target plant, like poison ivy!

Chemicals and Contaminants

Most foragers avoid areas likely to have been sprayed by pesticides, herbicides, and other contaminants. These usually include roadsides, waterways, some public parks, and urban areas. Some wild edibles (e.g., dandelions) are more likely to be sprayed by herbicides than others.

In The Weeds

Your wild edibles list should be based on your local landscape, wild edible habitats, harvesting seasons, culinary usefulness, and palatability relative to your needs. The edible's sustainability (ability to create future generations) should also be considered. All of these factors will impact which wild edibles are added to your list.

Since I'm focusing on "weed-like" outdoor edibles, fruit, nuts, fungi (mushrooms), and wild game won't be referenced. Once collected, all wild edibles should be washed thoroughly before consuming. Unless noted otherwise, "leaves" refer to young and tender, as older leaves tend to be bitter and used less. However, exceptions exist; refer to a reliable guidebook (see resources). Finally, each plant's harvesting season may vary by location; please consult an almanac specific to your area.

Amaranth (*Amaranthus spp.*)

Alias: pigweed

Edible parts: seeds, leaves

Found: sunny fields

Taste: nutty, "soapy" with crunchy texture

Uses: seeds—raw, roasted, toasted, baked (topping), ground (flour), puffed (popcorn), gluten-free beer, pasta/rice substitute; leaves—raw, chopped, cooked, spinach substitute

Note: seeds are high in protein and lysine (amino acid)

Recipe: Tabouli (http://www.eattheweeds.com/amaranth-grain-vegetable-icon)

Burdock (*Arctium minus*)

Alias: common burdock, lesser burdock

Edible parts: leaves, roots, seeds

Found: roadsides, riverbanks, vacant lots, fields

Taste: roots—starchy; seeds—mildly sweet, savory, artichoke-like

Uses: leaves—salads, tea; leaves, roots—stews, prepare like potatoes; roasted roots—caffeine-free coffee

Distinctive feature: burrs (prickly flower heads) stick or cling to clothing and animal fur

Caution: don't confuse with the toxic cocklebur.

Recipe: Burdock Root (Gobo) Stir-fry (http://ledameredith.com/wild-burdock-gobo-stir-fry)

Cattail (*Typha latifolia*)

Alias: bulrushes

Edible parts: roots, shoots, stalks, catkins, pollen

Found: wetlands, swamps, ditches, moist fields

Taste: similar to corn

Uses: eat early picked catkins like corn on the cob; cattail pollen used as high-protein flour; for more: www.farmersalmanac.com/cooking-wild-edible-cattails-25374

Note: early shoot texture is crunchy; later shoot texture is pithy

Recipe: Honey Cattail Cookies (https://www.ediblewildfood.com/honey-cattail-cookies.aspx)

Dandelion (*Taraxacum officinale*)

Edible parts: leaves, roots, flowers

Found: sunny gardens, pathways, grassy areas, yards

Taste: earthy, slightly bitter; similar to endive and arugula

Uses: leaves, roots—boil, soups, salads, sandwiches, stir-fry; flowers—wine; roots—roast as coffee substitute

Distinctive feature: bright yellow flower heads attract pollinator bees

Caution: often sprayed with herbicides; forage only areas you know

Recipe: Dandelion Beer (http://ledameredith.com/dandelion
-beer-recipe)

Fiddlehead Ferns (*Matteuccia struthiopteris*)

Edible parts: curled fern "scrolls"

Found: near creeks, very wet soil

Taste: root similar to horseradish; fern grassy, artichoke, similar
to asparagus in taste and texture

Uses: sautéed, steamed, boiled, pickled, frozen; may be toxic if
not cooked fully

Caution: choose fiddleheads that are completely curled up to
avoid gastric upset

Sustainability: don't over-forage; leave at least three fronds
remaining per plant for continued sustainability

Recipe: Szechuan Fiddleheads (https://edibleottawa.edible
communities.com/recipes/szechuan-fiddleheads)

Garlic Mustard (*Alliaria petiolata*)

Alias: hedge garlic, Jack-by-the-hedge

Edible parts: leaves, flowers, roots

Found: full sun/shade, along hedges

Taste: horseradish-flavored root with garlic-onion scented
leaves/flowers

Uses: substitute root for horseradish in sauces, marinades, sandwiches, and/or leaves/flowers for garlic/onions in seasonings,
sauces, etc.

Distinctive feature: S- or L-shaped root, garlic-onion scented
leaves/flowers

Sustainability: unlike with fiddleheads, take too much! Garlic
mustard is extremely invasive; foraging extra actually helps the
ecosystem

Recipe: Foraged Garlic Mustard Pesto (http://ledameredith.com
/garlic-mustard-pesto)

Mallow (Common) (*Malva neglecta*)

Alias: button weed, cheese plant/weed

Edible parts: raw leaves/shoots, roots, young/older leaves, dried leaves/flowers

Found: disturbed soil, vacant lots, field edges, woodlands

Taste: leaves, shoots, flowers—mild, nutty flavor

Uses: roots—egg white substitute, meringues; dried leaves/flowers—herbal tea; shoots/leaves—salads, soup thickener; older leaves—hot dishes

Distinctive feature: flower's shape resembles a cheese-wheel, earning it an alias or two

Note: common mallow resembles Carolina geranium, which is also completely edible

Recipe: Mallow Leaf and White Bean Burgers (Vegan) (http://ledameredith.com/mallow-leaf-white-bean-burgers-vegan-recipe-2)

Pineapple Weed (*Matricaria discoidea*)

Edible parts: flowers, leaves

Found: dry, disturbed soil (e.g., dirt roads)

Taste: tropical, sweet

Uses: raw, dried—salads, herbal tea, syrups, jellies, with cheese

Distinctive feature: flower head resembles an acorn

Caution: a close relative to ragweed, this plant's pollen may cause allergic reactions in people with hay fever

Recipe: Pineappleweed Flan (http://ledameredith.com/pineappleweed-flan-recipe)

Purslane (*Portulaca oleracea*)

Alias: duckweed, little hogweed, moss rose

Edible parts: leaves, stems, seeds, buds, flowers

Found: sunny sidewalk/driveway cracks, yards

Taste: slightly savory and sour

Uses: raw, cooked; thickener for soups/stews, okra substitute, compatible with meats, vegetables, salads, sandwiches

Distinctive feature: thick, succulent leaves; plant has gelatinous texture

Note: high in omega-3 fatty acids

Recipe: Purslane Relish (http://ledameredith.com/purslane -relish-recipe)

Ramps (*Allium tricoccum*)

Alias: wild leeks, spring onions

Edible parts: leaves, bulbs

Found: shady forests, moist soils

Taste: onion crossed with garlic

Uses: raw, sautéed, julienned, pickled; leeks or onion substitute

Sustainability: don't over-forage; harvest only 1–2 leaves from the plant; leave bulbs

Caution: lily-of-the-valley is a toxic look-alike: if leaves smell like onion/garlic, it's ramps; if not, leave it

Recipe: Spring Pesto Recipe of Wild Ramps, Garlic Mustard, and Basil (https://thepeasantsdaughter.net/spring-pesto-recipe-wild -ramps/)

Rose of Sharon (*Hibiscus syriacus*)

Edible parts: leaves, flowers, unopened buds

Found: moist, well-drained soil, urban hedging, suburban gardens, forests, forest edges

Taste: mild; similar to lettuce

Uses: raw/cooked leaves—lettuce substitute, salads, sandwiches, soups; leaves/flowers—tea; unopened buds—okra substitute, thickening agent for soups/sauces

Note: invasive, will crowd and displace native plants

Recipe: Goat Cheese Stuffed Hibiscus Blossoms with Chipotle Wild Berry Coulis (https://www.wildedible.com/blog/goat -cheese-stuffed-hibiscus-blossoms-chipotle-wild-berry-coulis -recipe)

Thistle (*Cirsium spp.*)

Edible parts: leaves, stems, thistle head, roots (first-year)

Found: variety of habitats, fields, backyards

Taste: leaves/stems—celery; roots—artichoke

Uses: leaves/stems—raw, boiled or roasted, steep for tea; roots—boil/fry like potato; young thistle head base—cook like artichoke

Distinctive feature: spikes! Use thick gloves. (Protective eyewear also recommended.)

Note: thistles offer pollinators food and shelter

Recipe: Thistle Soup (https://www.motherearthnews.com/real -food/thistle-soup-recipe-zmaz71mjzgoe)

And the one that started it all…

White Clover (*Trifolium repens*)

Edible parts: leaves, flowers, stems

Found: lawns, grassy fields, gardens

Taste: similar to vanilla

Uses: immediate use in salads, sandwiches, or as garnish; "dried" in baked goods; steep in tea; don't ferment!

Distinctive feature: tiny, white flower clusters

Note: forage plant for wildlife, attracts pollinators (bees)

Caution: fermentation of white clover may produce cyanide; warmer climates cause the plant to ferment naturally because of the heat, so be careful

Recipe: Clover Blossom Spoonbread (http://ledameredith.com /clover-blossom-spoonbread-recipe)

Recommended Foraging Supplies

Foraging bag/pack: May be hiking backpack (any size) depending on your needs.

Wild edible identification book or app: See resources for suggestions. Try Amazon or your phone's app store for other options.

Clothing/attire: Long pants (with pockets), long-sleeved shirt, long socks, comfortable and waterproof shoes, face masks, thick gloves, protective eyewear.

Plant containers: Food storage containers; I used plastic bags of different sizes, as I found them easier to label with a marker.

Tools: Knife, small shovel, scissors, trowel, marker (black).

First aid/survival kit: Water, sunscreen, bandages, bug repellant, first aid kit, baby wipes, antihistamine, EpiPen, any "just in case" medications.

Optional: Flashlight with batteries, sun-blocking hat, towels.

Above all, use common sense. Forage with a trusted friend in good weather during daylight. Inform reliable people of your plans, general location, and expected return time. Aside from the above, bring charged cell phones and anything needed for medical conditions that require monitoring during the day (e.g., diabetes). These recommendations are not one size fits all. In my case, mosquitoes and gnats love my repellant, sweating requires many sunscreen reapplications, and long pants are much more useful with many pockets. But face masks prevented bugs from flying up my nose!

Only you can decide if foraging for wild edibles is worth your time and effort. If you're still unsure, see eattheplanet.org for foraging tours, classes, and groups in your state. An experienced foraging guide can help you decide.

Animal Competition

If wild edibles are easy to find, taste good, and provide decent nutrition, wildlife will find them too. Though Woodchunk and pals aren't starving, they don't have our access to chain grocery stores and food delivery. Humans having knowledge to forage doesn't take precedence over wildlife's actual need to forage. I've whined about the picked-clean cherry or blueberry branches when I didn't make time to harvest them myself. My perspective now is that my lack of motivation provides food resources to wildlife, and I'm okay with that.

Getting Back To My Roots

While my experiences as an amateur forager haven't completely sold me on harvesting my own wild edibles, I learned a great deal about the natural world, I let go of significant amounts of anxiety and regret, and I feel more empowered (if grimy) than when I began. At the very least, I now appreciate the wealth of wild edibles readily available in my own backyard. After learning more about my animal neighbors, I don't mind sharing with them, including Woodchunk. When I tripped and fell into white clover, I took a chance with something new, didn't second-guess my abilities, and felt my confidence return. I accomplished my goal and know I can do it again in the workplace.

With any luck, that'll be a setting with no poison ivy, sweating, and flying bug parts.

Suggested Reading

Kallas, John. *Edible Wild Plants: Wild Foods from Dirt to Plate*. Layton, UH: Gibbs Smith, 2010.

Meredith, Leda. *The Forager's Feast: How to Identify, Gather, and Prepare Wild Edibles*. Woodstock, VT: Countryman Press, 2016.

Meredith, Leda. *The Skillful Forager: Essential Techniques for Responsible Foraging and Making the Most of Your Wild Edibles*. Boulder, CO: Roost Books, 2019.

Thayer, Samuel. *Incredible Wild Edibles: 36 Plants that Can Change Your Life*. Ogema, WI: Foragers Harvest Press, 2017.

Thayer, Samuel. *Nature's Garden: A Guide to Identifying, Harvesting, and Preparing Edible Wild Plants*. Ogema, WI: Forager's Harvest Press, 2010.

Foraging tours, classes, groups: www.eattheplanet.org

General foraging information: www.eattheweeds.com

Global urban foraging sites: www.fallingfruit.org

Foraging recipes: www.ledameredith.com

Wild edible database: www.wildedible.com

Phone app: Wild Edibles Lite

References

"Category Archives: Educational Resources." The Forager's Path School of Botanical Studies. Accessed August 11, 2020. www.theforagerspath.com/category/educational-resources.

Davies, Wilder. "Why Modern-Day Foragers Want You to Eat Weeds for Dinner." Time, November 7, 2019. https://time.com/5431240/foraging-for-weeds.

Kirkconnell, Andrew. "WTF Is Modern Foraging and Why You Should Try It." Accessed August 10, 2020. https://spoonuniversity.com/how-to/what-is-modern-foraging-and-why-you-should-try-it.

Disclaimer

About the Contributors

Elizabeth Barrette has been involved with the Pagan community for more than thirty-one years. She served as managing editor of *PanGaia* for eight years and dean of studies at the Grey School of Wizardry for four years. She has written columns on beginning and intermediate Pagan practice, Pagan culture, and Pagan leadership. Her book *Composing Magic: How to Create Magical Spells, Rituals, Blessings, Chants, and Prayers* explains how to combine writing and spirituality. She lives in central Illinois where she has done much networking with Pagans in her area, such as coffeehouse meetings and open sabbats. Her other public activities feature Pagan picnics and science fiction conventions. She enjoys magical crafts, historic religions, and gardening for wildlife. Her other writing fields include speculative fiction, gender studies, and social and environmental issues. Visit her blog *The Wordsmith's Forge* (https://ysabetwordsmith.dreamwidth.org/) or website PenUltimate Productions (http://penultimateproductions .weebly.com). Her coven site with extensive Pagan materials is Greenhaven Tradition (http://greenhaventradition.weebly.com/).

Mireille Blacke, MA, LADC, RD, CD-N, is a registered dietitian, licensed alcohol and drug counselor, and adjunct professor at the University of Saint Joseph in West Hartford, Connecticut. She has written numerous articles for Llewellyn's annuals series since 2014. Mireille worked in rock radio for two decades before shifting her career focus to behavioral health nutrition and addiction counseling. She remains fascinated with the city of New Orleans, her beloved (and insane) Bengal cats, criminal psychology, music that would surprise you, and the works of Joss Whedon. Someday, Mireille plans to complete a doctorate in Behavioral Health Nutrition when such a program actually exists.

Pam Ciampi was a professional astrologer from 1975 until her passing in 2019. She served as president of the San Diego Astrological Society and was President Emeritus of the San Diego Chapter of NCGR. Pam was the author of the Weekly Forecasts for Llewellyn's best-selling *Daily Planetary Guide* since 2007. Her latest contribution was an astrological gardening guide titled *Gardening by the Light of the Moon*. In its fourth printed edition, it is now available in a calendar format.

Sally Cragin is the author of *The Astrological Elements* and *Astrology on the Cusp* (both Llewellyn Worldwide). These books have been translated and sold in a number of countries overseas. She serves on the Fitchburg (MA) School Committee and is the founder/director of Be PAWSitive Therapy Pets and Communication. She does readings (astrological and tarot). Visit "Sally Cragin Astrology & TaroT" on Facebook, text or call 978-320-1335, or email sallycragin@verizon.net.

Vincent Decker, a native New Yorker, has been actively studying planetary influences on the weather for over thirty years. His forecast method relies on the work of the main modern and ancient contributors to the field of astrometeorology. At the same time, Vincent has incorporated many new techniques discovered from his own rewarding and fruitful study of planetary influence on weather patterns. His analyses of important past weather patterns have appeared in several astrological magazines. His forecasts and their results are available on his blog at www.theweather alternative.blogspot.com.

Shelby Deering is a lifestyle writer from Madison, Wisconsin. She specializes in writing about home décor, natural wellness, and mental health, contributing to publications like *Better Homes & Gardens*, *The Pioneer Woman*, *Naturally, Danny Seo*, and more.

When she's not writing, you'll find her hiking Wisconsin's many trails, shopping flea markets, or going on road trips around the country.

Alice DeVille has been enthusiastically writing articles for Llewellyn annuals since 1998. She is a graduate of George Mason University, Fairfax, VA (BA in sociology). Her contributions have appeared in the *Sun Sign Book*, the *Moon Sign Book*, *Starview Almanac*, and *Herbal Almanac*. Alice discovered astrology in her late teens when browsing the book section of a discount department store. Alice is known internationally as an astrologer, consultant, and writer. She specializes in relationships of all types that call for solid problem-solving advice to get to the core of issues and give clients options for meeting critical needs. Numerous websites and publications such as Star IQ, Astral Hearts, Llewellyn, Meta Arts, Inner Self, ShareItLiveIt, World Famous Quotes lists, and Twitter feature her articles. Contact Alice at DeVilleAA@aol.com or alice.deville27@gmail.com.

Amy Herring has been an astrologer for twenty-five years. Her background is in psychological, archetypal, and evolutionary astrology. She holds a master's level in Steven Forrest's Astrological Apprenticeship program and a bachelor's in psychology from Central Washington University. Amy has written two books on astrology: *Essential Astrology* and *Astrology of the Moon*. She is a long-time contributor to the *Moon Sign Book* and numerous other publications. She has lectured at several astrology organizations and conferences such as the Northwest Astrological Conference; however, as a self-professed introvert, her primary love is one-to-one client work and writing. Learn more at HeavenlyTruth.com.

Penny Kelly is a writer, teacher, author, publisher, consultant, and naturopathic physician. After purchasing Lily Hill Farm i southwest Michigan in 1987, she raised grapes for Welch Foods for a dozen years and established Lily Hill Learning Center where she teaches courses such as Developing Intuition and the Gift of Consciousness, Getting Well Again Naturally, and Organic Gardening. She is the mother of four children, has cowritten or edited twenty-three books with others, and has written seven books of her own. Penny lives, gardens, and writes in Lawton, Michigan.

Lupa is a naturalist Pagan who has been exploring the wild places of the Pacific Northwest since 2006. She is the author of several books on nature-based Paganism and vulture culture and is also the creator of The Tarot of Bones. She creates a wide variety of art with hides, bones, and other natural materials. She may be found online at http://www.thegreenwolf.com.

Michelle Perrin, aka Astrology Detective, has built a reputation as one of the world's most trusted and sought-after astrologers for more than ten years. Her work has appeared in some of the most influential titles online and in print, making her one of the few astrologers who has garnered respect from both a mass audience and the astrological community. Her horoscopes have appeared on the websites for Canada's W Dish and Slice TV Networks, Tarot.com's Daily Horoscope site, and *Dell Horoscope* magazine, among others. Her writings have also been featured in *The Mountain Astrologer*, the leading trade journal for the astrological community, and astrology.com. She also contributes to Llewellyn's *Moon Sign Datebook*, *Moon Sign Book*, and *Daily Planetary Guide*.

Kim Rogers-Gallagher has been a professional astrologer, writer, and lecturer for over twenty years. Based in Florida, Kim is the author of *Astrology for the Light Side of the Brain* and *Astrology for the Light Side of the Future*. Her monthly, weekly, and daily columns appear in *Dell Horoscope* and other astrological websites. She served on the board and edited the quarterly journal for the

International Society for Astrological Research and was a Steering Committee Member of AFAN (Association for Astrological Networking).

Christeen Skinner D.F.Astrol. S., FRSA, is director of Cityscopes London, which specialises in future-casting. She taught for the Faculty of Astrological Studies in London, was chair of the Astrological Association of Great Britain, and is a trustee of the Urania Trust. She is chair of the advisory board for the National Council for Geocosmic Research and a director of the Alexandria iBase Library, working to preserve texts and documents. She has spoken at many major conferences (UAC, AA, NCGR and ISAR) and is author of *Exploring the Financial Universe*, *The Beginner's Guide to Financial Astrology*, and *Navigating the Financial Universe* and a regular contributor to Llewellyn publications. In 2019 she was honoured with the prestigious Charles Harvey Award for services to astrology. Christeen is a fellow of the Royal Society of Arts.

Charlie Rainbow Wolf is happiest when she is creating something, especially if it can be made from items that others have cast aside. Pottery, writing, knitting, astrology, herbs, and tarot are her deepest interests, but she happily confesses that she's easily distracted, because life offers so many wonderful things to explore. She is an advocate of organic gardening and cooking, and she lives in the Midwest with her husband and special-needs Great Danes. Follow her at www.charlierainbow.com.

Moon Sign Book Resources
Weekly Tips provided by Penny Kelly, Shelby Deering, and Lupa
"The Methods of the *Moon Sign Book*" by Penny Kelly
"Gardening by the Moon" by Pam Ciampi

Notes